A Guide for Parents and Teachers

THE NEW LANGUAGE OF TOYS

3rd Edition

Teaching Communication Skills to Chil... ...eds

Third edition

All rights reserved. Published in the United States of America by Woodbine House, Inc.,
6510 Bells Mill Rd., Bethesda, MD 20817
www.woodbinehouse.com

Photographs by Valentine Sapcariu

Library of Congress Cataloging-in-Publication Data

Schwartz, Sue.
  The new language of toys : teaching communication skills to children with special needs / by Sue
Schwartz.— 3rd ed.
      p. cm.
  Includes bibliographical references and index.
  ISBN 1-890627-48-8 (pbk.)
  1. Language acquisition—Parent participation. 2. Toys. I. Title.
  P118.5.S38 2004
  649'.15—dc22

Manufactured in the United States of America

10   9   8   7   6   5   4   3   2   1

To the hundreds of deaf and hard-of-hearing
children who first taught me the value of play;

to Debra, Jeff, and Barry who continued the
learning and enhanced the fun;

and finally, most of all, to Anna and Geena who
allow the future to grow

Table of Contents

Acknowledgements vii

Foreword ix

Introduction xi

Chapter 1 Language: An Introduction 1

Chapter 2 Language Development in Children 5

Chapter 3 Playing and Learning 25

Chapter 4 Toy Dialogs 33

Chapter 5 Toy Dialogs for the First Year 43
           Birth to Three Months
           Three to Six Months
           Six to Nine Months
           Nine to Twelve Months

Chapter 6 Toy Dialogs for the Second Year 77
           Twelve to Fifteen Months
           Fifteen to Eightenn Months
           Eighteen to Twenty-Four Months

Chapter 7 Toy Dialogs for the Third Year 101
           (Twenty-Four to Thirty-Six Months)

Chapter 8 Toy Dialogs for the Fourth Year 121
           (Thirty-Six to Forty-Eight Months)

Chapter 9 Toy Dialogs for the Fifth Year 147
Forty-Eight to Sixty Months

Chapter 10 Toy Dialogs for the Sixth Year 171
Sixty to Seventy-Two Months

Chapter 11 Teaching Language Throughout the Day 193

Chapter 12 Computer Technology and Language Learning 199

Chapter 13 Videotapes, DVDs, and Television 209

Chapter 14 Toy Safety 213

Appendix A Alternate Sources of Toys 217
Appendix B Materials List 219
Appendix C Sources for Information about Children's Books 221
Appendix D Resource Guide 223
Appendix E Toy Manufacturers Cited in This Book 231
Appendix F Other Sources of Toys 235
Appendix G References 239

Index 245

Acknowledgements

Thanks to:

The staff at Woodbine House for their continued faith in my abilities to help children develop their language skills through play.

The parents and children who agreed to be photographed during their playtime:

A.Ivelisse Aviles
Lexi Brantley
Jacqueline, Eric, and Danielle Cannady
Robin, Gary, William, and Matthew Carter
Kristal and Kendall Dickerson
Aja English
Jennifer and Declan Hurley
Bonnie and Ethan James
Stephanie, Nicholas, and Morgan Johnson
Brad, Samantha, and Max Kappalman
Fran Katz
Sara Kaufman
Charlene McKelvin
Kyle, Wesley, and Dawn Muller
Steve, Maggie, Anthony, and Grace Neff
Nicholas and Nicky Paulter
Aimee, James, and Brandon Pennington
Salvador and Christina Rivera-Casiano
Daniel Vara Rivera
Debra, Val, and Anna Sapcariu
Jennifer, Barry, and Geena Schwartz
Robyn, Evan, and Samantha Schwartz
Annamarie and Graham Skinker
Adrienne, Kaely Maire, and Clare Mairead Sturges
Manuel Vara Caballero, Emanuel Vara, Saray Vara

viii | Acknowledgements

Emilio Vara
Delores and Alyssa Wallace
Elaine Weinstein
Susan, Kenneth, Justin, and Ryan Wilhelm
Kathy, Matthew, and Samantha Wooten

Additional thanks to:

Fran Katz for taking on some of the tedious jobs and
for seeing it through.

Marty Long for longstanding support and clever new ideas.

Valentin Sapcariu for his excellent photographic eye and
endless patience.

Sid Schwartz for constant support for the intricacies of
the computer

Debra Sapcariu, Jamie Schwartz, and Carol Sanders for
adding that degree of calmness to the photo shoot.

Meghan Blickman for venturing into Amazon.com
and finding it fun!

Barry, Jenny, Geena, and Jeff for always being there
with support.

All of my friends and colleagues for their advice and
encouragement for this work.

Foreword

By Nancy S. Grasmick, Ph.D
Maryland State Superintendent of Schools

"**P**lay is the highest expression of human development in childhood for it alone is the free expression of what is in a child's soul," said kindergarten inventor Friedrich Froebel. But Froebel understood that play is more than just free expression. To a child, play is work. It helps build his mind, body, and behavior. And when it comes to playful learning, the experts agree: the earlier, the better.

Long-term studies show that children's early experiences have a decisive impact—a dramatic and specific impact—on how their cognition and language develop and mature. And, as you're probably already aware, early stimulating experiences are even *more* critical for children with language delays.

While *The New Language of Toys* is widely used by speech-language pathologists and occupational therapists, the book was written foremost for moms and dads—a child's first teachers. By including such a wide variety of toys (and, in many cases, common household items that can easily double as toys), the book helps parents seize every opportunity to stimulate language. The brief, instructive scripts accompanying the toy ideas show parents that every day provides plenty of fun, teachable moments.

Of course, there's a lot more to be gained from these games than language development. Play connects children with the wider world and helps them understand their place in it. By interacting with you and others, your child begins figuring out how she fits in, and how her actions trigger reactions.

But perhaps most gratifying to those with whom I've spoken is the fact that play forges a deep and lasting bond between parents and children. And the confidence children accrue from a strong, loving relationship is as critical to their healthy development as anything else.

There's a reason *The New Language of Toys* is in its third edition. The book is an outstanding resource for parents and teachers—for anyone, in fact, who believes that learning can be, and should be, fun.

Introduction

Developing communication is as much a basic human need as seeking food and comfort. For many children this is a relatively simple process, while for others there may be significant delays. There are a wide variety of causes for language delay in children. Regardless of the cause, however, the results are usually the same: a child with delayed language development and concerned parents.

These concerned parents want to help their children with special needs learn language skills but often don't know the best way to go about it. An amazing amount of language can be pulled from even the simplest toy. This book, *The New Language of Toys,* shows you how to use toys and other play activities to aid your child's language development.

The first and second editions of this book showed thousands of parents how to use toys and other play activities to enhance their child's language development. Since their publication, many new and exciting toys have come on the market and some of the older toys have disappeared from toy store shelves. Therefore it is time to offer the third edition *of The New Language of Toys.* In this third edition, dozens of new toys and activities have been added. In addition, the chapters on language-enriching video and computer activities have been expanded and updated. Finally, the old photographs have been replaced with new photographs of children playing with the toys recommended in the book.

While you are playing with your child, you can be helping him increase his language skills. And you can have fun together at the same time. Your child can benefit from these times with Mom and Dad. This play/work time is dramatically more important for children with delays in their language development. They will need the extra effort that their parents can give them to help develop their language skills.

When speech and language therapists or teachers work with children with language delays, they use toys they think will encourage certain words or sounds. There is no "magic" to the toys they use. Rather, the toys are chosen carefully to be teaching aids. This book will help you to choose and to use toys like the professionals do to enhance the development of language in *your* child. Although certain toys have been selected for this book, be assured that there are many other toys that can be bought or made which can serve equally well.

The New Language of Toys, third edition, is divided into three parts. In the first part, important background information about language is explained: its sequential development, some of the causes of language delay, the value of play, how play can enhance language development, and your role in all of this. In the next section— which is the heart of the book—toys have been recommended that have been found useful in stimulating language development and show you how to use these toys in playing with your child. For each toy in the book, sample language dialogues are provided to help you get the most from that toy. Use these ideas in your play as well as to go beyond and devise new ways of playing to encourage language development. In the last section of the book, general issues related to toys and learning are discussed that will help you choose and use toys and learning materials wisely.

The book has been designed to be used with *any child who has a language delay, whatever the cause may be.* Guidelines have been given which should help you decide which toys your child would be most interested in playing with and most ready to learn from. Each child has his own unique profile for all developmental areas, including cognition, motor, social, self-help, *and* language. A child may make progress in different areas at different rates. The result is a wide variation in the developmental picture for each child, regardless of his chronological age. For example, a three-year-old child with a twelve-month language delay may have "normal" cognitive development or motor skills but speak on a two-year-old level. Alternately, a four-year-old child with "normal" language may have very delayed motor skills.

Individual suggestions have been made for modifying your play to accommodate the specific learning needs of each child. Every possible need may not have been discussed; you will be able to adapt my suggestions to your own child.

The toys and exercises in this book are arranged by language developmental ages. Each section covers several months and presents toys and dialogues that are appropriate for your child's particular level of language development. There are similar guidelines throughout the book to help you pick toys that are the most appropriate for your child's level of language development.

In addition to suggesting toys you can buy, at least two home-made toys for each language developmental level have been included. Many people enjoy making toys, and for children with disabilities, homemade toys can be designed to adapt to their specific needs. There is a lot of benefit in making your own toys—including saving money. Children and parents treasure these homemade toys long after other toys have been packed away.

Remember, suggestions are only suggestions. Expand and create. There are many books in libraries and in bookstores that will tell you more about homemade toys. Several have been included in the reference list at the back of this book.

Parents often ask, "When should we start?" You can start the fun in this book even before your child's language delay has been formally diagnosed. If you already know that your child has some special needs, you have to consider the possibility that he is language delayed too. Do not wait until you have a specific diagnosis of language delay to begin. Often your child's diagnosis has to wait until you are able to test him and in many cases that doesn't happen before age two. You can always work on his language skills even before getting a diagnosis. It can only help him in the long run. As you will see in the chapter on language development, you would not expect your child to be talking in understandable language much before one year of age. Enrich your child's language long before that time.

If your child is an older preschooler and you have just gotten the diagnosis of a language delay, then you can start this book at whatever level your child is placed and work from there. You might even be working with a therapist or school at this time. Show them this book and explain how you want to integrate these ideas with your child's specific plan. You will probably find that these examples fit right in with your child's individual education plan.

You are not expected, or wanted, to turn into a teacher for your child or to lose your role of being a parent. However, you can combine the two roles in a way that is fun for both you and your child. There is also no need to occupy your child's every waking moment with the exercises in this book. There are times when children should play alone because that is when they build independence and develop imagination. However, parents, grandparents, teachers, families, babysitters, and others can enhance the development of richer language by playing with toys with children for *part* of the child's playtime.

Follow your child's lead. If he is interested in farm animals, explore that area in your play. If you see that he has no interest at all in cars and trucks, then put that idea aside for a while. Your play should be fun, interesting, and meaningful. Experience your childhood again and enjoy the time you will spend in playful learning with your child.

Language: An Introduction

Language is everywhere. It is everywhere we live and work, and it will be everywhere our children live and work too. There is almost nothing we or our children do in this world that does not involve some type of communication. It is one of the most important life skills our children can acquire.

This chapter reviews some of the basics of language: what language is, its importance to society, and how it develops.

The Need for Language in Our Society

Society could not function without language to explain complex inventions, convey ideas, or relay information. History, science, law, technology, and mathematics are all based on information. And that information can only be communicated through language. We use language to record our past, to chart our present, and to prepare for our future. Our children will need language in order to participate fully in all of these activities of our society. They will need language to participate fully in their own personal worlds as well.

Through language, we explain our feelings. How could we express our deepest emotions without language? Fear, anger, happiness, and sadness are all communicated using language. All through life people use language in forming relationships, expressing love, and sharing thoughts and feelings.

Language, with its many nuances, is more art than science. How often have we found ourselves trying to explain our way out of situations caused by faulty communication? "That is not what I meant: you misunderstood what I said." Did he or she misunderstand, or was our language not clear enough? Language is an area most vulnerable to misunderstanding.

Through language, we transmit our values from one generation to the next. We need to communicate concepts for morality, concepts for religious beliefs, and concepts for family expectations. Language gives us a way to express things we've never seen but want our children to know about.

Through language, we transmit our cultural heritage to our children. Long before there were ways to write things down, language passed on legends from one generation to another. Telling vivid stories of people and places our children have never seen and never visited passes on a cultural heritage. Many years ago, the powerful story of *Roots* gave us insight into black culture that we would never have known otherwise. The graphic retelling of the events of the Holocaust keeps that part of our history alive. Each year at Christmas and Easter, the retelling of the story of Jesus fascinates a new generation.

Language is a vital tool for our children with special needs to have, for it is through language—whether spoken, signed, pointed to, or combinations of all three—that they will reach their fullest potential. In order for us to help our children reach that potential, it is important that we understand how language develops. With that knowledge, we can decide how to best help our children.

Children with special needs should be evaluated on an individual basis and have learning goals set specifically for them. When you learn how language develops, you can decide where on the continuum your child is now and begin working to strengthen her language skills from that point. Understanding the basics of language development is the first step.

Language Development

The development of language in young children is exciting. Parents everywhere share the excitement of that first coo or gurgle that actually sounds like "mama" or "dada." The long distance telephone companies profit from countless phone calls to Grandma and Grandpa who wait in breathless anticipation as the little one breathes into the phone for ten minutes and finally gurgles out that "first word." How do we get to that first word? Is the first coo or gurgle a "true" word? Did we teach our child that "first word" or did she develop language on her own? This section will answer these and many more questions about the development of language.

Receptive Language, Expressive Language, and Speech

The question Grandmas and friends ask often is, "Is she talking yet?" What they are really asking is "Does she have expressive language yet?" We can't answer that question until we learn what *receptive language, expressive language,* and *speech* mean.

Receptive language is the information that your child takes in by hearing sounds, seeing gestures and formal sign systems, or perhaps "reading" common signs around her. It is what she hears all around her. It is what she understands. For example, if a child is asked, "Where's the doggie?" she will look around and point to Rover. This

will show that she understands what was asked, even though she may not yet be able to say "Rover" or "doggie."

Children must be exposed to receptive language in order to develop communication skills. The language they are exposed to early in life is crucial to developing these skills. Fortunately, most young children are surrounded daily by language which they hear from brothers, sisters, neighbors, TV, radio, and YOU. Even when you don't think you're "teaching" your child language, you are. You are because you are communicating and she is taking in information! Basic human communication can be as simple as this, or it can be enriched in ways talked about later.

Expressive language begins with the birth cry. As air rushes across your newborn's vocal cords, she announces her arrival in the world. You receive her message and understand, so you have your first communication with your newborn. Expressive language is the communication of one person to another. It can be through crying, through laughter, through words, through gestures, through a formal system of sign language, through assistive devices such as communication boards, computers or through combinations of any of these. If we go back to our example of the child and the dog, we would expect that if the child has expressive language she would be able to point to the dog and in some manner produce the word for "doggie" or "Rover." This is now expressive language.

Although a newborn's crying *is* technically a form of expressive language, children need to have receptive language before they have anything more than the most basic expressive language. So, before you can answer that question, "Is she talking yet?" with a proud "YES," your child must be able to understand language. After many hours and months of listening, you'll be rewarded with that first precious word. Be sure to call everybody you know with the good news and tell them that she is "talking." You'll know that what she is really doing is using expressive language.

Speech, as mentioned above, is one way of conveying expressive language. Speech is the physical production of certain sounds and combinations of sounds, which, when uttered together, make a word that communicates meaning. It combines our understanding of language (receptive language) with our ability to produce sound (expressive language) in order to communicate intentions, questions, and information. Speech is only a tiny part of how people communicate. Has anyone ever said to you, "It isn't what you said that upset me but the WAY that you said it?" We communicate as much with our body language, our smiles or frowns, and the tone of our voices as we do by speech.

Conclusion

At this point, you may be wondering why you need to know all this terminology related to communication. Perhaps you are inclined to skip over the introductory chapters and plunge into the language activities with your child. But understanding the distinctions between receptive language, expressive language, and speech will stand you in good stead. First, if your child has language delays, you will find that teachers, speech-language therapists, and others frequently use these terms in explaining your child's strengths and weaknesses. Second, in working on language skills with your child, it will be important to understand whether she has trouble with receptive language, expressive language, or both.

Understanding how language develops will also help you pinpoint and work on your child's particular problems. The more knowledge you have, the more you will be able to enrich your child's language experiences so that she can more fully communicate with her world. Chapter 2 explains the process of developing language in young children.

Language Development in Children

As children grow, their physical and mental abilities develop to handle more complex skills. You can see this in an infant absorbed with a rattle, a two-year-old playing with sandbox toys, or a five-year-old building an intricate structure with blocks. Each is playing within a different range of abilities that is appropriate for his growth at that age.

Language ability also develops over time. From a child's first "mama" or "dada" through complete phrases and sentences made up of several words, an amazing amount of language development occurs. Like other areas, language development varies tremendously between children.

Parents of children with special needs often ask, "What is considered 'normal' language development so I can gauge my child's progress?" Figure 1 shows stages of language development in children. Remember, however, there is a very wide range of what is considered "normal" development. For example, although the average number of words a two-year-old can say is 272, a child could say as few as 50 and still be considered to be developing normally. Or, although some children can say a couple of words by the age of nine months, other normally developing children do not say their first word until fourteen months or later. Likewise, there could be a wide variation in your child's language skills.

Parents, teachers, therapists, and other specialists want to be able to determine the level where your child is functioning so they can target what skills need to be worked on. His development in areas such as fine motor, gross motor, thinking, receptive language, expressive language, and speech are tested to determine his strengths and weaknesses. Extensive studies by experts have established ages where most of the children tested acquired each skill. By comparing your child with these

Figure 2

Language Development in Normally Hearing Children

Vocal Play ◄──►	Babbling ◄──►	Jargon ◄──►	Imitation ◄──►
0 months	6 months	12 months	18 months
	1 word	3 words	22 words

Phrases ◄──►	Sentences ◄──►	Paragraphs ◄──►	Nearly Correct ◄──►
24 months	**Questions**	4 years	**Grammar**
272 words	3 years	1870 words	5 years
	896 words		2289 words

Full Command of English

6 years

2568 words

Vocabulary numbers taken from *Diagnostic Methods in Speech Pathology*, p. 192. Samples taken from children of average IQ.

norms, the approximate age at which your child is functioning can be found. This is called a **developmental age.** Since there is great variation among children, most tests will give a range from the lowest age where this skill is acquired to the highest age where almost every child tested had the skill. This developmental range is the accurate way to find where your child is functioning at this time.

For parents of children with special needs, development can be complicated. Often these children are a mosaic of different developmental levels. A child may have six-year-old gross motor skills, two-year-old fine motor skills, and another level in language development. Because of these varying levels, deciding where your child currently is *developmentally* in his language skills can be a little tricky.

The next section presents summaries of different developmental ages that emphasize language development. These descriptions should help you to determine your child's current level of language development. We have also included summaries of physical development so that you can have a clear picture of your child's development overall. Remember, these developmental ages are general outlines only. No two children are alike. Far more important than comparing your child's behavior to other children's within the same range is comparing your child's behavior, accomplishments, and progress with his own earlier achievements. It is not critical that your child reach any given stage by a certain age. Quality of development—not just quantity—should be your goal.

In working with your child with developmental delays in language, use his developmental age and not his actual age to determine what skills to work on. For instance, he may be chronologically twenty-four months old, but his language may have developed to a twelve-month-old level. In your work with him, use the language developmental age of twelve months. He will function best at his developmental age and you do not want to frustrate him by working too far beyond his capabilities.

Developmental Ages

This section summarizes developmental ages of children during the first six years of life. This information will help you decide what language developmental age best fits your child now so you can choose appropriate language activities.

One way for you to decide which toys your child will enjoy is to see which category lists the largest number of skills your child has acquired. This level should be close to his developmental age. Using toys from this category should insure that you and your child will benefit from the activities presented. These selections should not limit you but should be used as a guide. Choose any toy that you think he will enjoy playing with and learn from.

Birth to Three Months

A newborn is primarily interested in his most basic needs for food, comfort, and love. He spends most of his day being nourished, being kept clean, and being loved. During this time he is developing an understanding of trust and warmth from those who care for him.

Language Development

During his first weeks of life, your baby is most likely to communicate only through crying. The people taking care of him will soon be able to tell what his different cries mean. Is he hungry? Is he wet? Is he tired? Does he want company? Each of these cries has a different tone to it that can be understood easily in a short time. In a few weeks your baby adds cooing, squealing, and gurgling to his repertoire. You can see that he enjoys making all these different sounds as you talk to him, tickle him, and make those favorite silly faces that we enjoy making with little babies.

The little noises that infants make in these first months are called vocal play. Most infants, even deaf ones, will engage in vocal play. The sounds are vowel-like and can vary in loudness as well as in the pitch of high and low sounds. In these first few months babies often make sounds that are heard in languages other than their own. An American baby might produce an inflectional tone of an Asian language, a guttural sound from a Germanic language, or a tongue click from an African dialect. Because these sounds are not reinforced by the sounds he hears around him, he quickly stops playing with them and focuses more on the sounds that are reinforced in his own language. It is in this way that babies begin to learn to speak their native language.

Physical Development

During the first three months of life, you may see that your infant is developing an awareness of his sense of touch. You can get a response from him by rubbing his hands, arms, legs, and feet with smooth, scratchy, fuzzy, and soft materials. By the third month, he will be able to hold onto objects and will enjoy rattles and stuffed animals.

• • • • • • • • • • • • •

Three to Six Months

Your baby is now becoming more active and is awake for longer periods of time. He's ready for more playtime with you. Instead of spending most of your time just caring for your newborn, now you can increase both the amount of time you spend playing with him and can focus this play more on his language development.

Language Development

Around the fourth month, we begin to hear more of the consonant sounds emerging in a baby's vocal play. He will practice with sounds that use only his lips, such as /m/b/p/, as well as sounds using other parts of his mouth, such as his tongue, which produce /t/g/k/.*

Physical Development

Your baby is now able to grasp and hold onto things and will enjoy rattles, stuffed animals, and objects that he can explore with his hands like those textured rattles and animals you bought when he was a newborn. He is able to reach out for things and bring them to his mouth to explore them.

• • • • • • • • • • • • •

Six to Nine Months

Your infant is now on a fairly regular sleep and play schedule. He will be more interested in activities with you and awake longer to enjoy them.

Language Development

You will discover that his attention span is increasing and that he will enjoy longer periods of play and longer periods of looking at books and pictures with you.

---

* Speech-language pathologists use slashes to indicate the sound made by an individual letter or combination of letters.

Beginning at about six months, your baby's random sounds of vocal play will begin to become repetitive. You'll hear more combinations of sounds that he will repeat over and over again. This is called babbling. You may even hear some combinations of sounds that resemble actual words. They rarely hold meaning for him at this point. Gradually, at around eight months of age, these babbling sounds get more refined and begin to represent words to your baby. Around this time, you may hear his first true word, which will usually be a combination of consonant and vowel sounds that he has played with along the way. For example, he may combine the /a/ and /m/ sounds to produce "mama," or may combine /a/ with /b/ to produce "baba."

Physical Development

He is becoming more physically active and may be ready to crawl very soon. By the end of this time range, he may well be crawling along. He can sit up by himself, which makes him more available for different games that you can play. His fine motor skills are becoming more refined and he is able to pick up things using his thumb to help him. He'll be able to pick up blocks and help you in stacking them and in knocking them down! He'll enjoy stacking rings, but at first he will be more interested in taking them off than he will be in putting them back on.

By the end of this time period, he will probably be pulling himself up to a standing position, so be sure to lower the mattress in his crib and put away that crystal vase!

· · · · · · · · · · · · · ·

Nine to Twelve Months

Language Development

As he moves along toward his first birthday, you will see a dramatic rise in your baby's comprehension (receptive language). He will enjoy playing games of "Show me." "Show me your eyes." "Where's the kitty?" "Can you find your ball?" He will enjoy showing off how much he understands and may even try to imitate some of the key words he hears you say. So be careful of what you say!

His attention span is still increasing and he will enjoy listening to books, CDs, tapes, and videos. He may even be able to point to some known objects in the books as you tell him the names.

Physical Development

By now you've noticed how very physically active your baby is. He will be holding on and walking around furniture. He may even strike out on his own and walk by himself. He will enjoy active outdoor play. Make sure that his play area is fenced in or that you are with him all the time. He may be scooting around but he has no idea of danger at this time. He is able to roll a ball with two hands and if he is standing alone by this age, he may even be able to kick it as well. Balls are fun and a great way to encourage physical agility.

His fine motor skills are developing and he is able to pick things up, put them into containers, and gleefully dump them out again. Babies will often do this over and over for incredibly long periods of time. He is able to manipulate small switches, dials, and slides. He is able to clap his hands together and will enjoy imitating you in pat-a-cake type games.

Twelve to Fifteen Months

Language Development

By now there is much more babbling going on with many sounds strung together into phrase-like and sentence-like series. This babbling will have tone and inflection and many people say, "If I just knew what language he was speaking. . . ." This phase is called *jargoning.* You will occasionally hear a word tossed in among all of his singsong jargoning.

Physical Development

One of the play skills your toddler will find most interesting is turning "dumping" into "pouring." If he has been walking and is steady, he will now be able to walk sideways and backward and will enjoy walking with pull toys as well as push toys.

Up until now you have been rolling a ball to him. Since he is now steadily standing, he will be able to throw the ball to you. He probably will not be able to catch it yet but he will enjoy kicking and chasing it.

His fine motor skills are well developed enough now that he can turn the pages of a book and do other fine motor activities.

Fifteen to Eighteen Months

Your baby's imagination is developing and he will like playing with toys that are representational of his world. He will enjoy acting out many scenes that he sees in his own life.

Language Development

Jargoning continues while words develop. By eighteen months, you'll be able to distinguish more and more recognizable words mixed in the jargon. If you are keeping a list of words for which he has true meanings, you'll probably find that he says somewhere around 22-25 words. These are certainly not absolute numbers—some children may say more and some fewer—but this number is an average for an eighteen-month-old baby.

Physical Development

During this stage, your child is able to climb stairs and expand his world on his own. He now has the physical abilities he needs to indulge his curiosity. He will explore your home inside and out. Be sure to provide a safe environment for him.

Eighteen to Twenty-Four Months

At this age, your child's interest in books continues and now he is able to "read" the pictures himself. He will enjoy "reading" to you out of homemade books that you may have made for him earlier. He can even help select pictures for new books.

Language Development

At this age, your toddler enjoys imitating your words, tones, and actions. Now is a great time for finger plays and games like peek-a-boo and pat-a-cake. If you check the language development chart, you will see a dramatic rise in the number of words your little one is now able to use. Although there is wide variation, an

average number of words a child with no language delay might be using by twenty-four months of age is about 272. This number is shared with you so you are aware of the vast number of things he can identify by name. He also will be combining these words into short phrases. You'll hear him say, "Bye bye car" or "Daddy go work." You'll also hear many incorrect grammatical combinations such as "Tommy falled down" or "car go me." You'll begin to hear pronouns being used, although he will still refer to himself by name most of the time. His pronunciation of words and phrases can often be very hard to understand.

Physical Development

Your young child is probably very active at this stage. He is walking steadily, running constantly, and climbing, and now adds jumping to his repertoire.

His fine motor skills are developed to the point where he can open and close containers. He will be able to place puzzle pieces if there is one piece for each space.

Figure 2

Earliest Ages (in years) At Which Sounds Were Correctly Produced, In the Word Positions Indicated, by 75% of 208 Children

Consonants	Beginning Position	Middle Position	End Position
m	2	2	3
n	2	2	3
ng	–	6	3
p	2	2	4
b	2	2	3
t	2	5	3
d	2	3	4
k	3	3	4
g	3	3	4
r	5	4	4
l	4	4	4
f	3	3	3
v	5	5	5
th (uv)*	5	–	–
th (v)**	5	5	–
s	5	5	5
z	5	3	3
sh	5	5	5
h	2	–	–
wh	5	–	–
w	2	2	–
y	4	4	–
ch	5	5	4
j	4	4	6

Vowels and Dipthongs	Age
ee (beet)	2
i (bit)	4
e (bed)	3
a (cat)	4
u (cup)	2
ah (father)	2
aw (ball)	3
oo (foot)	4
oo (boot)	2
u-e (mule)	3
o-e (coke)	2
a-e (cake)	4
i-e (kite)	3
oy (boy)	3

* (uv) = unvoiced (using only breath to produce the sound, as in the word <u>th</u>ree)
** (v) = voiced (using the voice to produce the sound, as in the word <u>th</u>e)

Figure 2 (continued)

Consonant Blend	Age	Consonant Blend	Age
pr	5	–ks	5
br	5	al	6
tr	5	sw	5
dr	5	tw	5
kr	5	kw	5
gr	5	ngk	4
fr	5	ngk	5
thr	6	–mp	3
pl	5	–nt	4
bl	5	–nd	6
kl	5	spr-	5
gl	5	apl	5
fl	5	str-	5
-ld	6	skr-	5
-lk	5	skw-	5
-lf	5	–ns	5
-lv	5	–ps	5
-lz	5	–ts	5
sm-	5	–mz	5
sn-	5	–nz	5
sp-	5	–ngz	5
st-	5	–dz	5
-st	6	–gz	5
sk-	5		

(Powers, Margaret Hall, "Functional Disorders of Articulation/Symptomatology and Etiology." In *Handbook of Speech Pathology and Audiology*, edited by Lee Edward Travis, p. 842. Englewood Cliffs, NJ: Prentice Hall, 1971.)

Twenty-Four to Thirty-Six Months (2-3 Years)

Language Development

This is a fascinating time for you and your child in many ways. Language development is certainly one of the most exciting things happening during this year. This is the year where the phrases of 2-3 words turn into sentences of 4-5 words. The sentences then turn into questions. This is the year of "why," "what," and "where." Sometimes these questions are really for the purpose of getting information and sometimes your child just enjoys hearing himself talk.

You can expect your child to make many errors in the use of words and how they fit into sentences. He really does not understand the rules of grammar yet. He will also mispronounce many sounds at this age, and for the next few years. Figure 2 shows you when each of the speech sounds usually develops.

Physical Development

By this age he has many of his large motor skills under control. He may be able to pedal a trike, but more likely he will push with his feet on the ground. He will probably discover the low-seated plastic cars that children enjoy at this age.

His fine motor skills continue to develop and he will be able to play with interlocking block systems to create endless imaginative designs. He is comfortable handling puzzle pieces and enjoys showing off his skills.

Thirty-Six to Forty-Eight Months (3-4 Years)

During this year, most young children are involved with other children on a regular basis. Your child will continue to be very active both in and out of doors with playmates and alone.

Language Development

As your child's world begins to expand beyond your doors, new people will be adding to his receptive language. He will begin to have new playmates in the neighborhood and at his preschool or daycare center. He will pick up new and different words and phrases from them.

You will notice that he is able to tell you more complicated stories about things that happen to him when you aren't around. He can tell you about his activities at school and about his play with friends outside.

One disturbing development in his expressive language that may happen during this year may be the occurrence of *nonfluency or dysfluency.* Nonfluency usually happens like this: Your child has many things he wants to tell you. They are all very important to him and often he is overwhelmed with excitement at telling you about them. His thoughts may come so quickly that his oral muscles may not be able to keep up with the speed of his thinking.

Give your child time and attention during these moments. Do *not* comment about his nonfluency. Do *not* suggest that he calm down and slow down. Do *not* give him the words he is stumbling over. The problem will usually evaporate in time if you do not focus on it. There are differing opinions about the subject of nonfluency in young children, but it is the opinion of most people in the field of language development that the less you make of it the better. A note of caution: If the nonfluency continues past age five or if your child develops some other behaviors to go along with it such as a nervous twitch, or stamping his foot as he is talking, or any other involvement of other parts of his body, you will want to have an evaluation done by a speech-language pathologist, a trained professional familiar with the normal patterns of language development in young children.

It is important for you to note that this problem is technically called "nonfluency" or "dysfluency." You may want to call it stuttering or stammering, but these are loaded terms and do not accurately represent what is happening at this stage. What you actually hear is a nonfluency and this happens for normal reasons.

Physical Development

His fine motor skills are developed enough that he can hold small markers for games. He will begin pedaling his tricycle, may enjoy pulling and being pulled in a wagon, and will use playground equipment such as swings and slides. An outdoor sandbox is a great toy and can be used with his cars and toy people to act out play scenes.

Forty-Eight to Sixty Months (4-5 Years)

Language Development

He will be using well over two thousand words by the end of this developmental age. He will be talking in complete paragraphs and you will begin to see that most of his grammatical errors have straightened themselves out. He may still make a few errors in the speech sounds themselves but if he is generally easy to understand by you and others outside your family, you do not need to concern yourself with these few errors. Complete sentences and phrases continue to proliferate.

Physical Development

By the time your child is five, he will be able to walk on a line, hop on one foot for about ten seconds, jump over a rope, and catch a large ball when you bounce it to him.

Sixty to Seventy-Two Months (5-6 Years)

Language Development

By the end of this developmental period, your child may be able to comprehend 13,000 words: five times the amount of receptive language from the year before. He is able to use pronouns consistently, understand opposites, and can answer questions beginning with, "What happens if…?" He is now able to understand time concepts such as before and after, a.m. and p.m., yesterday and tomorrow, now and later, this month and last month, and days of the week. The average length of his expressive language is 6.6 words, and his *syntax* (the ability to put words together in the right order) is more refined than one year ago. He enjoys beginning printing when copying from a model, although letter reversals and inaccuracies in writing abound. A desire to read begins to emerge at this time as well. Your child begins to recognize numbers one through ten, letters of the alphabet, and written words such as his name and other very familiar words like Mom, Dad, cat, dog, up, and go.

In a nutshell, your child at this stage makes the leap from the spoken, signed, or cued word to the written word, and then to reading words. The play activities in this section will give you many, many opportunities to enrich your child's blossoming language skills. Be sure to offer lots of praise and encouragement for effort, and, overall, remember to keep the fun in your child's language-learning toys and games.

Physical Development

By the end of this developmental age, your child's physical abilities, both large and small, are greatly improved from one year ago. His better-developed fine motor skills allow him to grasp a pencil and print with a nice degree of legibility when copying from a model. He can color inside the lines of a picture quite well, and can copy a simple shape accurately. He can also learn to tie his shoes, although he may need a lot more extra practice in these days of Velcro closures. He can also button his own buttons, dress himself, and comb his hair.

Your five-year-old loves to use his large motor skills. He loves to jump and hop longer distances. He loves to run fast, skate fast, bike fast. Speed is a big part of this age. His eye-hand coordination has also greatly improved, and now your child can throw and catch a ball with greater accuracy.

Five-year-olds are interested in learning rules to help organize their play, and they like the idea of being part of a club, group, or team. Belonging to a group outside the family will help foster your child's self esteem. This also explains their newfound interest in participating in team sports such as soccer and tee-ball, either as a player, coach's assistant, or a spectator. Do not expect perfect adherence to rules. Fives like the idea of rules, but have been known to sway from playing by the exact rules when it is to their advantage. Great language learning opportunities arise directly due to this moral conflict. Playing fair, emphasizing teamwork, and cooperation versus competition are key elements necessary to govern the play of five-year-olds.

No time of life is as full of as much development and growth as the period from birth to age six. It is almost magic for parents—including parents of children with developmental delays—to observe as their children grow, change, and learn. But parents of children with a delay in language development need to know what may cause this. The knowledge of language development that you have learned is your foundation for understanding problems that may occur in this area.

Possible Causes of Language Delay in Children

Receptive language, expressive language, and speech evolve in a child who is moving along the developmental milestones in a typical fashion. How does this differ if there are developmental delays of one kind or another? There have been volumes written on this subject and it is not the intent of this book to focus in detail on specific disabilities. However, a variety of developmental disabilities will be discussed that may have an effect on language development, and adapted teaching techniques for individual special needs will be offered.

In reading about each of these disabilities, bear in mind that each child is unique and his abilities are unlike any other child's even if he shares the same generic label of a particular disability. We have seen children with profound mental retardation who were not expected to walk or talk do both under guidance from professionals and parents who believed in their potential. But while we need to keep our expectations high, we should not close our eyes to the obvious. In spite of our greatest efforts, some of our children may never achieve the level that we would like to see for them. Reach for the stars but make them stars you can see, not just hope to see. Rejoice in what your child is able to achieve, in the potential he is able to realize.

Cognitive Delays

The relationship of intelligence to language development is a most complex issue. Once again, it should never be assumed that a "low IQ" is an absolute predictor of language development. Many articles have been written about the accuracy of IQ measurements and there is no clear-cut evidence that an IQ is a very good predictor of anything, especially language development. When we speak of an average IQ, we do not mean that a child with an average IQ should only be expected to acquire average language development. We know that experiences and exposure to interesting and exciting vocabulary, as well as personal motivation, can enhance anyone's language development.

If, however, we are talking about children who have been diagnosed as having specific disorders such as Down syndrome, brain injury, or other conditions that can cause mental challenges, then we know that language development will probably be slower than for children of the same age without these conditions. This does not mean, however, that we stop speaking to this child or stop giving him enriching language experiences. Just the opposite is true: this child needs more language stimulation than other children. Remember that receptive language must come first, and if he has nothing to talk about, it is certain that he will not have expressive language.

The child with mental challenges will acquire language at a slower rate than a child of average or higher intelligence, but in most cases, he *will* acquire language. Remember that language need not be "spoken" to communicate with another individual. He may use a form of sign language, a communication board with pictures, a computer, or other assistive devices to help him express himself. It will be necessary for you to work at the developmental level of your child rather than at his chronological age. When you read the chapters on toys, find a toy that fits with your child's developmental age rather than his chronological age. You will both derive more pleasure from playing this way than if you try to interest him in something that is beyond his abilities.

Physical Disabilities

A child who has severe physical disabilities may be delayed in his language development because so much of his time is spent working with his physical limitations that he simply doesn't have the time to spend enriching his language. He may require many hospitalizations, reducing the amount of time that he is in his own home. This can produce stress for him as well as for you. Neither of you may have much energy left for playing with toys or games. Additionally, he may not have the physical ability to manipulate toys in ways that will facilitate playing. If the physical problems that your child has interfere with the small muscles that are necessary for the production of speech, he may have excellent receptive language and yet be physically unable to produce the sounds necessary for speech. It is at this point that you must find alternative ways of communicating: sign systems, communication boards, computers, and other new technology.

Today's technology allows people who are unable to verbalize to communicate. As discussed in Chapter 12, computers have voice synthesizers as well as the ability to communicate visually with another person. Although speech is the goal for every child, remember that it is only one form of expressive language.

Sensory Deficits

Children who have sensory deficits in the area of vision and hearing are sometimes at a disadvantage in learning language. Visual impairments limit what the child can actually experience for himself but in no way limit the input that an adult can supply to overcome that deficit. It is important to remember also that not all children with visual impairments are totally blind. Many partially sighted children can see bright colors as well as high contrast colors such as black on a white, or, in many cases, white on black background. Colors, though difficult to describe to someone who has never seen them, can be adequately described in terms of how they relate to objects the child knows or can learn about that remain constant. For example, a lemon is yellow, apples are red, and potatoes are brown. Use consistent color references often with your visually impaired child. There is a wonderful book called *Hailstones and Halibut Bones* by Mary O'Neill which uses poetry to describe colors and is appropriate for preschoolers ages 3-5. Using other senses can help children with visual impairments to understand, if not entirely know, the concepts of things they cannot see.

Hearing impairment, on the other hand, almost always produces a deficit in receptive language. Without the ability to hear a spoken language, it is very difficult to build a receptive base of language in the critical language-learning years. Many volumes have been written on the "best" way to convert spoken language into visual language. There is no clear "best" way. You will have to explore to find the best way for your child. To help you make that decision, you may want to consult the book *Choices in Deafness: A Parent's Guide* by Sue Schwartz (published by Woodbine House).

Environment

Your child's language-learning environment is one final factor to consider in unraveling possible causes for language delays.

Studies have compared how children are raised in families with how they are raised in institutions. Looking at families, it is often, but not always, found that firstborn children begin to speak sooner than their siblings. This is probably because parents may have the time for more interaction when they only have one child. Subsequent children may be given less parental time. On the other hand, there are equally as many studies that have shown that children in large families talk early as well because they have many more people to interact with and often learn more from their brothers and sisters than they do from their parents. The key, of course, is that someone must be talking to the child so that receptive language can be built.

By contrast, children who are raised in institutions where there are more children than adults are often delayed in language development. These findings have had a profound impact on modern daycare centers. More and more centers are making it a priority to have low adult-child ratios and to encourage language development among the children through stimulating activities. These studies underscore one important point: It is essential to language development to provide children—particularly children with special needs—with a rich receptive language environment.

The language a child hears in the environment should closely resemble the language that will be used in the school he attends. This has raised questions about bilingual families. Current research shows that children can learn both languages—the native family language and the one he hears in the environment. It is true that these children may have more catching up to do when they enter the school environment than those children who speak the same language as the instructional one. In no circumstances, however, should parents who speak a different language speak no language to their child for fear of him having problems in school. If the child has a rich receptive language background, regardless of the language, he will be more successful than if he has no receptive language at all.

Whatever your child's special needs may be, it is important that you determine the nature of his language delay as early as possible. The earlier you find out how he is delayed, the earlier you can begin to help him catch up. Use the following checklist to help you determine if your child has a problem in his language development.

Recognizing Speech and Language Problems Early

If your child exhibits any of the following fifteen problems, you should consider consulting a speech-language pathologist to evaluate your child's language development.

1. Your child is not talking by the age of two years.
2. His speech is largely unintelligible after the age of three.
3. He is leaving off many beginning consonants after the age of three.
4. He is still not using two- to three-word sentences by the age of three.
5. Sounds are more than a year late in appearing in his speech according to their developmental sequence.
6. He uses mostly vowel sounds in his speech.
7. His word endings are consistently missing after the age of five.
8. His sentence structure is noticeably faulty at the age of five.
9. He is embarrassed and disturbed by his speech.
10. He is noticeably nonfluent after the age of six.
11. He is making speech errors other than /wh/ after the age of seven.
12. His voice is a monotone, too loud, too soft, or of a poor quality that may indicate a hearing loss.
13. His voice quality is too high or too low for his age and sex.
14. He sounds as if he were talking through his nose or as if he has a cold.
15. His speech has abnormal rhythm, rate, and inflection after the age of five.

(Checklist reprinted from: *Teach Your Child to Talk,* by David Pushaw, published by CEBCO Standard Publishing, 104 5th Ave., New York, NY.)

Assessment

If you have been concerned that your child has a delay in language development, you will want to have an assessment done by a trained speech-language pathologist. An assessment is a complete evaluation of the speech and language skills that your child has acquired. His strengths and needs will be determined, which then will be used in planning how to help him.

You should ask your pediatrician if she can recommend someone to do this assessment. If she doesn't know of a speech-language pathologist in your area, contact a national organization such as the American Speech Language Hearing Association (see Resources for Speech and Language Disabilities in the Appendix). This association will be able to give you names of certified speech clinicians in your area. If you are unable to make this contact for any reason, try your local college or university and ask whether they have a department that trains future speech-language pathologists. They will be able to refer you to someone for an evaluation. Additionally, every school system has an early identification program. Call your local school district and ask for the program that helps to identify young children with special needs.

Taking a History

When you come for your child's assessment, the speech-language pathologist will want a complete history of your child's growth up to now. If you have kept baby records, bring them with you to help you remember important milestone events in your child's life. If you have medical information about his special needs, you will want to bring this along with you as well. The more information you can provide about your child, the more the clinician will be able to help you determine where your child might be in his language development.

Testing

Clinicians use a variety of assessment tools and tests to help determine where your child's language development is. Some tests will ask you for information about your child, while others directly ask your child to respond to various questions that will indicate his understanding and expression of language.

Testing Receptive Language. Your child's receptive abilities will be tested by asking him to point out objects or pictures when they are named or to choose between sets of pictures in response to a word or group of words that is presented by the therapist. In one test, for instance, your child will be shown a small doll and will be asked to point to various facial and body parts. "Where is the dolly's nose, eyes, ears, etc.?" His responses will be recorded on a testing sheet that will later be used to determine his language development level. If your child is unable to point to the object because of visual impairment or physical disability, he can be given two or more objects to explore with his hands and then touch or hand you the object requested.

In all of these tests the questions get increasingly more difficult, and your child will begin to be unable to respond. The clinician will keep testing to reach the level where your child is no longer able to respond. This will indicate the upper level of his understanding. It will let the clinician know what level to focus on when working with him later on.

Testing Expressive Language. Almost all of the language tests that are used with young children use objects or pictures to encourage children to respond in certain expected ways. For example, on the Structured Photographic Expressive Language Test (SPELT), your child will be shown pictures of modern everyday situations. He will be asked questions such as "What is the girl wearing?" The expected response is "A dress" or "A red dress." These items are structured so that all the parts of language are tested. Single nouns, plural nouns, possessive nouns, possessive pronouns, and so on are all tested. This and other language tests will give the clinician a good idea of areas where your child might need help and where his strengths are.

Oral Mechanism Exam. The speech clinician will want to check inside your child's mouth. She will want to check the roof of your child's mouth (palate) to see that everything is formed correctly. She will check the size and movement of your child's tongue and see the alignment of his teeth, lips, and jaw. All of these parts of the mouth area are involved in the production of speech. Your child's ability to control drooling will be examined, as well as the tone of the muscles in the mouth area.

Speech Sounds. If your child is talking at all, the clinician will want to systematically check to see which sounds he pronounces correctly and which he has difficulty with. Again, pictures will be used for the stimulus. The pictures will be of objects that show the sound wherever they generally occur in words. For example, for the sound "B" the pictures might be:

beginning: **b**ed

middle: ba**b**y

end: tu**b**

Your child may have some substitutions or omissions of sounds. For example, he may say, "fum" for "thumb" (substituting "f" for "th") or "cah" for "car" (omitting the "r"). The significance of these errors will depend on your child's age.

To ensure a complete picture of your child's language development, be sure to tell the clinician of your child's language experiences at home. Your input is important for a complete assessment.

Immediately after the evaluation of your child, the speech clinician will be able to tell you a few specific things that she noticed. Usually, however, you will need to wait longer for a final and more complete report. Be ready to return to review the findings and to follow through on the suggestions that the clinician will make.

Conclusion

Children with language development delays are still like other children. They go through most, if not all, of the language development stages that all children go through. You may need to spend more effort, however, helping your child achieve language skills.

Understanding language development in children is essential to understanding where your child might have a problem. Knowing what some causes of language delay are can help you understand your own child's particular problem. Finally, an assessment by a speech-language pathologist can identify the type of language delay your child has and help you get to work to overcome that delay. That work is, in reality, play for your child, and understanding how your child will approach that work/play is vital to teaching him language skills. The next chapter explains this fascinating world of child play.

3

Playing and Learning

Why Play Is Important

In our technological society where we are busy trying to cure cancer, land men on Mars, and live in harmony with countries of clashing political viewpoints, can we allow our children to relax, have fun, and play? Of course we can! More than that, we *should* encourage them to play. Why? Because play is important for children—it is a way for them to learn and be creative.

It is through play that children learn about the world around them. While playing, children test ideas, ask questions, and come up with answers. For instance, in playing with nesting blocks, your child learns about size relationships—she learns that smaller blocks fit inside larger ones. She learns cause and effect as she builds her blocks higher and higher until they come crashing down. When her blocks come tumbling down, she can link that to the world of experiences and ideas by using the language we are teaching her.

Play begins in infancy. There are simple games you and your baby play as you interact during feeding time. Your baby sucks on the bottle or breast and if you pull the milk source away, the baby will suck harder, wiggle her toes and fingers, and give you the message that she wants her bottle back. Trading smiles and fake coughs is another early game played between infants and parents. Through these basic games, your baby learns that her actions have an effect on the people around her. She learns early basic ways to control those larger people in her life.

As your baby gains more and more control over her environment, her idea of who she is and what she can accomplish develops in a positive way. She learns self-confidence as she sees that what she does influences what happens to her. She can use this vision of herself as the sturdy foundation from which she can explore what life has to offer. She can try new experiences without being overwhelmed at the prospect of failure. Yes, she will fail sometimes, but sometimes she won't. Without self-confidence, she wouldn't try at all.

The Value of Play

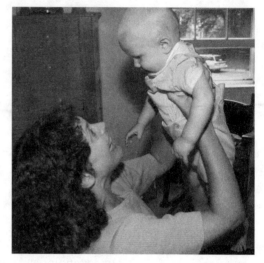

Playtime is more than just "fooling around" time. Playing with toys with your child can help her develop emotionally, physically, socially, and cognitively. Let's look at how you can help her grow in each of these areas through play.

Emotional Development

If your child has a language delay, she may have some frustrations to work out. It is emotionally difficult for children not to be able to adequately communicate their needs. The inability to communicate is hard on any child, but when you add a disabling condition with its special needs, the frustration level can be almost intolerable.

By carefully watching your child play, you will be able to see areas of frustration that she may have. She will give hints by the way she handles her dolls, the actions she has play-people perform, or her reactions to stories you read her. For example, through play your child can work out some of her feelings of anxiety or concern. If, for example, she sees a physical therapist twice a week and these visits cause her discomfort, you might want to structure a play situation with her where the toy "therapist" comes to the house to help the little girl feel stronger in her legs, arms, or wherever the difficulties are. Your child can then work out some of her feelings during this playtime and you can point out what is positive about what the "therapist" is doing.

In a similar way, if your child had a disagreement with a friend a little while ago, you might want to structure a play situation where you help her work out a solution to the problem. This will keep you from interfering when the friend is there, yet give you a way to show your child what to do the next time she is in a similar situation.

You can encourage positive emotional growth in your child when you interact through play. She will see that you are interested in spending time with her and that you respond to her needs. Children need to feel loved and valued in order to grow. The time you spend with her reinforces her vision of herself as a person who is worthy of your time and love.

As your child gets older, she does not lose her emotional need for some control of her world. By playing with your child, you can allow her to have the control in play that she may not be able to have in real life. If we go back to the example of the physical therapist, you can allow your child to have one of her toy people refuse to see the "therapist," whereas in real life she cannot refuse. She will learn that she can control some areas of her life but not others.

Physical Development

Your child may be language delayed, but it is possible that her physical skills are right on target. This will be very encouraging to you as well as to her. She can do things with her hands and feet that perhaps she just is not able to do with language. She will feel confident if you pick up on those physical strengths that she does have and encourage language development around them. For example, you can ask her to shake her rattle. As she does this, you can say, "Good! You are doing a great job of shaking the rattle." You can emphasize specific sounds like "sh" and encourage her to imitate you.

You can stress how well she plays with her toys. You can remind her that she is getting so big that now she can hold the block in one hand. Toys can be a way to give her a sense of pride in what she can accomplish physically.

If your child also has physical limitations, you will want to make sure to use toys that she can handle and to encourage her by making adaptations in the toys. For example, if she has small motor difficulties and loves to play board games, you might want to add Velcro to the board and the bottoms of the markers so that she can easily move her marker along and play the games.

Social Development

The social play of children passes through three stages. At first, the very young child plays alone. She does not like to interact with playmates her own age, although she will interact with you. Gradually, she will move into parallel play and play nicely alongside a friend doing similar kinds of things but not involving each other. In the final stage of social play, the children play together with each contributing something to the play situation. If your child has a language delay, this could be the stage that presents some difficulties for her. By the time children are ready to engage in social play, they need language to communicate ideas. You will then see that you can use your playtime to give her the vocabulary that she will need in order to play with her friends.

Your child learns from you that sharing her toys is a fine way for you to play together and that each of you can take a turn. She learns that when her friends come over it is okay to share with them and wait her turn. These are difficult skills for children to learn, but you can practice with her when you are alone. Through imaginative play, you can play out a situation that your child may need some help understanding. For example, you can re-enact a scene in the park in which another child was not being very nice to your child. You can show your child how to be sensitive to another person's feelings through this kind of pretend play.

Many more children today are exposed to men and women in nontraditional career roles. They will see more women doctors than you did when you were growing up. They will see more men in jobs that previously only women seemed to perform. Your daughter can use toy cars and trucks to play mechanic, while your son is using the play kitchen to fix lunch. Playing with these toys in nontraditional ways encourages your child to accept society's move away from stereotyping. This is another example of the way that toys can represent our world to our children.

Cognitive Development

Swiss educator Jean Piaget identified four stages of cognitive development in children. How does knowing them help you interact with your child and her toys? Your child's ability to think, understand, and eventually reason things out is a dynamic process. With each new toy, game, or experience that you introduce, your child is taking in all the information and knowledge her brain is capable of assimilating depending on her level of development. Although each stage is separate, they are all dependent on each other for success. With the exact same toy, game, or sample dialogue provided in this book, your child can extract from it what she is capable of understanding at any given developmental point in time. Later on she will derive something different from the same toy. As a parent you can help challenge your child's ability to her potential within each stage as well as looking ahead to what comes next.

The first stage of cognitive development is the **sensorimotor stage.** It lasts roughly from birth to two years of age. Your child will be learning about her environment through her muscles and her senses. By watching, hearing, touching, and feeling, she will learn about things around her. You will be giving her language for things that she sees in her daily life such as water, spoon, and ball. She will experience them by touching, seeing, and physically interacting with them.

The second stage, which is the **representational stage,** occurs from approximately two to seven years of age. Your child will begin to be able to represent things by using symbols (pictures, objects, words) instead of the real thing. For example, she can use a play farm and plastic animals to reenact a visit to the farm. It is during this stage that her receptive language will increase rapidly and you will begin to notice a big leap in expressive language at this time as well.

The third stage, the **concrete operations stage,** usually occurs from about age seven to eleven. During this stage, your child is able to think through a situation without having to actually act it out. She is able to see the consequences of her actions and think about what may happen before it actually happens.

The fourth stage, the **formal operations stage,** begins around age eleven. Children who have reached this stage are able to do serious problem solving. They are able to reason with abstract thoughts and do not need to depend on concrete observations.

As a child progresses through these stages of cognitive development, her ability to play will become increasingly sophisticated to the point that it ceases to be merely "play" and begins to resemble concerted problem solving, exploration, and analysis. Let's look at how play with a ball might change through each of these stages.

In the earliest sensorimotor stage, a parent would want to expose her child to the idea that the toy they are playing with is called a ball. "Look, Tyrone, this is a ball. It is round. It is hard. Can you hold it? Can you roll it to Mommy? Look. Mommy can catch the ball. Now Daddy will help you catch it. Let's see if we can throw it way up in the sky."

At such an early stage in infancy, a child might not understand any of the words Mother is saying. However, the child is receiving an invaluable language learning experience. Through Mother's words, Tyrone can begin to understand what the word ball really means— what a ball feels like, how it can be thrown and caught, that it is round and smooth, that it moves apart from his hand when he lets go of it, and that it can land in his lap when someone throws it to him.

In the early preoperational stage, the child would understand the game even better based on his earlier, sensorimotor experiences. Tyrone would now begin to understand that when Mom asks, "Do you want to play ball?," it is a give-and-take, back-and-forth arrangement that involves the two of them playing together. When Mom asks, "Can you roll it?" or "Can you throw it?" or even, "Can you bounce it?" each word means something different and has a different action associated with it.

Finally, an older preoperational child has often developed enough logic to know that after Mom throws the ball into the air and yells, "Heads UP!," he can go scurrying after it, trying to follow its course so that it will fall straight down into his hands. Although Tyrone would understand this once he enters the preoperational stage, at the younger sensorimotor stage he would not have understood that "what goes up must come down." That's why we don't play a hearty game of catch with a nine-month-old still operating at a sensorimotor level. But that doesn't mean we shouldn't play ball with an infant at all. Earlier action experiences and the language a child learns set the stage for more complex actions and later learning.

It is easy to see that to a child—especially a child with special needs—"play" is very important. It helps her express herself, develop a positive image of herself, and learn to interact with the rest of the world. But how can you as her parent involve yourself in her play effectively? The next section discusses using toys to help with language development.

Playing with Toys to Help Develop Language

With toys, we can teach our children about our world and how to live in it. We can teach them how to interact with other people and their environment. And toys can substitute for the world while they are learning how to interact. Playing with toys is particularly important for children who have problems in adjusting to their world.

Since one of the primary goals of play is to teach your child about her world, you need to understand how toys can help her with this goal. When she is young, you represent the world for her. If she can learn to interact with you, she can take those learning experiences with her when she begins interacting with the rest of the world.

Toys Are Interactive

You, the significant adult, are your child's first plaything. She reaches out and touches your body as she nurses. She grabs at your nose or Uncle Sonny's glasses. These could be called her first toys. When she grabs you and you respond with a kiss as you remove her hand, the two of you are interacting. She is learning that what she does can have an effect on you. You begin giving her language for her use of these toys.

> *"Be careful, those are Uncle Sonny's glasses. Let's give them back. You touched Daddy's nose—where is your nose? Ouch, it hurts when you pull Daddy's hair. See how gently I stroke your hair . . . ."*

Because you want to encourage interaction but not at the expense of your nose or glasses, you can substitute toys. You can play with stuffed animals and talk about noses and other facial features. You can hang toys in your child's crib and when she is ready, she can reach out and touch and play with them. The toy will "respond" back as it swings or a small bell rings.

Toys Are Representational

The most significant value of toys may be the way they represent a wider world for your child. Although we encourage you to go on many outings with her to see and experience real-life situations, toys can bring these things into your home. You can use toys to prepare children for experiences that are about to happen and then use the toy again after the experience to reinforce what she saw. Let's use the Fisher Price Farm as an example. You have decided that tomorrow you and your family are going for a ride out to a farm. You can use the Fisher Price Farm to talk about all of the animals, buildings, and people that you *will* see on the farm. At the farm, you can remind her that the cow is the same color as the toy cow at home or that the real horse is certainly much bigger than the toy horse at home. Later, when you have come home from your outing, you can go back to the toy farm and talk about what you *saw*. Did you know that you are also teaching verb tenses?

Children with special needs usually spend a lot of time seeing doctors, therapists, and specialists of one kind or another. They are *very* busy children. We don't want you to become one of those parents who is always pushing her child to do one more task; yet you need to spend time to help her develop her language. You can do this through play. You can pick toys that are both fun and can be used to develop her language. The toys in this book are both amusing and educational. It is easy to capitalize on the natural and pleasurable activities associated with toys to help your child with her language development. Just remember that no child learns well under pressure. If you feel that your child has had enough for one session, quit! You can always play with her another time.

Conclusion

In the next section of the book, you will be taking all the information you have just read and putting it to good use as you try the dialogues that have been written for you. Remember to pick the developmental age that best describes your child, then gather some toys that will work with the dialogues you want to use, and start talking and playing.

4

Toy Dialogs

Maintaining our children's interest in learning is one of our primary jobs in teaching language. We want to send our children off to school well prepared *and* as excited about learning as they were as infants when they loved our first imitation games. Many an educator has said that if we could maintain the enthusiasm that young children have for learning before they come to school, many of our educational problems would be solved. The dialogs in this section have therefore been designed to teach basic language in a variety of interesting ways.

How to "Teach" with the Dialogs

As you read the dialogs, you may wonder why there are so many repetitions of key words and concepts. Did you know that a baby must hear thousands of repetitions of a word before he can produce it? As you play with your baby, most of this talking will come naturally.

Some people don't talk enough to little children and other people talk on and on, never really giving the child a chance to absorb what is being said. As you speak with your child in the short little sentences described in the dialogs, you will want to pause ever so slightly between sentences so that he will have the chance to take in what you are saying and then to respond. If you keep talking on and on, he will only be processing a jumble of meaningless words.

As your child gets older, you can increase the length and complexity of your sentences, but still make sure you give him enough time to understand what you are saying. It just takes a little extra time and patience to learn to talk this way to a young child. Realize that the brief phrases I suggest in the toy dialogs are only examples of what you could say to pull language from any given toy. Feel free to substitute other similar words or ideas that feel comfortable for you.

Children, particularly children with language delays, will benefit more from toy play carried out in a repetitive fashion. It may take days, or even weeks, for a child to grasp the concepts of *up* and *down* or *back* and *forth*. Repetition is not boring for your child and can be of tremendous benefit for your child's learning.

A number of *single concept* dialogs have been included in each developmental age grouping. These focus on one idea at a time and give you the repetition you need to work with your child, stressing just that one idea. The single concept dialogs are of special help to children who may need intensive emphasis in one area.

There are ways to vary the repetition necessary to teach your child. When you are working on the concepts of *back* and *forth*, vary the type and size of the ball. Change the location. With this type of varied repetition you and your child will have the advantage of new play activities within the structure he needs in order to learn.

If you want to make playtime something your child will look forward to, then you need to be very careful about how you interact with him when the two of you are playing. If your child's tower falls because he has put too many blocks on it, try to be positive instead of giving him negative criticism. Toy play should have the same goals as other interactions with your child—the goal of helping your child develop a good self-image. "Josh, this time you built the tower higher. Isn't it fun to watch all the blocks tumble down when it gets too high?"

Another way to make sure that your child looks forward to his playtime with you is to instill in him the joy of learning. This really isn't very hard to do because children are born curious and eager to learn—if the learning is fun. It's up to us to make sure it is. If you sit down with your child and say "OK, Josh, today we are going to talk about colors. There are three primary colors. Now repeat after me…" Josh will probably be halfway out of the room before you finish the sentence. The toy dialogs are specifically designed to avoid that regimented teaching style. When you use the dialogs, put some enthusiasm into your voice; move around and use gestures. If your child sees that you are having a good time, he will enjoy himself more and find learning fun.

Focus on one toy at a time. Imagine doing a special type of crossword puzzle designed so that all the clues must be examined simultaneously. It would be impossible. This is how your child would feel if you overwhelmed him with a variety of toys and activities all at the same time.

When your child is very young—say, under two—you should have as much of your language playtime as you can with him in a highchair. A highchair is handy because there is a tray to put toys on and the children are at eye level with us. Additionally, this helps your child focus on one toy at a time so that he doesn't become distracted by other toys around him. If you can, you might want to have two highchairs in different rooms so that one is associated with eating and the other with playing. If you have only one, that's okay. Some people also like to use the Sassy Seats™ that attach to the table. These are fine.

Also make sure that you spend time on the floor with your child. That is the natural play environment for a child and you can get down to his level with him. This is particularly important for some of the toys that are discussed further along in this book. The key is to be at your child's eye level. That way, he is getting additional cues about language from your face. This is particularly important for a deaf or hard of hearing child.

As your child's receptive and expressive skills continue to improve, use the actual names of things as much as possible rather than generic terms such as "cars." Talk about station wagons, convertibles, vans, or campers. With repetition and developmental maturation, your child will learn to *generalize*. He'll learn that each of these vehicles, for example, fit under the broader category of "cars."

The richer the language that you put in, the richer the language your child will use later on. It is not necessary that he have perfect or even intelligible speech to use rich and powerful language. With the increasing use of computers today, even the most severely disabled child can communicate his thoughts. With a computer he can use a head stick as a pointer, eye gaze, and voice commands. We will talk more about computers later on.

Try to play for a few short periods of time each day to try out the dialogs. A good time is right after a nap or after snack time when your child is refreshed. Begin with five- or ten-minute sessions and gradually increase the amount of time as your child is able to handle it.

While playing with your child, there will be many times when you will want to "test" his comprehension by asking him to hand you various objects or name them for you. You know your child and you will know when he has had enough. Even though we are talking about playtime as "teaching" time, it still must be fun and your child must think of it as *play* or he will not stay interested for very long.

Special Considerations

There are a few things to keep in mind for children with different special needs. If your child is deaf or hard of hearing, keep the toy near your mouth so that he can see your lips as you speak to him about the toys. If he has visual impairments, have him hold the toy with you while you describe it and move his hands to each part as you talk to him about it. Add Velcro and other textures to different parts of the toy so he can begin to associate that texture with that particular part. If your child is physically not capable of holding a toy on his own, hold it with him as you describe it to him. Present challenging opportunities to improve motor coordination at the same time you are choosing toys that are set into action with easy-to-press switches, buttons, and dials.

If your child's speech muscles are impaired, or if he has a disability such as Down syndrome that is associated with significant speech delays, you may want to teach him sign language. This will give him a way of expressing his needs and wants to you. Your speech-language pathologist, audiologist, or pediatrician can direct you to an introductory sign language course. There are also CD-ROMs and videos that can help you learn sign language. You may also want to begin teaching him to point to items on a communication board. Another way of having him demonstrate to you that he understands what you are asking is to have an "eye gaze frame" so he can simply shift his eyes to indicate the object or picture of an object that you are referring to. (See photograph below.)

An eye gaze frame can be made with simple materials obtained at a hardware store. Buy three lengths of PVC pipe about 12 to18 inches long. Then purchase two elbow connectors and two round pipe connectors that fit the size of pipe that you bought. Buy or make two blocks of wood about 3" by 5". Hot glue two round pipe connectors to the wood base. Fit the three pieces of pipe together with the elbow connectors and then fit the entire structure to the connectors on the wood base. Purchase stickyback Velcro strips and cover the piece of pipe running horizontally between the two uprights with the fuzzy part of the Velcro. (Instructions provided by the Center for Technology in Education.)

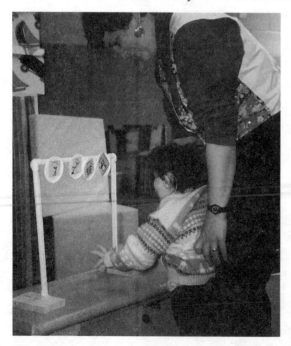

To use this eye gaze frame with your child, you can put Velcro on pictures or small objects and attach them to the Velcro-covered pipe. At first you may want to put only two objects or pictures on it at opposite ends so the child is very definite in his eye gaze as to which object or picture he wants.

These types of nonverbal communication will still help your child build language skills. More importantly, they will help him to communicate with you. Be assured that learning a nonverbal system first will not inhibit the later development of speech.

Summary of Teaching Techniques for Any Child with a Language Delay

1. **Start with simple words and phrases**—A strong receptive language base must be built first as a foundation for expressive language which emerges later.
2. **Use actual names of things when teaching language**—Say "bottle" not "ba-ba."
3. **Using varied repetition of key words and single concepts is crucial**—This is one of the best ways to pour in all of that extra language that is necessary for learning and is a great tool to aid memory.
4. **Speak in short sentences**—Increase sentence length and complexity of meaning as you see your child's language skills improve.
5. **Pause between phrases**—This allows your child to process the meaning of each word in the phrase.
6. **Focus on one toy or activity at a time to prevent distraction**—Keep other toys out of sight and keep background noise and activities to a minimum.
7. **Play with your child at his eye level**—Sit your child in a highchair or at a table or sit or lie down on the floor when playing with your child and his toys.
8. **Play for a few short periods of time**—Five to ten minutes a few times a day. Increase length and frequency of sessions as your child's attention span increases over time.
9. **Know when it is the best time for instructive play**—After naptimes or mornings are the times when children are generally the most refreshed and eager to interact with you.
10. **Know when to end play sessions**—If your child grows restless, stops paying attention, or becomes fatigued, it is time to take a break.
11. **Offer praise and encouragement**—Children love verbal and physical rewards. Saying "Great job!" or giving a big hug works wonders.
12. **Most important: Keep the fun in learning! Be enthusiastic!**

Behavior Management

Behavior management is a major issue for all children but especially if you have a child who is developmentally delayed in any way. You may feel that your child has enough to handle without making his life more difficult with a lot of rules. If you look further down the road toward raising a responsible and independent young adult, however, you will realize that catering to his every whim will not help him in the long run. We encourage you to establish consistent guidelines for his behavior and to expect him to abide by them.

During this time, one of your most important roles as a parent will be to teach your child how to behave properly. I've heard parents say how much easier it is just to let their three-year-old walk out of the grocery store with the small package of candy he's picked up off the shelf than to have a big discipline scene in public. Similarly, it is easier to buy two of every toy for your two children to prevent fighting than it is to teach them to share. I agree wholeheartedly that it is not always pleasant or fun to teach discipline to young children. In many instances, it would almost be easier to become invisible and let your child carry on with his antics until he finds a way to resolve things himself.

The fact is, children do not like it either when they misbehave, particularly if their parents value and encourage good behavior. It's a frightening feeling for them to be out of control and they need you to set limits for them when they are upset. Believe it or not, deep down inside, your child wants to be the sweet little angel that you know he can be. If you praise your child as many times for good behavior as you scold him for bad behavior, he will try his hardest to be good. Everyone likes praise.

When he does misbehave, there are many disciplinary methods that work. If you have found one or two that work for you, then simply stick with them. Many parents of three-year-olds, however, are still groping for suitable ways to manage misbehavior. We offer a couple of specific techniques for you here.

One key to good discipline is consistency. This is true for all children, but especially true for children with special needs. If your child has a condition that hampers his understanding, you may have to go over concepts many times before he has a clear understanding of what you mean.

Be firm and clear about which behavior you expect and be as gentle as you can. "Karen, do not grab that toy from Sarah. If you do this again, you may not play together."

If she does grab the toy again, you must stick with what you said and remove her from the play area. She can sit in your designated *time out* area until you feel she is ready to rejoin the other children. Repeat this technique again and again until you feel she understands the situation.

The theory behind the time out method of behavior management is that a child is disciplined when he cannot demonstrate pro-social behavior. Specifically, children must be taught that it is a privilege to participate within a group. The inherent reward for behaving in a pro-social way is being able to stay in the group and play. If the child cannot play nicely in the group, even after one or two verbal reminders, then the adult must ask the child to sit outside the group. Children should feel permitted to re-enter the group again whenever they feel they can act nicely. If you are alone with your child, the same theory applies and he must sit in his special time out spot until he feels that he is ready to be cooperative again.

Another technique is called the *wait technique*. Here's how it works: Let's say that Karen is playing with her friend Rachel. Karen looks over and sees Rachel playing with a Barbie Doll. Of course this looks like more fun than the book that she has been reading. She grabs the Barbie Doll and as they fight over the doll, she hits Rachel. It's time for you to step in. Karen needs to hear the cardinal rule: "There will be no hitting." Under no circumstances should you, the parent, come in and hit your child for hitting the other child! Firmly and gently state the rule, "no hitting," and insist that your child not play until she returns the doll. You can say, "Karen, I'll wait until you're ready." Once she returns the doll you can then help the two youngsters with the notion of taking turns or trading toys so that each gets a chance to play with the doll.

Social Skills

Many parents of children with special needs feel that neighborhood kids don't want to include their child. One way that you can help bridge that gap is to invite the children to your house and for you to involve yourself some of the time in the play. This way, you can help smooth the road if language gaps get in the way. In these situations, a good rule of thumb is that the maximum number of children who can comfortably play together should equal your child's age in years. For a three-year-old—two playmates, which would be three in total.

I encourage you to start your child in some kind of organized play group or nursery school. This is not to promote the concept of what David Elkind warns against called the overly programmed "hurried child." Instead, it is to expose your child to larger social situations than he would normally be involved in at home. For the language delayed child, play groups and nursery schools are excellent learning situations because the children they come in contact with can provide good speech and language models. You must be cautious, however, not to place your child in an environment where he has no possibility of being involved. If his impairments are so severe that he cannot interact in any way with this group of children, then he will only experience frustration and your expectations will not be met as well. Be cautious and realistic when you look for a peer group with whom he can interact.

Toy Selection

Just about anything can be a toy! Cardboard boxes, leftover ribbon, spoons—almost anything you can think of. In putting together this list, however, several important factors were considered.

The first consideration in selecting toys was safety. Each of the toys that is suggested for a particular developmental age is safe and has been approved by the United States Consumer Product Safety Commission. Secondly, I looked for toys that lent themselves well to parent-child dialogs that were rich in vocabulary and concepts. Finally, I considered how easily available the toys would be to consumers around the country.

The toys recommended are divided into developmental age categories. Once again, these categories are not absolutes. Many of these toys fit into several age groups and can be enjoyed by children beyond the ages mentioned here. Children will often use an "old" toy in new and creative ways as their world enlarges and their imaginations develop. In general, the lower age limit is the age where your child can begin to physically and mentally handle the toy, but the upper limits have no bounds.

Each toy has been selected so that you can interact with your child for the purpose of encouraging and developing expansive and exciting language. This does not mean that your child should not play with toys alone. He will need time to practice the language skills you have taught him. He may also find new ways to play with the toys that he can show you the next time you play together.

When you first use a toy to "teach" language, it's a good idea not to leave it around to be routinely played with. If you do this, your child may lose interest in your "teaching" activities sooner. Put the toy safely in a toy chest or on a shelf.

A word here about toy shelves and toy boxes. Shelves are recommended for two reasons. One is a safety factor. Often toy boxes have hinged tops, which can close on a child who has crawled inside. Or the lid can slam shut accidentally and perhaps injure your child's head or fingers. The second reason is that toys become lost in a toy box. The ones on the bottom are never seen again as they become buried under layers of other toys. Additionally, they do not have an orderly appearance when they are thrown into a box. A toy shelf that is sturdy and not very tall is encouraged. Your child should be able to reach the shelves himself and not have it topple over on him. The toys should fit easily on the shelves and there shouldn't be room for too many. This way, you can have a few toys accessible and keep the others packed away. If you rotate the toys that are on the shelf, your child will maintain his interest in them for a longer period of time.

Homemade Toys

At least two homemade toys have been included in each developmental age group. These tested, easy-to-make toys will provide your child with great language learning opportunities. Often, they are more fun and interesting to play with than many store-bought toys. They can also be less expensive!

Homemade toys give you the opportunity to create and adapt toys to meet your child's own personal needs and preferences. For instance, your child may have a visual impairment in addition to a language delay. You can meet his special needs by printing letters and pictures in extra large, extra bold type (computers are very helpful here) or adding texture to them. Additionally, you will want to simplify the picture by eliminating extra pieces of information like the background. You can cut out one object from the photo or the picture instead of using the whole thing.

Conclusion

Hopefully, you will enjoy using the toy dialogs presented in this book and you will try out the language experiences suggested. Remember, the toys, dialogs, and techniques you will be using are like the ones professional teachers and therapists use. You will find that as you use the dialogs, you will come up with some new ideas of your own that you can expand on from here. Enjoy your play with your child. This is a precious time of sharing experiences and of helping your child grow.

5

Toy Dialogs for the First Year

Birth to Three Months

During your baby's first three months, many new things will be happening. Your whole lifestyle will undergo a change. Your sleeping patterns will change and you may find that you are exhausted. Therefore you should sleep when your baby sleeps and play when she is awake. Save the housecleaning and other chores for another time. Believe it or not, the dirt will still be there waiting for you! Try to avoid getting overtired. You need rest so that you can be available to your baby when she needs you.

If you have learned that there is some delaying condition in your newborn, you will especially need this time for your own rest and care. The emotions associated with this discovery can be very exhausting. You may need to add visits to the doctor or special therapists to your daily routine. Try to add in time for yourself too.

Once you are no longer feeling quite so overwhelmed, you will be better able to concentrate on information that will help you optimize your newborn's early development. Researchers have spent a lot of time with young babies, studying how they learn and develop. For now, we will just summarize research about what the newborn is most interested in focusing on. First of all, you should remember that for the first three to six weeks, the optimal focusing distance for your baby is from seven to nine inches from her face and slightly to the right. Babies look to the right more than 90 percent of the time. Some studies have found that the newborn is most interested in bright primary colors such as red, blue, and yellow. More recent research has found that young infants focus best on objects that are black and white. Try them both and see which your baby likes the best.

• • • • • • • • • • • •

Mobile A mobile over your infant's crib gives the newborn something to focus on at a time when she is trying to drift off to sleep. Since infants are put to sleep on their backs, they are able to look up and see the mobile.

One of the newer mobiles is the Symphony in Motion™ by Tiny Love. It features a frog, a monkey, and a bird. In addition, there are shapes that spin and drop in different patterns. This mobile keeps your infant's attention for a long time. It plays 15 minutes of Mozart, Bach, and Beethoven as well.

"Hi, Geena. Watch your mobile. See how the monkey spins around. Where's the frog? There he is! Watch for the bird. Do you see it? Follow the bird. Down it goes. Here comes the monkey again. See it? Time to go to sleep now. Listen to the pretty music. Mommy will see you soon."

Notice that your sentences are short with long pauses in between to let the baby focus on what you are saying. You are not trying to teach specific vocabulary at this point but just to show her that what she is looking at has words associated with it and more importantly that you are interacting with her.

• • • • • • • • • • • •

Stuffed Animal: Octopus™
by Battat

Although your baby is much too young to be left alone with a stuffed animal, you can still play with one with her. While she is comfortable in a bouncy seat or on a blanket on the floor, you can talk about this toy. The octopus has facial features which usually interest very young babies and it has eight long dangly legs that will fascinate her as they flop around gathering her attention. She will be looking directly at you as you say,

"Look, Samantha. Look at the funny octopus. Do you see his eyes? His eyes do not look like yours. You have pretty blue eyes. Let's see... where is his mouth? You have a cute little mouth too. You are like the octopus in a lot of ways. But you do not have eight legs! Oh, no, you have two cute chubby little legs."

In this way you are talking a lot about body parts. Of course, we do not expect her to know what we are saying but the lilt and smoothness of our conversation will appeal to her. Lean over and be close to her as you are talking.

Safety note: Do not leave the octopus with her if you go away. One of the dangers is that she could move closer to it and not be able to move her head to get away from it and might have trouble breathing.

Discovery Circle™
by Small World Toys

You are always looking for a safe place to put your baby down when needed. Discovery Circle™ is an ideal place for a newborn to be. On one side of the enclosed circle are black and red features which babies love to look at. When she gets a little bit older, she will enjoy the other

side that has nursery rhyme characters on it and you can say the rhymes to her. She will enjoy listening to the rhythm of your voice. On the black and red side is a mirror in one of the spaces. Babies love to look at themselves.

At this age, they cannot differentiate themselves from the baby in the mirror but they enjoy watching nonetheless. You can talk about her facial features and reintroduce the language that you used when you were playing with the octopus mentioned above.

"I'm going to put you down on this nice soft circle. Look over here. There is a mirror. Can you see the baby in the mirror? That is you! See your cute little nose [touch baby's nose]? I see your little mouth [touch baby's mouth]. Where are your eyes? I see them right here [gently touch baby's eyes]."

Picture This Crib Bumper™
by Discovery Toys

Sometime during these very early months, your baby will lie awake in her crib looking around and discovering new things in her environment. This crib bumper can be used not only in the crib but also for floor time play with Mom, Dad, or any other caregiver. At this age, your baby is absorbing language. You don't expect a response from her except maybe a smile and an inquisitive look as you talk to her about this toy.

This crib bumper gives you textures and pictures to talk about and explore. On one side of the bumper are different panels with

different textures on each. The textures are satin, terry cloth, wool, corduroy, a raised bumpy pattern, and velour. You and your baby can explore these textures together. She loves to feel the different ones and absorb those feelings into her brain. If your child has a visual impairment, you will want to describe these patterns to her as she feels them with her hand. This is very early exposure but important.

On the other side of the bumper are panels with cards with interesting patterns on them. You can also insert your own pictures in the slots so that you can talk about baby's family with real pictures of them. One of the cards has a black and white picture of a face. Babies love to look at faces—yours is, of course, the most appealing. You can talk about this face as your baby stares at it.

"Look at this face. It looks like a girl just like you. Here are her eyes and here are your eyes. She has a nose just like you. Here is your nose. And she has a mouth with a big smile. Can you show Momma a big smile [around 6-8 weeks]? Where are her ears? Oh, I see her ears and where are your ears? Right there. I can touch your ears. And here is her hair. Her hair is short. You have black hair."

After a few weeks substitute some of the cards with pictures of your family. Don't forget the pets. They often get more attentive stares than the family members. Be sure to name each family member. Remember you are putting language **into** your infant. You do not expect language **out of** your infant at this age. However, it all builds into her language that she will begin to use around 14 or 15 months of age.

This crib bumper can also fold into a book which can be read at laptime or bedtime or whenever the mood strikes you both. Enjoy.

Homemade Toys

Texture Blanket

This homemade toy has been featured in each of the previous *Language of Toys* books. It is such a classic that it is repeated here for you.

For a homemade toy for this age group, we suggest that you make a texture blanket. Often we put a blanket down for our baby to lie on to protect her from dirt, dog hairs, or small particles embedded in the carpet. You can protect her with your homemade texture blanket and stimulate her at the same time. If you don't know how to sew or don't have a sewing machine, why not suggest this to one of your friends to make for you as a gift?

To make this blanket, visit the local fabric store and look through their remnant basket. Choose a variety of different textures. You should only need one-fourth to one-half yard of each fabric you want to use. I suggest that you not use wool for this project. Although the texture of wool is wonderful, it is possible that your infant could be allergic to it. Also, you will want to be able to wash the blanket frequently and you cannot always wash wool.

Take your materials home, wash each of the fabrics, cut them to the shapes that you want, and sew them together. You will enjoy putting your baby on this blanket and allowing her to experience each of these textures. When you have playtime, lie down with her and talk about each of the different materials that you used. What a treasure for you to keep for your infant as she gets older and can understand that this was made just for her.

> *"Oh, would you like to lie down on this nice blanket? Look over here. This is a nice soft blue piece of fabric [take her hand]. Can you feel how soft it is? It feels so nice and furry. Ooooh, soft! Look at this red part over here. This is corduroy and it feels bumpy. Can you feel how bumpy it is? . . ."*

Continue with each of the textures that appear on the blanket. Choose words that accurately describe the feel of the material. Don't be afraid to use the actual names of the fabrics when introducing the various textures to your child. Remember, she needs to acquire language receptively before she can expressively communicate back to you. When you label the corduroy "rough" as opposed to the satin "smooth," your child gains an understanding of these words as she feels the textures. This kind of sensory impression will help her understand the concept and remember it the next time you use the words "rough" and "smooth."

Make Your Own Mobile

What you will need is some string, some colored paper, and some juice lids. Collect about four juice lids. Clean and dry them. Then attach different colors of construction paper to them: one color to each lid. Glue a short length of string to each lid then attach them to the longer string. Tie the longer string to each side of the crib so that the lids dangle over the crib. Talk about the colors as your infant gazes at them. Obviously you are not teaching color names at this time but merely providing some language stimulation to your baby.

> "Look, Jack! Do you see the different colors hanging here? I see a red circle and look over there; there is a blue circle. Can you see the red circle? It is a bright color. Wow, look at all the different colors here! Daddy's going to touch the yellow circle. See it move as I touch it."

Safety note: Do not leave your infant alone in the crib with this toy. It is suggested at this age because your infant cannot reach the toy but you never can be sure so never leave your infant alone. Be sure and take the toy down before you leave your infant's room.

Three to Six Months

By the time your infant is three months old, you may be into an established routine. You will be feeling better after the adjustment in your schedule. You will have longer periods of sleep at night, and, in fact, your infant may be sleeping through the night.

She will be more alert and interested in playing with you during these three months of her early life than when she was a newborn. You can continue with some of the activities that we have already talked about and add the new ideas in this section.

Although your baby may not be quite ready to imitate you at this time, it is fun to imitate her. If she starts cooing, try to say back exactly what she says. You may be surprised to see that she'll wait for you to make your silly sound and then she'll make hers. This is the very beginning of imitation and turn taking and is a fun way to spend diaper changing time. It is also a good way to teach language since imitation is the way that we learn language. Therefore, the more that you and your child can play these babbling imitating games, the more practice she will have making the sounds of our language.

It's important that she have time alone to play around with different sound combinations. It is also important that she have you around some of the time to reinforce those sounds and to play babbling games with her. When you reinforce her "talking," she learns that she is communicating with you. It's up to you to provide the correct model for the word that she is saying. If you imitate back to her, she will enjoy beginning to play an imitating game with you. It is a good idea for you to reinforce her accidental combinations of sounds that sound like real words. This gives her a sense of competence in communicating something to you. Remember, she really doesn't know exactly what she is saying nor does she attach real meaning to your words.

Let's look at an example of how your reinforcement of her accidental combinations of sounds might happen. She's babbling away and accidentally latches onto the vocal combination of "mamamamama." You will want to jump right in with "You're right, little one, here's mama. Mama. I'm your mama." She may look at you quizzically and respond back with "tata." But rest assured, you have done your part. Each time she gets reinforced for saying a new combination that is meaningful, you will encourage her to vocalize more and more. She is just playing with sounds, but she is aware when she's listening to what you are saying.

Ocean Wonders™
by Fisher-Price

This crib toy is a wonderful way to lull your baby to sleep. It has two brightly colored fish, a clam, and a starfish in a background of bubbling water. Nothing is more soothing than the sound of bubbling water and the soft lights that are in this toy. When your baby is older,

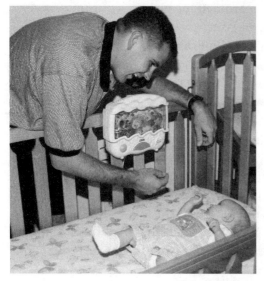

she can press a lever to make the starfish spin and activate a roller ball to make the clam open and shut. There are three lullabies that play when it is switched on.

"Oh, Anna, look at the beautiful fish swimming around. Do you hear the bubbles? Let's see where the starfish is. Oh, I see it, there it is under the seaweed. Watch the clam. Daddy will make it open and close. See, did you see the clam open and close his shell? Listen to the music. It is very soft and sweet, just like you. This is lovely music for you to go to sleep with. You sleep now, and Daddy will see you later."

This toy will last long into toddler stages as young children love to fall asleep to music. Don't be surprised if your toddler asks you to turn on the music well into her twos and threes.

Wrist Rattle™ Assortment
by Learning Curve

Your baby may be just starting to notice her hands as they wave about her. You can help her focus on her hands by attaching two of these wrist rattles to her wrists. As she waves her hands around, she can also hear the wrist rattles make noise. This will help her to focus.

"Listen, Kyle, do you hear the rattle making noise? Why, look! They are on your wrists. See where your hands are waving around? You have two hands. Watch: one—two. Let's shake your hand over this way. Do you see your hands over here?"

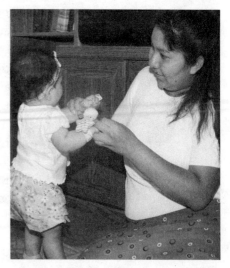

Safety note: Do not leave these wrist rattles on your baby when she is alone. She could manage to get them off and they could be a choking hazard. Always stay with your baby while you are playing with these rattles.

Sparkling Symphony Gym™ by Fisher-Price

This toy is just right for your baby at three to six months and will carry over to the "just standing up" age because you can tilt the board upwards for a standing child or down for the baby reclining on her blanket on the floor. When your baby kicks her feet and touches the toys that are hanging down, it activates the music and lights and teaches your child the first concept of cause and effect. When she kicks, music plays. This will teach her to keep kicking to get the satisfaction of the music. When she is standing, she can press each of the colored keys and make the music herself. Some language that you can use with your infant at this time is:

Single Concept

*"Let's see if we can make the music go on. Let me lift your legs and touch the toys. Oh, listen, you made the music go on. Can you **kick** some more? You are using your legs to **kick! Kick** the toys. Good job. **Kick** some more. Look at the pretty colors that light up when you **kick.** There's red and green and yellow, too. You like to **kick.** You can make the music play."*

Kick and Learn Piano™ by Fisher-Price

This is a crib toy that allows your baby to continue moving her legs and learning to kick and make something happen. Remember we talked about varied repetition. This is a toy that you can use to reinforce the language introduced in the toy above. There are three modes that you can control with a switch on the front of the toy. The first plays continuous music and as your child kicks and touches the toy, it plays a song.

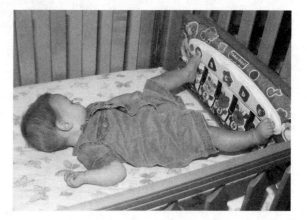

The letters at the top of the Kick and Learn Piano light up as the music plays. In the second mode, when your child kicks each animal, the toy says, "A is for ape," plays a little melody, and makes the sound that the animal makes. The other letters are B is for Bear, C is for cat, D is for dog, and E is for elephant. Each animal has a number on it so this gives you another opportunity for language input. Remember that you are not expecting your baby to learn these letters or the names of the animals but to take the language in and store it in her memory bank when the time comes that she is trying to talk.

This toy ties onto the crib so you can leave it in the crib even when you are not there. It is safe for your baby to be alone with this Kick and Learn Piano.

A dialog for this toy might be:

"I see you kicking and I hear the toy is playing music. Let me see. You kicked the ape and the letter A lit up. A is for ape. Now I see you kicking the elephant and the letter E lit up. E is for elephant. Why don't you kick and we can listen to some music? I like the music you are making while you are kicking. You are a strong little girl."

Sunshine Symphony™
by Neurosmith

This is another music-making toy that will teach your baby cause and effect. A simple touch anywhere on the face of the sun will make the music start to play. If you want to use it as a bedtime soother, you can put it in the play mode and it will play continuous music.

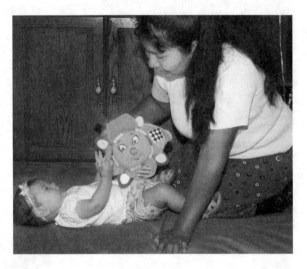

"Oh, Danielle, look at the beautiful shiny sun face. Can you make the music play? Touch his face right here. Listen, you made the music play. Wonderful music. Shall I hum along to the music playing? It is so pretty."

 Safety note: Make sure you take the toy out of the crib when your child falls asleep. She could roll over on it and not be able to breathe.

Homemade Toys

Flashlight Fun

Your baby will be able to track with her eyes in the earlier months so this will be an easy game for her to play at this time. Just use a flashlight that you have around the house—the one left over from the last blackout!! Turn off the lights in your baby's room and show her the light from the flashlight.

"Watch, Jill. Do you see the light? Oh, the light is on the ceiling! Where is it now? The light is on the wall. Watch carefully. Where is the light now? I see it. The light is on the ceiling. Follow the light with your eyes. Let's see where the light will be next. There it is—on the wall."

Safety note: Do not shine the light in your baby's eyes. Always keep the light directed away from her.

Tummy Time

Since babies should be put to sleep on their backs to avoid the danger of Sudden Infant Death Syndrome, you need to make sure your child gets some tummy time. Take out one of your rolls of paper towels and gently place her so that the roll is under her chest. Make sure you are right there all the time, as she could easily roll right off. Rock her gently back and forth and watch as she tries to keep her head up. This is good exercise for your young baby. Your touch on her back will keep her reassured as she tries this new game.

"Leah, I have a new game for us to play. I will hold you on this roll. I am watching you. I am rocking you back and forth. You are on your tummy. Oh, you keep your head up so nicely. Rock and rock. Back and forth. I am holding you tight. Time to get down? Okay. Nice job, Leah. We will try that again later."

Six to Nine Months

At this developmental age, your baby is able to do more and more things that she could not do before. If she has no physical limitations, she will be able to sit alone for long periods of time, which will give her a whole new perspective on the world and also make it easier for her to play with you. She is able to pick up and hold objects, which will allow her to be more involved in playing with you. You will begin to see more play that involves both of you, including times when she will initiate the fun.

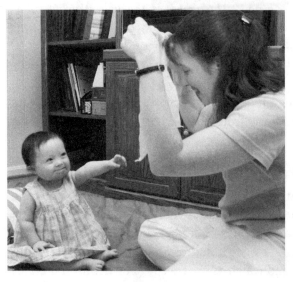

During this age span, your baby should be able to sit in a highchair comfortably. If she has physical limitations, she may be able to sit in a specially constructed chair with support. On the floor you might get a baby-sized swim ring and seat her in the middle. This will give her support all around yet allow her hands to be free to interact with you.

A word is in order here about "baby talk." It is my opinion that baby talk on the part of the baby is cute, but on the part of the parents, unnecessary. It is cute when a one- year-old asks for her "baba," but when the same child does this at age five, it is less appealing. When your baby asks for her "baba," you can respond with, "Sure, I'll get your bottle." You are telling her that you understand her communication but this is what the word really sounds like. If you start doing this now, you will have less correcting to do when she is older.

While your child is beginning to communicate with you by crying and cooing, keep in mind that she is also on the receiving end of the communication. Talk to her about your everyday activities and things you are doing with and for her. "Hmm, looks like you need your diaper changed. Shall we go and get you a clean one? Okay, off we go." Remember, receptive language must come before expressive language. She'll enjoy hearing your voice and begin to understand what you are saying months before she will be able to say any intelligible words.

Soft Cubes™
by Battat

Blocks are very versatile toys, and your baby can enjoy block play at different levels for many years. She can begin playing with them now and continue into her early school years, when she will build elabo-

rate roads and structures which will be the basis for a lot of her imaginative play for many years.

At this developmental age, your baby will be able to stack two or three blocks on top of each other. You will be able to teach the concepts of up and down with blocks, and we give you examples of dialogs for each concept.

Two sets of blocks are going to be discussed in this age group. Each of the sets can be used for teaching different language. The first is a set of six blocks that come in a plastic carrying case. The red block has the following language: a bear, a jacket, a sheep, an apple, the number 2, and the letter B. The green block has: a watermelon, a cow, a car, a ball, the number 3, and the letter C. The purple block has: a bunch of grapes, crayons, a sock, a cat, the number 5, and the letter E. The blue block has: a strawberry, a boat, a pair of pants, a dog, the number 6, and the letter F. The orange block has: an orange, a pacifier, a shoe, a chicken, the number 4, and the letter D. The yellow block has: a horse, some bananas, a bottle, an airplane, the number 1, and the letter A. Each of the pictures on the blocks are raised, so if your child has a visual impairment, you can help her feel and learn the different feel of each side of the block. Try not to overwhelm her by showing her too many new things at once. There is just so much rich language for you to share with your child. Two different ideas are discussed here and you can take it from there and be creative with this wonderful set of blocks.

Single Concepts

Now for introducing the concept of **up.** Take the blocks and show her how you can stack one on top of the other.

> *"Here's one block. Now I can put one **up** on top. See it go **up** on top. Here's another one—**up** it goes. Can we do one more? **up-up-up-up** on top. See, we made the block go **up**."*

This toy also lends itself to teaching the concept **down.** We suggest that you do not introduce this concept at the same play session that you introduce **up.** Otherwise, your child may be confused by the two concepts.

> *"Do you want to make the blocks fall **down**? It's fun when they all crash **down** to the ground. First let's make a tall tower. Let's make it as high as we can. Great—now let's knock it **down**."*

[Gently take your child's hand and knock down the tower.]

> *"Here they come **down**. Wow—they all fell **down**."*

As you stack the blocks, you can take the new one, start at the bottom of the stack, and say "up-up-up" as you pass each block that you have already put down.

The most exciting part of this game for your baby is when they all tumble down. She thinks that is great fun and you will hear her chortling with glee. This kind of fun will carry over to the times when she builds her own structures and watches them tumble down. She will remember from her infant days that tumbling down is half of the fun.

Now let's talk about some different vocabulary possibilities here. Remember that you are adding to her language bank at this time. You are not expecting her to say any of these words or to be able to point them out. Resist the desire to say, "Show me the_____." She is much too young for this kind of activity. Rather use the following language:

> *"Let's play with your blocks for a while. I can take them all out of the case. Here is the red one, now blue. Here's the yellow block and the green one. What's left? Oh, there is purple and green. Yay, now we have all of the colors out of the bag. I see a dog. The dog is on the blue block. Now let's find the cat. Oh, where is that cat? I see it. It is on the purple block. I think there are more animals. I see a sheep on the red block and a cow on the green block. Let's line up all the animals. Wait there are two more: the chicken is on the orange block and the horse is on the yellow block. Now we have all the animals. Let's line them up. Help me count the animals. One, two, three, four, five, six. There are six animals here. Are you ready to put them back in the case? In goes the sheep, now the cat, here's the cow. Let's put the dog in and the chicken. I think there is one animal left. That's right. We can put the horse in the case too."*

Remember that you are using these blocks for different purposes so you will only want to use one language concept at a play session. You will also be able to put these blocks away after several weeks of play and bring them out again when she is older and ready to talk about more advanced concepts.

Musical Activity T.V.™ by Tolo

This toy has multiple activities on it. There is a button to be pushed, a roller to be rolled, small discs to be slid, and finally the musical T.V. The musical TV is what we will focus on for this toy. You turn the dial (a parent must do this at this age) and the screen moves across the

window showing two each of many animals. As the screen moves slowly across, you will have an opportunity to talk about the pairs of animals. The animals depicted are pigs, horses, sheep, dogs, cows, and ducks.

"Watch, Nicole, can you see all of the animals? I see a pig and there are two horses. Now I see some sheep and two dogs playing in the water. There are two cows and a mother duck and her ducklings. Let's see if they come by again. Here they come. I see a pig and some horses. And there are the sheep and dogs. Finally here are the cows and the mother duck. Shall I turn the dial and make it play again?"

Musical Surprise Bear™ by Small World Toys

This brightly colored little music box is great fun for this age group. When you push the button on the front of the box, the lid pops open and a little bear turns around to the music. This will keep your baby focused for a long time as she watches the bear turn around. The bear is three dimensional; so, it will help your baby to feel it and learn that it is a bear. The music is pleasant to listen to and helps to keep the focus. It is a newer version of the old jack-in-the-box. It is fairly easy to push

the button that makes the lid pop up but you may have to help your baby to push it. If your baby is just starting to crawl, you can hold the toy a little distance away and play the music to encourage your baby to crawl over to it.

Single Concept

*"What's in this box, Ethan? Watch, I will push the button. Whoops—the top flipped open. See the little bear? He is going **round and round** Do you want to touch him? See it going **round and round** Uh, oh. The bear stopped going **round and round** Shall we turn the dial and see him go **round and round** again? Let's see. Yes, the bear is going **round and round** Listen to the pretty music. The music plays while the bear goes **round and round** Can you close the top? There, you did it! The bear stopped going **round and round** Push the button and then you can see the bear going **round and round** again. Hooray, you pushed the button. There he goes **round and round** again."*

• • • • • • • • • • • • • • •

Knock Knock Blocks™ by **Small World Toys** This is a darling set of blocks that feature windows and doors on each of the blocks. For babies in this age category, these blocks provide a new way of playing peek-a-boo. Your baby (or you) can open the door or window and see what lies behind it. Some examples are babies, puppies, a fire station, balloons, and other interesting scenes. The set also contains some triangle blocks that can go on top of the square

block to make a little house. The blocks are textured and some have jingling sounds. These sounds and textures will help if your child is visually impaired. Of course the most fun of all is to build the houses higher and higher until they topple over. Lots of laughter follows this activity! One of the blocks has a mirror hidden behind the door and babies love to look at themselves. Let's talk about a peek-a-boo game with this toy.

"Here are our blocks, Michelle. I see a little door here. Can you open the door? Let me help you. Look there is a boy holding a fish. I think he caught the fish. Throw the block. Yay, you threw the block. Here's another one. What will we see behind the door? Peek-a-boo! Who's there? Wow, a baker. He has a pie in his hands. Throw the block. Can you throw it far? Hooray for you. Let's see what else we can find. Open the door. Peek-a-boo! Who's

*there? A boy with some sailboats and he has a sailor hat
on. Close the door. Throw the block. This block has two
doors. Open the doors. Peek-a-boo! Who's there? Wow,
two children at a party. They have party hats on."*

You can continue in this way with the other four blocks. Remember to point out the textures to your child. If she has a visual impairment, she may remember which blocks have which doors when she gets a little older.

Homemade Toys

**Peek-a-boo
with Paper
Towel Roll**
Babies love to play peek-a-boo with you. Save one of your paper towel rolls and cover it with colorful contact paper or just color it yourself with markers. Get one of your colorful scarves and push it into one end of the paper towel. With your baby, pull it out slowly and say "peek-a-boo!"

*"What do we have here? Let's see what's hiding inside.
Can you look and see? Pull it out. Peek-a-boo! There is
a scarf. Push it back inside. Where did the scarf go?
Look on the other end. Pull it out. There it is. There's
the scarf. Peek-a-boo. It is fun to hide the scarf. I am
going to put it over my head now. Whoosh. Peek-a-
boo! I see you now. Shall I put it on your head? There
you go. Peek-a-boo. I see you now. Let's stuff the scarf
back in the tube. There we go."*

**Paper Box
Tunnel**
Your baby may be just starting to crawl around this time. You can make a tunnel for her to crawl through. Go to a large appliance store and ask if they have an empty refrigerator box. They usually do and if they do not, let them know you want one in case they will save the next one that comes in. Open both ends of the box and encourage your crawler to crawl through by putting her favorite toy at the other end where she can see it.

Single Concept

*"Look at this big box. I see your toy at the other end. Can you **crawl** through?
You can go through to the other end. Let's see you **crawl** through. Wow, look
at you **crawling** through. Did you get your toy? Yeah, you did it. You
crawled through the tunnel. Let's put your toy over here at the other end.
Now you can **crawl** through again. Hooray. You **crawled** through the tunnel.
You are very good at **crawling** through this tunnel."*

Nine to Twelve Months

If this is your first child, you will be astonished at how active your baby becomes in this last part of her first year. You will look back in amaze-

ment at all that she has learned. You should also be pleased at how interested she is in playing with you. Her attention span is longer and she understands more and more of what you say to her. If she has started to walk, she will soon be running more than she will be walking.

If she has a visual impairment, she may not be as comfortable in another house as she is in yours. Don't hover over her, but help her adjust to this new environment. If she has never been there before, you can take her on a tour of the place and tell her where certain things are. For example, "You are standing in front of the couch and there is a small table next to you." Obviously, these directions are more than a child of this age will be able to understand, but you are giving her the language at the same time you are giving her a general feel for where things are. She may not understand "small," but "table" will alert her to a possible obstacle. Tell her where you will be and that she can call you if she needs you for any reason.

The toys suggested in this section are ones that your child will enjoy for many months to come. They include activities that will use many of her new skills and capture her attention.

Animal Tower™
by Discovery Toys

This charming stacker is sure to delight your baby. The cone is straight and round allowing the animals to be stacked any way your baby decides to do it. Additionally each animal provides opportunities for naming and describing. The animals are a yellow duck, a pink and white

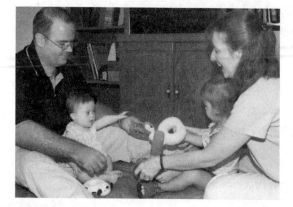

lamb, a purple cat, and a black and white dog. For children who have a visual impairment each animal is recognizable by its individual texture. Additionally the dog has a sweet vanilla scent to it.

There are many ways to play with this toy and the language possibilities will be presented here. Be sure not to overwhelm your child by introducing all of this language at one time. Add language concepts as your child is ready for them.

Naming

You can help your child take off each animal from the cone in turn. Your dialog will go something like this:

"Look, Cara. Look at these cute animals. Let's see. Here's the dog. What else do we have? See—a lamb. Where should we put the lamb? Good—next to the cat and dog. And here's the last one—a duck. Now they are all off."

Sounds

"Let's try and put them back on the cone. Which one do you want? Ah, you picked the lamb. A lamb says, 'baaaaa baaaa.' Can you say that? Good try. Which one do you want next? Great—you picked the duck. The duck says 'quack-quack.' Let's hear you say that. Good for you. There are two left. Which do you want? The cat? The cat says 'meow meow.' Did you try that? You said, 'meow.' I heard you. And the last one is the dog and he says, 'woof, woof.' Can you be a dog? Hooray, you said it. Now they are all back on the ring."

At another time, you can talk about the textures each animal represents. You can talk about which animals can be pets and which animals live on a farm. Later, you can talk about the different sizes the animals are and how they fit on the cone.

This is a toy that you can go back to time and again for language concepts. Your child will enjoy this toy for many months to come. It is a little challenging to put cloth rings onto a cloth cone so she will need some help until she is a bit older. To make it easier you could cover the ring with something slippery like aluminum foil.

It is a good idea to put toys away for a while and then bring them back at a later date. They will have much more appeal than if there are just a part of the toy barrel. Some friends exchange toys and their children find it much more exciting to play with this "new" toy which was actually theirs just a few months ago!

• • • • • • • • • • • • •

Smart Magnets™
by Fisher-Price

Your child may be just pulling to stand at this age and cruising around the furniture. Many times your child will reach up and pull anything she can reach off the table. One fascinating place for your child to be is with you in the kitchen. Do you keep things on the refrigerator as

reminders? These are great attractions for a baby who is beginning to stand. These smart magnets by Fisher-Price are just the thing to keep her attention in the kitchen. There are three magnets that come in the set. One has shapes: circle, square, and triangle. When your baby presses the shape a voice says the name of that shape. "This is a circle." There is also a music button that plays when your child pushes that button. The other two feature A, B, C and 1, 2, 3. It is fun for your child to be able to play with something of her own on the refrigerator. Put them down low where she can reach and put your items of importance up higher where they are safe.

You will be in the kitchen with your child and you can provide the language for these toys as she plays with them.

> *"Oh, I see you are playing with your magnets. That one has shapes on it. Can you find the circle? Push it. Listen, I hear her say, 'This is a circle.' Good for you. You found the right one. Where is the triangle? Oh, listen. She said, 'This is a triangle.' Wow, you are learning your shapes. Let's listen to some music. Can you press the right button? Great. I hear some lively music playing. You are dancing to the music."*

You can continue to feed your child the language as she explores each of these magnets. The other nice thing is that she can pull them off and they very easily go back on when placed close to the refrigerator. In a subtle way she will be learning about magnetism.

Balls We will be talking about two different kinds of balls that are fun to play with at this age. One is a magnetic ball distributed by the Lillian Vernon catalog (ordering information can be found in the Appendix) and the other is a play ball by Play Sports.

The magnetic ball is just the right size for tiny hands, but the fun part is that it comes in four sections or wedges that can be pulled apart. Magnetism was mentioned in the toy above and this is another way for your child to experience this force. Won't it be a surprise for her when you show her how to pull apart the wedges! As you take them apart, you can count the number of wedges.

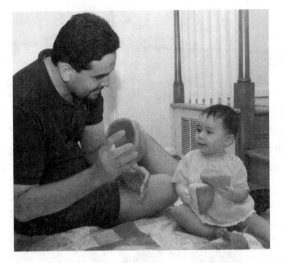

"Sonya, look at this fun ball. Watch. Uh oh. It comes apart. Can you pull it apart? That's right. We have one piece of the ball. Let's try another part. Wow, now we have two pieces. We have half of the ball. And now we can pull apart the last two pieces. It's all apart! Where did the ball go? We have to put it back together again. Let's see how many pieces we have. One, two, three, four. Okay, now let's put it back. Now we have half the ball back again. Now the third piece and now the fourth. It is all back together. Shall we play with the ball? I can throw it up in the air. Wheee. Now it comes back down."

Remember that you are only exposing your child to rich language experiences. She is not expected to know about magnetism, halves, or thirds and fourths. It is just a natural way to get sophisticated language into your child. You will be surprised in another year or so how much of this language begins to come from your child.

Large Play Ball
by Play Sports

Any large play ball is fun to play with. You will want to find one large enough that your child can grab it easily. You can play with her and show her how to roll, bounce, and throw the ball. Your child cannot do these easily by herself but you will be there to show her how.

Single Concept

"Here's your ball, Tommy. Can you **roll** it to Daddy? Watch, Daddy will **roll** it to you. Here it comes. It is **rolling**. Catch the ball. You did it. Wonderful. Now **roll** it back to Daddy. Push with your hands. That's right. **Roll** the ball. I've got it. You **rolled** the ball to me. Now I can **roll** it back to you. Look out—here it comes. You got it. Great. **Roll** it back to me."

Sparkling Symphony Star Beads™
by Fisher-Price

You have seen the bead frames that seem to be everywhere that children are: in toy stores, in pediatricians' offices, and in waiting rooms. This is a variation that is a lot of fun for babies this age to play with. The toy can be held and has different strands of curved wire with blocks on them. Your child shakes the toy and it lights up and plays music. She can move the blocks

around the different strands and shake, shake, shake the toy. This is one of the early exposures to cause and effect that will make your baby feel very powerful. She can make the music happen on a toy!

Single Concept

*"Let's see what we have for you to play with, Christina. How about this toy with the beads? Watch. I can **shake** the toy. Listen! When I **shake** it, the music starts to play. Can you **shake** it? I will help you. Here, we can do it together. **Shake, shake, shake.** Good. Listen to the music. Try it yourself. **Shake** the toy. **Shake, shake, shake.** You did a good job. Let me help you. You have to **shake** it a little harder. That's right. Now you've got it. You can **shake, shake, shake.** See the lights. Oh, that is pretty. When you **shake** the toy, the music plays and the lights light up. I like this toy."*

Sherberts Hippo™ by Learning Curve

Stuffed animals are usually a young child's favorite plaything. You can introduce these toys at any age but it is important to remember not to leave a stuffed toy in your child's crib or play pen until she is about 9 to 12

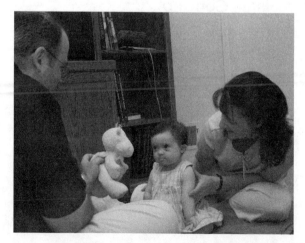

months old. Before that, it is possible that she may roll over on the toy and not be able to breathe. As long as you are with your child, it is fine to play with stuffed toys. The Hippo featured here is very soft and cuddly. It is nice to hold and look at. You can talk about how this stuffed animal feels. Let's see how that conversation might go.

"Here is a purple hippo for you to play with. Isn't it cute and so soft? It feels nice to hold. I like its soft body. Does it feel soft to you? Squeeze the hippo. He is squishy and soft. Watch, I can rub him on my face. It feels so soft. Let me rub him on your face. How does it feel? Soft and sweet. Would you like to hold the hippo? See how soft it is. You can take the hippo to sleep with you if you want. He is soooo soft."

Large Stuffed Mickey Mouse™ by Disney Products

This Mickey Mouse toy is almost as large as your baby! But what great fun to snuggle up to a big Mickey Mouse. If your child is able to stand and push a toy cart, she will be able to put Mickey in the cart and push him around the house. Great practice for walking.

"Wow, look at this big Mickey Mouse. Can you hold him? He is very big. Is he too big for you? You can put the Mickey Mouse in your cart. I'll help you. Here he goes. In the cart. Now let's see if you can push him. Oh, great, look at you—you are walking with the cart and Mickey is in the cart. Can you push him into the kitchen? Good job. You are walking with the cart and Mickey."

Duplo Blocks™ by Lego

These blocks have stood the test of time. They are as popular today as they were years ago. These blocks encourage your baby to use the fine motor control she is beginning to have to manipulate and build with them. They are also very colorful and are a great way for you to begin to match colors with your child. She may not yet have the ability to discriminate colors but it is a good start.

Keep your blocks together in a container so your child will be able to find them easily and also learn to put them away when she is finished playing with them. One inexpensive container is a plastic laundry basket. It is easy to store them in this container and easy to see them to play with them.

Single Concept

*"Let's play with your colorful blocks today. I see many pretty colors. Here is a **red** block. Can you find another one just like it? Here it is. Another **red** block. This is **red** and this one is **red**. Let's stack them on top of each other. Two **red** blocks. Let's see—where is another **red** block? Look, look all around. Over there, I see another **red** block. Put it on top. Now we have three **red** blocks. Wow, can you find more? Good for you, you found another **red** block. Up it goes. Let's count, one, two, three, four. Now we have four **red** blocks."*

Continue in this way with the blue, yellow, and green blocks. This is early exposure to colors. You are putting language into her receptive word bank at this time.

Push Toy
by Playskool

This is a wonderful first walker for youngsters who are just struggling to stand and walk. Your child can push this little toy and walk with it or it folds down to a little car that she can push with her feet. Either mode, it is a fun toy to play with.

"Wow, you are walking with your push toy! Wonderful, you are pushing it around the kitchen. Look how well you are walking. Soon you will be walking by yourself. Push, push, push!"

Books We have not talked very much about books yet, but you will want to expose your child to books from her very early days. You will find an

annotated list of books at the end of every developmental age section. Making reading part of your life and part of your child's will help her to develop her love of books as she gets older and can manage them herself. We know one young mother who read the complete original version of *Peter Pan* to her infant as she nursed her in the very early days of her life. Perhaps it is only coincidental that this little girl was reading by herself at the age of the three. We do know, however, that early and consistent exposure to books is important for young children because it instills an interest in reading, shows that you value reading, and is an excellent vehicle for expanding language experiences and vocabulary.

Homemade Toys

Newspaper Fun* Who has time to read the newspaper, you might ask? Hopefully, you have time to read a section or two. When you are finished with the newspaper, leave a section on the floor for your baby to play with. Babies this age love to play with the newspaper—to hear the rattling sound of the paper and to squish it up in a ball. You should be with her, however, because you must make sure she does not put it in her mouth or accidentally swallow a piece. Your play might sound like this:

> *"Jocelyn, you found the newspaper. Can you squish the paper? Listen to the sound it makes. I like to hear that sound. Oh, you tore a piece of paper. Here, give it to Daddy and let's put it in this bag. Can you tear some more? Wow, you did tear some more. Give it to me and I'll put it in the bag. Good girl. Thanks for giving it to me."*

A variation on this would be to give her a stack of old magazines. The colorful pages are even more fun to play with. If you sit and play with her, you can minimize the mess that the torn paper will leave all over your play area.

Danielle's Story This would be a good time to make a book about your child. Take actual photos of your child doing her daily activities: in her crib; at nap time; eating breakfast; taking a bath; playing outside; going in the car; at a therapy session. Whenever. Put these pictures in a sturdy

---

* Idea inspired by Geena Nicole.

book such as a photo album with easy-to-turn pages or a loose leaf notebook that can be added to over time. You will find these books to be a treasure as a chronicle of time and your child will enjoy looking at them over and over again even as she grows older.

If your child has a visual impairment, use high contrast "mug shots" (faces only). Use pictures that are taken against a solid background and show only a close-up of the face. Start with pictures of family and friends. Connect the person or object with the picture and use the language to describe who they are. If you cover the pictures with clear contact paper or photo album pages be sure to hold the book so that the light doesn't make a glare on the pages. Also look for books in the library that have high contrast pictures of everyday objects. Examples include *Black on White* and *White on Black* by Tana Hoban.

As you talk with your child about the picture, paste it into the book and then write a sentence about it. We know that she is not reading words yet, but exposing her to print early gets her thinking about the printed word.

> *"Look at this picture, Danielle. This is a picture of you upstairs in your crib. Are you sleepy? There's your rabbit. Time for a nap. Danielle is taking a nap in this picture. Let's paste it in your book. Can you help? I'll put the paste on and you can turn it over and pat it down. Now, let's see—we'll write 'Danielle is taking a nap.' Okay. Let's see Danielle's other pictures. . . ."*

Continue in this way as long as she stays interested in what you are doing. Add pictures of relatives so that they are available when these people are about to visit. Preparing your child ahead of time allows her time to think about unfamiliar people coming into her life. If she is going to therapy, be sure to take a picture of her therapist so that on the days when she is going to see her, you can refer to this picture. You can even have a second picture to put up on the calendar on the days when she will be going so that she can see the relation of the calendar to her activity. Again, remember, this learning is at a receptive level. She is not expected to be at all aware of days of the week at this age.

Summary

Here we are at the end of the first developmental year. Can you believe how many things your baby is able to do for herself? This is a time of rapid growth and all of the months of building her receptive language will start to pay off. She is probably saying or signing at least one or two words by now and soon this number will increase dramatically.

Toy Summary

The following is a list of the toys we have worked with in this developmental year. Asterisks indicate homemade toys.

Discovery Circle™—Small World Toys
Octopus™—Battat
Ocean Wonders™—Fisher-Price
Symphony in Motion™—Tiny Love
Discovery Toys crib bumper™—Discovery Toys
Kick and Learn Piano™—Fisher-Price
Sparkling Symphony Gym™—Fisher-Price
Musical Activity TV™—Tolo (distributed by Small World Toys)
Moon Assortment Wrist Rattles™—Learning Curve
Sunshine Symphony™—Neurosmith
Soft Cubes™—Battat
Musical Bear™—Small World Toys
Knock Knock Blocks™—Small World Toys
Sherberts Hippo™—Learning Curve
Animal Tower™—Discovery Toys
Musical Stacker™—Fisher-Price
Star Beads™—Fisher-Price
Magnetic ball—distributed by Lillian Vernon
Stuffed Mickey Mouse™—Disney Products
Play ball—Learning Curve/Play Sports
Duplo Blocks™—Lego
Push toy—Playskool
* Make Your Own Mobile
* Homemade Texture Blanket
* Flashlight Fun
* Tummy Time
* Paper Towel Peek-a-Boo
* Paper Box Tunnel
* Newspaper Fun
* Experience Story

Vocabulary and Concepts

The following list will give you an idea of the vocabulary and concepts that your child has been exposed to during this first year:

- *action words:* push, turn, slide, dial, fill, pour, roll, kick, throw, catch, bounce, fill, dump, crawl, walk, jump, run, shake, peek-a-boo
- *animal names:* sheep, horse, kitty, puppy, rabbit, bear

- *animal sounds:* moo, baa, quack, meow
- *baby's belongings:* cup, bottle, high chair, playpen, crib, spoon
- *body and facial parts:* eyes, nose, mouth, head, tummy or stomach, arms, legs, fingers, toes
- *child's name*
- *clothes:* pants, shirt, hat, sweater, shoes, socks, mittens, coat
- *colors:* black, white, red, green, blue, yellow, purple
- *common familiar objects:* fruit, toys, foods
- *daily activities:* play in crib or playpen, riding in a car, going to the doctor or therapist, taking a nap, taking a bath, changing diaper, drinking a bottle or nursing
- *descriptions of animals:* fluffy, tail, hops, soft
- *emotions:* happy, sad, laugh, cry
- *familiar video characters:* Big Bird, Ernie, Barney, Thomas the Tank, Bob the Builder, Baby Einstein characters and animals
- *family members' names*
- *goodbye*
- *hello*
- *lullabies*
- *materials:* corduroy, satin, felt, plastic, cotton
- *opposites:* up/down, in/out, on/off, back/forth, sleeping/awake
- *shapes:* such as round and square

Books

It is never too early to introduce books as a quiet activity before bedtime. Usually bedtime is not a problem at this age, but it is a nice ritual to begin.

You will find that your child is much more interested in sitting still for a quiet session of book reading now than when she was younger. She will not be able to follow a complicated story, but will enjoy pointing to pictures and perhaps naming a few in some of the early picture books.

A word here about the format of books for this age. If you are reading to your child, then any kind of book will do. However, if you want her to participate in the activity, you might want to use books with sturdy cardboard pages that are easier for her to turn. These are also nice for her to explore on her own.

ABC: An Alphabet Book. Thomas Matthieson. New York: Platt and Munk. Photographs of common objects that will be familiar to a young child. A is for apple, B for Balloons, G for guitar. The photos are clear with only one to a page. The facing page has the letter and a brief paragraph using the word.

Animal Crackers: A Delectable Collection of Pictures, Poems, Songs, and Lullabies for the Very Young. Jane Dyer. Boston: Little, Brown.
> A wonderful collection of songs for the youngest child. The rhythm of the words is very soothing as bedtime stories.

Animal Signs. Debby Slier. New York: Checkerboard Press.
> Sturdy board pages show 14 animals and the sign language equivalent for each one.

Babies. Gyo Fujikawa. New York: Grossett and Dunlap.
> Board book showing babies being washed, changed, eating, laughing, crying. Babies enjoy seeing pictures of others just like themselves.

Baby Einstein books. San Diego, CA: The Baby Einstein Company.
> The Baby Einstein books follow the characters in the videos and most young children are entranced by these books as well as the videos. For all of the titles of books and videos check out www.babyeinstein.com

Baby's First Words. Lars Wik. New York: Random House.
> Board book of photographs of clothes, objects, and actions in a young child's life.

Black on White. Tana Hoban. New York: Greenwillow Books.
> Beautiful photographs of everyday objects in black silhouetted against a white background. Babies love this book.

Board Books by Sandra Boynton. New York: Little Simon/Simon Schuster.
> This set of board books, which includes *Horns to Toes* and *In Between*, introduces your child to animals, colors, parts of the body, and daily objects.

Early Words. Richard Scarry. New York: Random House.
> Cardboard pages with little clutter. The objects are easily recognizable. The objects are of daily activities of waking up, washing, dressing, eating, playing, and bedtime.

The Everything Book. Denise Fleming. Henry Holt.
> This is a book filled with words to name everyday things. There are simple and bright paper illustrations. A fun first book.

Faces. Barbara Brenner. Photographs by George Arizona. New York: E.P. Dutton.

Pictures of many faces showing features that are all the same but illustrating that we all look different. Introduces the senses that we use with the facial features.

Family. Helen Oxenbury. New York: Wanderer Press.
This is a board book that talks about members of the immediate and extended family.

Goodnight Moon. Margaret Wise Brown. New York: Harper and Row.
A classic tale for young children in which the little mouse says goodnight to all the objects in the bedroom and also to the moon. An all-time favorite with children. Now available as a board book.

Hush Kittens. Emanuel Schongut. New York: Little Simon Books.
Two little cats making different sounds, such as crackling leaves, popping balloons, breaking dishes, ripping paper.

Mama Mama. Jean Marzollo. Illustrated by Laura Regan. New York: HarperCollins.
Gentle lullaby verses about how animal mothers care for their young with portraits of mother and baby pairs.

The Me I See. Barbara Shook Hazen. Illustrated by Ati Forberg. New York: Abingdon Press.
In a lovely, rhymed text, parts of the body, senses, and functions of each are shown.

My Animal Friends. New York: Grossett and Dunlap.
A board book with pictures of familiar animals.

My First Soft Learning Books. New York: Nasta.
These are plastic tub books. One talks about numbers and the other about letters of the alphabet.

Pat the Bunny. Dorothy Kunhardt. Racine, WI: Western Publishing Co., Inc.
A hands-on touching book with activities for babies to do: play peek-a-boo, pat the soft cotton on the bunny, look in the mirror, feel daddy's scratchy face, read a small book, put a finger through a ring, and wave bye-bye. A long-time favorite that will interest young children for many years.

Pat the Cat. Dorothy Kunhardt. Racine, WI: Western Publishing Co.
A brother and sister play with their cat, shop with Daddy, eat snacks, and prepare for bedtime. Scratch and sniff labels, textures to feel, flaps to lift, and things to move.

Playing. Helen Oxenbury. New York: Simon and Schuster.
Simple pictures of babies with different toys such as a block wagon, drums, books, teddy bear, and sitting in a box.

Say Goodnight. Helen Oxenbury. New York: Macmillan Publishing Co.
Gorgeous pictures and lovely rhyming text to accompany pictures. Will help lull your baby to sleep.

Spot's Toys. Eric Hill. New York: Putnam.
Vinyl book that can go in the tub with pictures of the little dog Spot playing with toys.

What Is It? Tana Hoban. New York: Greenwillow Press.
Excellent photographs of everyday objects in a baby's life.

White on Black. Tana Hoban. New York: Greenwillow Books.
Horse, baby bottle, sailboat, on a black background.

Word Signs. Debby Slier. New York: Checkerboard Press.
Objects babies are familiar with are pictured along with the sign language equivalent for each one.

Summary of Your Child's First Year (0-12 Months)*

LANGUAGE

Developmental Milestones	Date Achieved	NOT YET	PROGRESSING
cries to express needs			
makes vowel-like cooing sounds			
responds by smiling to friendly faces			
turns to sound			
laughs out loud			
vocalizes when spoken to			
uses her voice to express needs			
babbles several consonants			
"talks" to toys			
"talks" to mirror			
responds to name			
stops action when "no" is said			
waves bye-bye			
nods head for "yes"			
responds to "yes/no" questions			
enjoys music and rhymes			
one or two words			

This chart lists skills acquired by babies who have reached the developmental age of twelve months. Children who have developmental delays may be chronologically several months to several years older before they acquire these skills.

PHYSICAL

Developmental Milestones	Date Achieved	NOT YET	PROGRESSING
follows a moving person			
follows a moving object			
focuses on hands			
brings hand to mouth			
can hold on to rattles			
plays with fingers			
plays with hands			
can move object from one hand to another			
can crawl			
can sit alone			
can clap hands			
can drink from a cup			
can roll a ball			
can creep upstairs			
can walk with one hand held			
can walk alone			
moves body to music			
can build a tower of blocks how many?			
can put objects into containers			
can dump objects out of containers			
can pick up small objects			

COGNITIVE

Developmental Milestones	Date Achieved	NOT YET	PROGRESSING
responds to visual stimulation			
responds to touch stimulation			
responds to sound stimulation			
focuses on faces			
discriminates between family and strangers			
enjoys being with people			
raises arms when told "up"			
responds to name			
discriminates between friendly and angry voices			
understands bye-bye			

can follow a single direction
   "come here"
   "stand up"			

has exposure to colors:
   red
   green
   blue
   yellow
   black
   white			

has exposure to facial parts			

has exposure to vocabulary of texture:
   smooth
   scratchy
   bumpy
   rough
   soft			

6

Toy Dialogs for the Second Year

Twelve to Fifteen Months

During this developmental period, you will begin to see your play with the dialogs pay off. Your toddler understands more and more of what you say. He should be able to go and get an object that you ask him for, such as his ball or doll.

"Bring me the doll. Good! I'll put the doll on the shelf. Now get the big giraffe with the long neck. He goes on the top shelf because his neck is so long. Can you reach the top shelf or shall I lift you up? Oooooo, he's tall and so are you. Up it goes. Now we have all of your nice toys ready to go to sleep and ready to play with you tomorrow. Let's choose our story now. . . ."

It is fun to listen to a child of this age with a toy telephone because you will hear him using your tones and your inflections. Once you have realized how easily your child can imitate tones and inflections, you will want to pay attention to how you use your voice with him. Your tone and your inflections carry a lot of meaning for him. He will need to learn to understand your tones of love and caring as well as the tones you use when you disapprove of his actions. While he is learning to communicate, walk, and interact with you, he is also learning about his feelings. You can teach him about his feelings by telling him how you feel at different times. Repeat in meaningful ways how much you love and care for him, your pleasure in him, and your joy in being with him. Communicating feelings of love will help him to grow with confidence and self-esteem.

Physically, your child will be on the go all of his waking hours. Be sure to encourage his participation in clean-up time. Make this a ritual before bedtime or whenever it is convenient for you. If you join him in the clean up and make it a language-learning time, it will be enjoyable for both of you.

Big Band Set™
by Battat

Children and music. Music and children. They are inseparable. Be sure to sing to your children all the time. In the car, in the house, before bedtime. They love to hear the melodic tone of your voice. Don't worry if you can't carry a tune. They have no idea and just love to hear your voice. Children will pick up on the words in such a short time.

This toy introduces your child to several rhythm instruments and, nice for you, it all comes packed in the big drum so clean up is no problem. Take each instrument out one at a time and allow your child to explore it. If he does not automatically do so, show him how to use it. As he uses the rhythm sticks, sing a melody with him. "Bang bang bang go the rhythm sticks. Bang bang bang, I hear the music."

"Here's the rainbow maker. Shake it up and down. See the beads falling. Rain rain falling everywhere makes a swishing sound. Turn it around and see the beads fall again and make the swishing sound. Shall we sing a song? Round, round, round we go up and down and round we go. I like making music with you. We are having fun."

"What is this over here? A tambourine. Yeah, let's shake the tambourine. Shake, shake, shake. It makes a different noise than the rainbow maker. But we can shake shake, shake the tambourine."

"Your turn. What do you want to play with now? Ah, yes, the big drum. Boom! It makes a booming sound. Turn around and listen. Can you hear that? A big booming sound."

Do not be concerned about playing with this toy if your child has a hearing loss. He can be taught to listen for the different sounds and it makes a great auditory training game to get him listening for sounds he will listen for when he has a hearing test.

See N' Say Animals™
by Fisher-Price

Variations of this toy have been around for decades but this newer version is easier for the young child to operate. The lever is big and easy to hold and to pull down. At the later part of this age range, your child should be able to play with this toy with your help. It is a great way to develop language and speech sounds as your child hears and imitates animal sounds. He is well on his way to speech by this time and this will be a fun activity for him.

"Let's turn the arrow and see what animal we can hear. I see a cat. Pull the lever. What do you hear? I hear the cat say 'meow, meow.' Can you say that too? Let me hear you say 'meow.' Do you want to hear it again? Okay, turn the arrow round and round and point it to the cat. Now listen. Meow, meow. I hear it again. Can you be a cat and say meow?"

Your child will enjoy this toy with you for long periods of time. If you are working on animal sounds specifically, you will want to put the toy away for special play times with you. Later, when you have taught those sounds, you can have the toy out for his play time.

Homemade Toys

Large Boxes

When you watch your child unwrap his gifts at holiday or birthday time, you may have been amused to see that he loved the boxes the gifts came in almost as much as the gifts themselves. Keep some large boxes around for your toddler to play in, on, under, and anywhere else he can get himself into. One favorite has always been the boxes that refrigerators come in. You can usually check at a new home construction site and talk with the site manager. He can let you know when they will be delivering the home appliances. Your child will enjoy making his box into a play house, boat, car, airplane, and whatever else his imagination leads him to. Your child can help you draw the windows, doors, and flowers in a flower box under the window. Your play with him might be like this.

> *"Come here, Alison. I have this huge box for you to play in. Let's make a house for you and your dolls. Be careful here. I'm going to cut a door so you can get inside. Okay, here is your door. A house needs windows. You draw a window over here. Now, let's see, maybe we can make a flowerbox right under this window. Remember, Grandma has a flower box under her window. Those are pretty flowers that you are drawing. Good job. What else shall we make on your house? Here are some stickers you can put on your house. Oh, it looks so pretty. Now you and your dolls can play inside."*

Pouring Practice

Put two paper cups on your child's highchair tray. Fill one cup halfway with Cheerios or a similar cereal and show your toddler how to pour from one cup to the other. No harm done if he spills a few, especially if he has a dog to help clean up! After he tires of this activity, he can have the Cheerios for a snack.

Single Concept

*"Let's play with these Cheerios. Watch, I will **pour** some in the cup. Watch me **pour**. Now it's your turn. **Pour** the Cheerios into this other cup. That's right. You **poured** the Cheerios into the cup. Can you do it again? **Pour** the Cheerios. Great— you **poured** them right into the cup. Oops, some spilled out. No problem. You can put them in the cup or eat them. Let's **pour** some more."*

Fifteen to Eighteen Months

You will notice your active toddler becoming even more active during these few months. He can climb now, so you need to be careful of dangerous things, not only on the floor but at any other level as well. There is no place that he cannot get to at this time. Safety first. If you think he can't, he will. He is also walking well by this time. He rarely falls. When he is running, he still may fall because his feet tend to get ahead of him. He enjoys moving in time to music.

Your child will also enjoy scribbling with crayons and markers. When buying crayons and markers, get the kind that are rather fat. These are easier for him to hold. At this stage, he will be holding the crayons in his fist rather than as you would hold a pencil. That is fine for this developmental age.

You will want to keep crayons under your control. They often end up being used to decorate walls and furniture. We do not recommend coloring books at this age since your child is most comfortable with scribbling and may be frustrated because he cannot color within lines. He will be able to color within lines by the time he is five. For now, large blank pieces of paper or rolls of white shelving paper are perfect. He may go off the paper, so make sure the surface that he is coloring on is washable or covered with a layer of newspaper.

You will notice that he is interested in helping you when you dress him. He can be most cooperative. He is also very capable of taking off his shoes and socks even though he will not be able to put them back on. Encourage these self-help skills. After all, your goal is to turn your toddler into a full-fledged adult one day. These early signs of independence should be encouraged.

You are still the main source of receptive language building for your child. You'll want to begin to use more specific and descriptive words for things. Talk about how things taste, how they feel, and the sounds that things make. You'll want to talk about shapes, sizes, and colors. Remember that his receptive language is more highly developed than his expressive language. You can feel comfortable using words like "fuschia" for "pink" and "huge" for "big." Talking about foods in a positive way gives your little one the idea that all foods are acceptable and may prevent some of his "I hate spinach" attitudes. For example, say, "These peas are a glowing green color." Using exciting and descriptive words doesn't mean that you want to bury your toddler in an avalanche of words, however. Keep your phrases directly related to objects and activities around your child.

At this age, you will see a great increase in your child's expressive language. He is making even more rapid gains in his receptive language and you can help him with this by keeping your phrases short. Don't be afraid to repeat the same words over and over; your child learns by hearing the same words again and again. You will probably find that by the time your child enters the next developmental age, he will be understanding and repeating more of those same words back to you.

First Blocks™
by Fisher-Price

Children this age love to play with shape sorters. You may have to help in the beginning, but this toy only has three shapes and most children this age can "sort" it out. Start with the round one because it is the easiest to place. When you first play with the toy, use only one shape at a time. This will lessen your child's frustration.

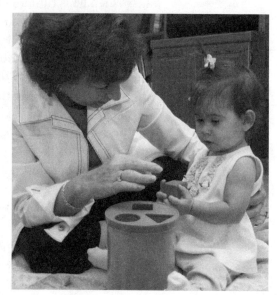

Single Concept

*"Let's play with this bucket. I found some shapes. Look, this one is **round**. Can you find the **round** hole? Where does this **round** block go? I see. Over here in the **round** hole. Can you put the **round** block in the **round** hole? You did it. Wonderful. Do you see another **round** block? I see one right here. Here is a **round** block. Let's see you put it in the **round** hole. Terrific. It goes in the **round** hole. I see one more **round** block. Can you put that round block in the **round** hole? And dump them all out. Hooray, let's play again."*

Continue on another day or at another time with a different shape until he is able to place all of the shapes correctly. It is lots of fun to dump them and start again.

Spin-a-Shape Elephant™
by International Playthings

When you are playing with your child and teaching new concepts, varied repetition is the key. This cute little toy will allow you to continue talking about shapes and sorting without using the same toy over and over. This toy gives your child additional practice in

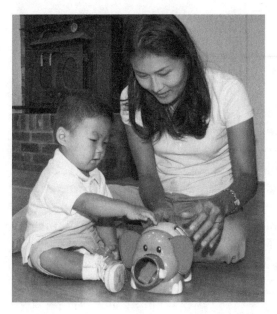

sorting shapes. The elephant has different shapes around his body and the body turns to show the shape on top that the child is supposed to place.

Try this toy after you have established that your child can place the shapes in the easier shape sorter described above. Then you can vary the activity by having him pick out the shape from two or more in front of him.

"I see two shapes there. One is round and the other is square. Can you spin the elephant and put the square shape in? Okay, that is the round one. Now let's find the square. Good, you got it. You put the square and the round shape in the elephant. Spin it around. What can we find? Okay, there is the triangle. Good for you. Put it in the elephant. Now watch. I have two shapes. Which one is the triangle? Right, you got the right one."

Bubbles

Bubbles are great fun at any age. They are a wonderful speech practice tool. Toddlers love to chase the bubbles and they may be the only way to elicit "voice" from some children as they get into the carefree "pop pop" of popping the bubbles. You can buy bubble solution very inexpensively at lots of stores. Once you have the container and the bubble wand, you can continue the fun by mixing your own bubble solution in the same container. To make your own bubble solution, mix one cup of water with ¼ cup liquid dishwashing detergent and a teaspoon of sugar. You can also use pipe cleaners and bend them into the shape of a wand.

At first, you may want to blow the bubbles yourself. Small children often lack the breath control to do it themselves. They will enjoy running about and popping the bubbles. Try having your child imitate the word "pop" as he pops the bubble. As in any speech game, accept whatever sound he gives you and model the correct way for him. Give him the opportunity to try to blow the bubbles also. When he blows too hard, take his arm and blow gently on it. He will feel the difference between a gentle stream of air and a hard one. You will just love seeing his face the first time that he is successful at getting a good stream of bubbles out.

I have never seen a child who was not fascinated with this activity. You may also find that your older child will enjoy blowing bubbles with his younger brother or sister.

Besides helping your child learn breath control and to use his voice, you can also introduce the ideas of "all gone" and "disappeared" as the last of the bubbles drifts away. Talk about how the bubbles go "up, up, up" and then back "down, down, down." If you blow some bubbles for him he might enjoy blowing them away with his own breath. This is a great exercise for any language-delayed child who needs some work on getting more breath behind some of his sounds.

If your child has a visual impairment, blowing bubbles is a good activity to encourage visual tracking. If he has a significant vision loss, however, remember that he will not be able to follow the bubbles much beyond 8 to 12 inches.

Safety note: Be careful that your youngster does not swallow the bubbly water as he puts his mouth close to the wand to blow it. Do not leave him unattended with the jar of bubbles. You also may want to blow bubbles outside or on a floor that can be mopped. It is inevitable that the bubble mixture will spill! Even if it doesn't spill, if you play for a long time, you will have a soapy film on the floor and furniture.

Homemade Toys

Tugging Fun All you need is a large dish towel. Sit facing your child and give him one end of the towel and you hold the other end. Pull back and forth as you sit facing each other. Sing, "Row Row Row Your Boat" as you do this. In a subtle way, your toddler is learning to take turns as you go back and forth.

"Let's play a game. You sit over there and I will sit here. Take this end of the towel. Hold on tight. I am going to pull. Don't let go. Now you pull me. That's right. You are pulling me and I am pulling you. Listen, let's sing. "Row row row your boat, gently down the stream. Merrily, merrily, merrily, merrily, life is but a dream." Can you sing with me? Wonderful. I love to hear you singing. Let's do it again."

. . . .

Tennis   Do you or a friend play tennis? Ask him or her to save you a can of
Time   used tennis balls. Your baby will love to spend time filling and empty-
ing the can of tennis balls.

Opposite Concepts

*"Look what Aunt Fran gave us. This is a can of tennis balls. Watch. I can dump
them out. Now the can is* **empty***. You put the balls back in the can. Now it is* **full***.
Out again. The can is* **empty***. Now fill it up. The can is* **full***. Dump again. The can
is* **empty***. Wow, you like to* **empty** *and fill the can. Sometimes it is* **full** *and
sometimes it is* **empty***."*

Eighteen to Twenty-Four Months

As your toddler nears the developmental age of two years, you will notice an incredible leap in his expressive language. If you remember our discussion on language development, we talked about how he may comprehend approximately three hundred words and use approximately fifty words by the end of this time frame. All of the hard work that you have put in will be worth it as you hear him come out with more and more recognizable words.

This is where your months of playing imitation games will begin to make sense. You don't want to correct your child when he says phrases incorrectly or uses the wrong tenses of verbs. What you want to do is model the correct way to say them and hope that he will want to imitate you. When he says, "car go me," you say, "You want to go in the car? Okay, we're leaving soon."

Remember that you are continuing to build your child's receptive language at the same time that you're admiring his growing expressive language. Reading books, playing with him and with his toys, and using descriptive and novel words are great activities for this age. While you are looking at books together, involve him in the "telling of the story" by asking him to supply the endings to familiar sentences in a story. We know a youngster of this age who was "reading" the Madeline books because of the rhyme and repetitive nature of the story.

His love of jumping at this age may spell big trouble for your bed and his. Do you have an old mattress? Put it in his playroom and let him jump about to his heart's content. Put his indoor slide next to it so he can slide down onto a soft place. Having an indoor slide gives you a lot of opportunity for language input of action words and prepositions like "up," "down," and "under." He is ready to learn this now and you can count on his love of active play to stimulate his interest in this type of language development.

Outside, he needs a fenced area or you need to supervise him closely. This is the time when you can begin talking about safety regarding cars and setting limits of where he can play. Don't expect him to follow these rules without supervision. He is endlessly curious and may set off in any direction at any time. If you have a driveway, tell him that he can go to the end of the driveway and stop. You may want to put some type of barrier up there to visually remind him. You can line your trash cans up across the drive. If you have a sidewalk in front of your house or apartment, he can play on your sidewalk but not the neighbors'. Once again, a trash can at either end of the boundary will help to remind him. If he moves beyond those boundaries, you will be there to gently remind him of the rule.

Take advantage of his energy level and take a trip to the park. There you'll find many physical activity toys such as slides, swings, and seesaws that provide great opportunity for language building. I urge you to use the language that you think of as you push your child up and down on the swings and as he goes way up in the air on the seesaw.

> *"You want to go on the swing now? Okay, up you go.*
> *Let's put this bar down so you don't slip out. Here we go.*
> *[If this is a new experience for your child, stay in front of*
> *the swing and gently push it back and forth.] You're*
> *swinging now. The swing goes back and forth, back and*
> *forth. You're swinging. Back you go and forward you*
> *come. Back and forth. You're swinging! Do you want to*
> *go higher? Up you go. Down you come. Up and down."*

> *"This is the seesaw. When you go up, Johnny goes*
> *down. [If this is your child's first time on the seesaw,*
> *stay on his side with him. If you have no playmate for*
> *the other end, you can make it go up and down by*
> *pushing him down and lifting his side up.] Here you*
> *go, up in the air. Look how high you are. You are up in*
> *the air. Shall we go down? Down, down, down. Now*
> *you are back on the ground again. You came down.*
> *Do you want to go up again? Up, up, up; way up high.*
> *And now it's down, down, down again."*

Step-a-Sound Mat™
by International Playthings

If your youngster is walking by now, this will be a fun activity for him. You can also use it to "teach" the "wait a minute" game. The mat lies flat on the floor and as your youngster stands on it (or crawls on it) a sound will come from one of the footprints. Your child should be able to run freely over and over the mat when you first introduce it to him and then you can play a game.

> *"Come over here, Justin.*
> *Let me show you how to*
> *play this game. Stand*
> *tall. Okay, when I say*
> *"go," you walk on the*
> *first number. Ready—go.*
> *Good for you, you stood*
> *on the first number.*
> *Listen, did you hear that*

sound? Let's try it again. Okay, go. On to the next
number. Wow, that's a different sound. What fun! Can
you run all the way down the mat? Hooray for you.
You did it! Do you want to play again? Okay, can you
wait at the top right next to number one? That's right.
Now step on the mat. Ah, listen to that sound. Okay,
move on to number two. One-two. Good for you."

Puzzles

Puzzles range from very simple to incredibly complex. The primary skills that they teach are eye/hand coordination and the ability to visualize abstract shapes. Additionally, for the young language-delayed child, they can be used to teach the vocabulary that is on the pieces themselves.

The simplest puzzles have one space per object. Some are made of wood and have knobs to aid in taking out and putting in the pieces. I recommend the wooden puzzles since they are very sturdy and your child can use the pieces in a variety of other play situations without fear of damaging the pieces. Puzzles increase in complexity until you reach adulthood and encounter puzzles with hundreds and thousands of small pieces and very complicated designs. When my children were small, we always had a puzzle out on a table where anyone passing by could add a piece or two. We often sat together at the table and TV was quickly forgotten when we were spurred on by someone finding just the right piece of blue sky. It is a great family activity for people of all ages.

The Basic Skills™ puzzle described here is made by Lights, Camera, Interaction and has many activities within the puzzle to help your youngster begin to do some selfhelp skills. He will need your help in the beginning with this puzzle. Use it as a tool to introduce these skills. There are six objects in the puzzle. A backpack with a buckle, a coin purse with two snaps, a windbreaker with a zipper, a pair of pants with a belt buckle, a shirt with two buttons, and a shoe with laces. The shoe is the most difficult one to do and may have to wait a little bit before your child can conquer this one. The backpack buckle is the easiest and one that children are familiar with from their strollers and car seats. Many children this age can buckle themselves in with a little help. It is a little more difficult skill to unbuckle than it is to buckle! Besides the basic skills that are the point of this puzzle, there is a lot of language that can be discussed. Under each object is a picture of what would be found in the backpack, under the pants, inside the shirt, under the windbreaker, and inside the shoe.

Your play may go as follows:

Sally, look at this cool puzzle. See all the things there
are to do? Which would you like to try first? Ah, yes,

the buckle. Can you unbuckle the backpack? Do you need some help? I can help you. Snap, the buckle is undone. Now I am sure you can buckle it back. See, I knew you could do it. Let's take the piece out. That is a backpack. What can you find in the backpack? I see a book, an apple, a sandwich, and a watch. This back-pack is for school. You have a backpack for school, too. What is in your backpack? Let's go and find it. Here's your backpack. Look, you have papers for school and there's your favorite ball. Your backpack is bigger than the puzzle piece. Do you want to buckle your back-pack? You can practice with the puzzle piece and then you can buckle your own backpack!"

Tea Sets Children this age are just beginning to appreciate and enjoy imagina-tive play. They love to prepare your "coffee" or "tea" and have you share a drink with them. You may even find that this is an activity that two children can enjoy together at this age. They are a little young still for playing together but tea sets just seem to lend themselves to sharing the fun. There are many tea sets available today. For this age, stick to the plastic sets, as there is likely to be much drop-ping and stepping on!

"Hi, Declan, I am glad you came to play today. Sara and I were just going to have some tea. Would you like to play? Here is a cup for you. It's a blue cup and Sara's is red. Can you find the saucer? It's over here. I will hand it to you. Here is a blue saucer for your blue cup. Sara, can you pour some tea for Declan? Isn't it good? Ummm, I want some more. Declan, can you pour some tea in my yellow cup? Thank you. It is delicious. Let's get some crackers to have with our tea. We can put the crackers on a plate. Sara, your plate is red. Declan, your plate is blue, and mine is yellow. Who wants some crackers? How many would you like? Great, here you are—one, two. This tea party is fun."

Homemade Toys

. . . .

Color
Match
You have been exposing your child to colors for a few months now. This activity will help him learn to match colors. He does not have to say the names of the colors to be able to match them.

You will need a dozen spring-type clothespins and a dozen index cards, white preferably. At your local office supply store, you can find round colored dots that are about a half an inch in diameter. Look for a set of dots with the basic colors: red, green, blue, and yellow.

Put three yellow dots on three index cards and three clothespins. Do the same with the other three colors. Now you are ready to play.

> *"Jamal, come and look at this new game I have for us
> to play. Do you see the index card with the yellow dot?
> Where is the clothespin with the yellow dot? Yes, that's
> right. You found the yellow dot on the index card and
> the yellow dot on the clothespin. Watch—I will show
> you how to attach the clothespin to the index card.
> See, now they match."*

Continue this way with all of the index cards and the clothespins. See if your child can match all four of the colors. Help him with the ones he has trouble with. You can play this game many times with your child.

. . . .

Cereal Box
Puzzles
Cut the front off an empty box of cereal. Cut it into three to six pieces. Give it to your child and help him put it back together again. If it is a cereal that he eats, he will more readily identify the picture.

> *"You are so good at puzzles. Let's try this one. It is
> your favorite cereal box. Watch how these pieces fit
> together. Can you find another piece of the puzzle?
> That's right. That piece goes right there. Only one
> piece left. Where does it fit? You did it. You put the
> cereal box back together again! Let's mix it up again.
> Now you try by yourself. Of course, I will help you if
> you need help. That's right, that is the first piece. Very
> good. Now can you find the second piece? See, you
> don't need my help. You did it all by yourself. Now find
> another piece. Only one left. Very good. There's the
> cereal box back together again."*

Toy Summary

The following is a list of toys that we have worked with in this developmental year. The asterisk indicates a homemade toy.

Big Band Set™—Battat
First Blocks™—Fisher-Price
Spin-a-Shape Elephant™—International Playthings
See 'N Say Farm Animals™—Fisher-Price
Creative Designs International
Basic Skills Puzzle™—Lights, Camera, Interaction
Step-a-Sound Mat™—International Playthings
Tea Set
* Bubbles
* Color Match
* Large Boxes
* Tugging Fun
* Tennis Time
* Cereal Box Puzzles
* Pouring Fun

Vocabulary and Concepts

The following list will give you an idea of the vocabulary and concepts that your child should be familiar with at the end of the second developmental year:

- *action words:* topple, fall, swing, pop, turn, push, pull, pour, twist, open, close, sleep, hide, float, fill, spill, turn over, squeeze, dump, pile, measure, touch, find, disappear, all gone
- *colors:* yellow, green, blue, purple, orange, red
- *commands:* bring me; find the; where is; get the; get it; give me the; show me the
- *community helpers:* firefighter, mail carrier, construction workers, farmer, pilot
- *expressions:* winking, smiling, surprised, happy
- *farm animals:* dog, duck, frog, horse, pig, bird, kitten, cat, rooster, cow, sheep, turkey
- *nouns:* sun, rain, stroller, tire, wheel, boat, balls, train, airplane, suitcase, seat belt, street light, bed, buckle, snap, backpack
- *numbers:* one, two, three, four, five
- *nursery rhymes:* Jack and Jill; Hey Diddle Diddle; Mary Had a Little Lamb; Eensy, Weensy Spider; Humpty Dumpty; Pat-a-Cake; Twinkle, Twinkle Little Star; Rain, Rain, Go Away; London Bridge is Falling Down; Baa Baa Black Sheep; Hush Little Baby

- *opposites:* behind/in front of; before/after; in/out; tall/short; up/down; under/over; high/low; dirty/clean; hi/bye bye; empty/full
- *playground equipment:* slides, swings, seesaw, merry-go-round
- *prepositions:* inside, top, on top of, over, under, up, down, out, in, through
- *questions:* where, what, when, who
- *rooms of the house:* bedroom, living room, kitchen, bathroom, garage
- *shapes:* circle, square, triangle
- *sizes:* small, smaller, smallest; big, bigger, biggest
- *video characters:* Barney, Baby Bop, Thomas the Tank Engine, Baby Einstein characters, Dora the explorer, Bear in the Big Blue House
- *zoo animals:* elephant, monkey, parrot, bear, kangaroo, tiger, lion

Books

Your child will enjoy books if you spend time reading with him every day. Books that name things are probably still his favorites. Now he should be able to name more and more of the pictures in his old favor-

ites. He also will be able to follow a simple story plot. Some of the picture books that have no words are also fun. Be sure to keep adding books to your child's library and to make sure books are readily available.

Since animals are of great interest to toddlers, several zoo animal books are suggested. You can read these both before and after you go to the zoo. Other titles you might be interested in also focus on animals. Be sure to choose others that you see in the library when you visit.

Remember the language books that you made a while back? Why not try making a new one? If you have a digital camera, you have instant access to pictures you could use in a book. You also could take advantage of the one-hour photo developing that is available today. At this age when you make a language book, have your child give you the language for each picture. For example, "I had French fries at McDonald's today." Then write what he says. It's wonderful to look back at these books as your children get older.

Ask Mr. Bear. Marjorie Flack. New York: Aladdin.
>An older book that has withstood the test of time. Its repetitive simplicity has appealed to children through the years. A young boy wonders what to give his mother for her birthday. He asks many animals for their suggestions until he finds the perfect solution.

But Not the Hippopotamus. Sandra Boynton. New York: Little Simon/Simon Schuster.
>A hippopotamus stands aside and watches as the other animals interact. Finally he joins in. A nice beginning to social interaction language.

Chicka Chicka ABC. Bill Martin, Jr. and John Archambault. Illustrated by Lois Ehlert. New York: Simon and Schuster.
>A wonderful alphabet chant book for even the youngest child.

Cleo in the Snow. Caroline Mockford. Cambridge, MA: Barefoot.
>When Cleo wakes up she goes outside and discovers the wonders of the first snow.

Daisy Is a Mommy. Lisa Kopper. New York: Dutton.
>Toddlers will enjoy seeing their own actions played out by Daisy and her puppies. A fun read-aloud story for this age.

Everywhere Babies. Susan Meyers. Illustrated by Marla Frazee. Orlando, FL: Harcourt Brace.
>Babies love looking at babies and pictures of babies, especially themselves! This is a fine book of babies doing all the things that babies love to do. A sure favorite with your baby.

The Farm Counting Book. Jane Miller. Englewood Cliffs, NJ: Prentice Hall.
>Colorful picture book that uses animals on the farm to teach the numbers one through ten. A different concept on each page. A nice way to learn and review the animal names. Halfway through the book, pictures of the animals are represented and the child needs to count them. Photos are simple, brightly colored, and clear. Numbers and words are bold and easy to read.

Hug. Jez Alborough. Cambridge, MA: Candlewick.
>A little chimp travels through the jungle in search of a hug. While he finds many other animals hugging, it is not until he finds his mommy that the little chimp is content. Also available as a board book.

Humpty Dumpty and Other Rhymes. Illustrated by Rosemary Wells. Edited by Iona Opie. Cambridge, MA: Candlewick.
> These are the tried and true rhymes that every generation should hear. Your baby will enjoy the rhythm of these age-old rhymes. Great for cuddling time.

Kipper's Kite. Mick Inkpen. Orlando, FL: Harcourt Brace.
> A touch-type book that features different textures on each page.

Little Blue and Little Yellow. Leo Lionni. New York: Obolensky.
> Talks about the activities of two friends, blue and yellow, and what happens when they are together (they make green). A fun book to read after you do your playdough activity with your child.

Little Red Hen. Paul Galdone. New York: Seabury.
> A hardworking hen tries to get her lazy friends to help her bake some bread. Young children get the message easily from this charming story of how they must help if they want to benefit.

Moo, Baa, La La La. Sandra Boynton. New York: Little Simon/Simon and Schuster.
> Lyrical verses about what different animals say.

Millions of Cats. Wanda Gag. New York: Coward McCann.
> A charming book that has endured for over fifty years. An elderly couple would like just one little cat to keep them company, but making the decision is hard and lots of fun.

Moo Moo Goes to the City. Jo Lodge. New York: Little, Brown.
> Moo Moo the cow takes a trip to New York City. Pull tabs show hats in the hat shop, an ice cream treat, birds in the park, and a boat in the harbor.

The Napping House. Audrey Wood. Illustrated by Don Wood. New York: Harcourt Brace.
> A clever and beautiful book for young children. A cumulative rhyme that adds a variety of sleeping people to the bed until the surprise ending at dawn. The lighting on the page cleverly shows the passage of time as the night turns into morning.

Peekaboo Morning. Rachel Isadora. New York: Putnam.
> From sun up a playful little toddler plays peek-a-boo on every page with all the important people and things in a toddler's life.

Play with Me. Marie Hall Ets. New York: Viking Press.
> A little girl makes friends with different animals: a frog, turtle, chipmunk. She learns she needs to sit quietly and wait for them to come to her. The illustrations are simply lovely and endearing.

Rainbow Candles. Myra Shostak. Illustrated by Katherine Kahn. Rockville, MD: KAR-BEN Copies.
> A rhyming book about every child's favorite activity at Chanukah time, lighting the candles. Teaches the concepts of numbers one through eight. Sturdy board book format.

Sam Who Never Forgets. Eve Rice. New York: Puffin Books.
> Sam is a zoo keeper who never forgets to feed all of the animals promptly at three o' clock until one day. . . .

Squeaky Clean. Simon Puttock. Illustrated by Mary McQuillan. New York: Little, Brown.
> Reluctant bathers will identify with these three little pigs who don't want to take a bath. Clever Mama Pig adds bubbles, ducks, and scrubbing brush to turn bath time into a treat.

Talkabout Bedtime. Margaret Keen. Illustrated by Harry Wingfield. London: Ladybird Books.
> A lovely book that talks about every aspect of bedtime. Different kinds of beds, different people sleeping—adults as well as children. Talks about some of the noises you might hear at bedtime and jobs that people have who work at night. As in the other "talkabout" books, there are activities for matching and finding similarities and differences.

The Very Busy Spider. Eric Carle. New York: Philomel.
> Different barnyard animals try to distract an industrious spider from building its web. Children can chime in with the different animal sounds that are described here.

The Very Hungry Caterpillar. Eric Carle. New York: World.
> Several language concepts can be built from this book. Days of the week, metamorphosis of a butterfly, different foods, numbers. An eternal favorite.

Wake Up Big Barn. Suzanne Tanner Chitwood. New York: Cartwheel.
> A delightful story of farm animals waking up with all of their unique sounds. Babies love to try and imitate these sounds.

What Baby Wants. Phyllis Root. Illustrated by Jill Barton. Cambridge, MA: Candlewick.

> Mama takes a nap and all the barnyard animals come to try and soothe the crying baby. The little brother is the only one who knows what the baby wants and solves the problem.

What Do Toddlers Do? Photographs by Debby Slier. New York: Random House.

> Beautiful, clear photographs show the everyday activities of young children picking flowers, swinging, climbing, and banging on kitchen pots.

Where's My Baby? H.A. Rey. New York: Houghton Miffin.

> This little book has a foldover page on each page. Shows the mother animals and then asks the question, "Where's my baby?" The foldover flap shows the baby animal that belongs to the mother. Gives an opportunity to talk about the actual names for the babies such as calf, colt, and lamb.

Summary of Your Child's Second Year (12-24 Months)

LANGUAGE

Developmental Milestones	Date Achieved	NOT YET	PROGRESSING
uses jargon			
names objects (which ones?)			
uses nouns with adjectives (e.g., big truck; little car; red ball)			
uses subject-predicate phrases (e.g., Daddy go car)			
uses two-word sentences			
can say own name			
knows at least one family member by name (e.g., Mom or Dad)			
asks for food at the table			
follows one direction at a time			
hums to music			
imitates your words			
listens to rhymes			
uses pronouns (which ones?)			
comprehends about 300 words			

PHYSICAL

Developmental Milestones	Date Achieved	NOT YET	PROGRESSING
can walk alone			
can turn pages of book			
can climb stairs on all fours			
can walk sideways			
can pull a toy			
can climb onto furniture			
can feed self			
can undress self			
can scribble			
holds crayon in fist			
can run stiffly			
can build a tower of blocks (how many?)			
can walk up stairs holding hand or rail			
can walk down stairs holding hand or rail			
can kick a ball			
can throw large ball			
can do single piece puzzles (how many pieces?)			

COGNITIVE

Developmental Milestones	Date Achieved	NOT YET	PROGRESSING

can point to facial features:
    eyes
    nose
    mouth			

follows simple directions:
    Give the ball to me
    Sit on the chair			

can name several nouns that are familiar objects:
    table
    bed
    toy car
    apple			

can point to pictures showing different action verbs			

can match colors without necessarily knowing the names
    red
    green
    yellow
    blue			

develops imaginative play			
has longer attention span			

can demonstrate understanding of prepositions:
    in
    out
    up
    down			

understands math concept of "one more"			

7

Toy Dialogs for the Third Year

The developmental period from two to three is the one in which your toddler strives to become more independent. This period is often called the "terrible twos." A few suggestions might help you ease your way through this time with a little less trauma for both you and your preschooler. One simple tip is not to ask a "yes" or "no" question. If you do, you are more likely to get a "no" than a "yes." A better approach is to offer two alternatives, both of which are acceptable to you. This gives your youngster a feeling of control over her life. Let's look at an example of how this might work. Say, "Would you like to have apple juice or orange juice for a snack today?" as opposed to "Do you want apple juice?" If your child responds to the first by saying, "I want a cookie," you can calmly say, "Cookies are not a choice today. Do you want apple juice or orange juice?" If you are consistent in this approach, you should experience fewer problems.

Consistency is another key issue in handling your youngster. Try to establish a daily routine for her. This does not mean that every day is etched in granite never to change, but as much as possible, give her a routine that she can latch onto. While toddlers are struggling to become children, they also need the stability of knowing what is happening so that they feel they are in control.

Control is one of the key issues that results in misbehavior from children. Often children want to show that they are in control and parents often give up in frustration or tiredness and the children "win" again.

Keep your youngster active. She will be more likely to demand your attention, fuss, and misbehave if she is bored. This doesn't mean that you need a three-ring circus going all the time, but try to arrange some time during each day when you have a trip to the store or the playground or a special trip to a museum. This will give her something to plan for and give you some leverage for keeping her behavior manageable. When you do go out, keep your trip short and have a definite purpose in mind.

The two- to three-year-old loves to play rhyming games and she will learn how to use different sounds by playing these rhyming games with you. Running errands in the car is an ideal time for these kinds of word games. Just think of words that rhyme—they don't always have to make sense. A lot of laughter can come from silly sounding rhyming words. This is great exercise for all of those speech sounds that our mouth muscles need to learn to say.

This is also a good time to begin teaching your child her full name, her address, and phone number. One mother used a familiar nursery rhyme and inserted her child's full name into the rhyme. Another time, she would add her address or phone number to the rhyme. Using this technique makes it fun and easy for your child to begin to learn this very essential information. For example, you can insert your child's name in the song, "Mary Had a Little Lamb" so that it would sound like this:

> *"Jenny lives on Jessup Road, Jessup Road, Jessup Road.*
> *Jenny lives on Jessup Road at 12604.*
> *Jenny lives in Mt. Sinclair, Mr. Sinclair, Mt. Sinclair.*
> *Jenny lives in Mt. Sinclair, it's in the state of Maine...."*

Your child will love having her own personal rhyme.

Where language learning is concerned, you need to continue the same modeling that you have done before. Use the same idea that she has said to you but say it back to her correctly. She says, "wheel falled off." You say, "Oh my, the wheel fell off your car. Do you need help fixing it?"

At this age, your youngster needs even more time to play alone. Many of the toys selected for this age group are perfect for stimulating your child to create on her own. At the same time, you want to remember that you are helping to build receptive language and expand the language she has.

Also, your child will recognize the similarities between toys at home and the real objects they represent in your world. As you go about your daily routines, be sure to point out these similarities. "Today we are going to get the car fixed. We need to take the car to the garage. The mechanic will fix our car." Then when you get home you can play with the toy garage that you have in the house and point out the things that are the same and different.

• • • • • • • • • • • • •

Fun Sounds Garage™
by Fisher-Price

You have just come home from the trip you made to the garage to have your oil changed. This would be a good time to bring out this garage from Fisher-Price.

"Do you remember when we went to the garage today? We had to have the oil changed. Let's play with your garage and see if we can change the oil in your tiny car. Where is the car? Okay, I see it. Drive it up the ramp and we'll see if we can change the oil. At the garage, the mechanic took out all of the old oil. Can you do that with your car? Put it up on the lift. Right, that's the way he did it. All the oil is coming out. Let's get a small bucket to put it in. I see one right there. You can't drive the car yet. You have to put some fresh oil in. Here is the mechanic. He is pouring fresh oil in the tiny car. Great, now it's ready to go. Oh, maybe we should wash the car before it leaves the garage. Here is the car wash. Now it is all clean and has fresh oil. Shall we put this little lady in the car and she can drive away? You remembered a lot about changing the oil and washing the car."

• • • • • • • • • • • • •

Little People School Bus™
by Fisher-Price

If your child has special needs, she may be in a preschool program where she rides the bus to school. Even if she doesn't ride the school bus, she sees them everyday when she is on the road with you. The Fisher-Price school bus is just made for little hands to play with. It even comes with a wheelchair that can roll up the back ramp of the school bus. It is a great toy for role play and imaginative play. If your child is just starting preschool and will ride the bus, this may be a useful toy to help her work out any fears she has about getting on the school bus. On the other hand, many young children talk longingly about the day they will ride the school bus.

"Jeff, look what Mommy has for you. This is a school bus. It is yellow just like the school bus that Craig rides on. Let's see what's inside. Oh, here are some children. They are sitting nicely in their seats. They

are waiting to go to school. Can you drive them to school? Off they go. Push the bus driver down. Listen, he is talking. What is this back here? It's a wheelchair, like the one James uses. The boy can go up and down the ramp here in the back. Can you push him up the ramp? You are such a big helper. The boy stays in his wheelchair for the ride. When you go to school tomorrow you can ride on the yellow school bus. Will you ride with James? No, he goes on a different school bus but you will see him when you get to school."

As with all the toys that are described and dialogs presented, you will want to make sure you give your child an opportunity to share the language that she has. The dialogs are written to give you an idea of the play value of the toy but be sure and pause often so she has a chance to offer her views also.

All Shapes and Sizes™
by Small World Toys

This is a beautifully constructed wooden toy that will last and last and provide hours of play time for you and your child. There are four of each basic shape: square, triangle, circle, and rectangle in the four basic colors: blue, yellow, red, and green. You have been talking about these attributes for some time now and your child will be able to recognize these shapes and these colors. She may be able to actually say the names of these shapes and colors at this point. Make sure that you give her plenty of opportunities to tell you what she knows.

In addition to shape and color, this toy also gives you the opportunity to talk about size. When lined up by color, the shapes are also lined up by size and you can talk about small, big, bigger, and biggest. This will be introductory language at this age but there is no reason that you can't introduce it. Start with the familiar concepts of color and shape and then move on to the more

Single Concept

The first round of play may go as follows:

*"I have a new toy to show you today. Look at all the bright colors (hold up one). This color is **red**. Can you tell me the color? Right, it is **red**. Let's find all the **red** shapes. Here is a **red** triangle. Here is a **red** square. Do you see the **red** circle? Good, there is the **red** circle. One more. What shape is this **red** one? It is the rectangle. Wow, you know all your shapes. Watch, I will show you how they fit here. Give me the **red** circle. See, it goes right here. It is round and it is a circle. Now find the **red** square. Give me the **red** square. What color is it? Right, it is **red**! Let's put all the **red** shapes in first. Wonderful, now that is done. What color should we play with next? Okay, let's do blue."*

At another time:

*"Let's find all of the **squares**. Do you see them? I see a red **square** and look over there. There is a blue **square**. Can you find another **square**? Good, that one is green. I think there is one more **square** left. Do you know which it is? That's right. It's the yellow **square**. Let's see how many **squares** we have now. Count with me. One, two, three, four. Right, there are four **squares**. Now let's find all the triangles...."*

challenging size concepts. This toy will be one that you will want to play with, put away, and then bring out again and again as your child grows.

Continue in this way giving your child plenty of time to say the words she knows and to fit the shapes in the appropriate places. If your child has a visual impairment, you can help her feel the shape of the wooden pieces and then finger the appropriate space that it goes in. You will want to tell her the names of the colors, but unless she has some vision, this may be a challenging concept for her. Nevertheless, you do want to provide the language.

If your child has a hearing loss, you can use this toy as you have with other toys at younger ages, to help her take a hearing test. At a different time, when you are not teaching shapes or colors, have her hold one of the shapes and listen to a noise you make behind her back. When she hears the noise, she can place the shape in the right spot. This will help her prepare for the type of behavioral hearing test in which she is asked to drop a block in a container or the like when she hears a sound. Many children pick this task up quite easily and you may not have to spend much time teaching her to do it. This toy is, however, a fun way to practice.

- - - - - - - - - - - - -

Farm House and Farm Figures™
by Battat

Children love animals and usually the first ones they are introduced to are the farm animals. These animals have wonderful sounds to make which helps young children with their speech development.

This toy farm is large and made to last. There is a farmer, a tractor, cows, sheep, chickens, pigs, and horses. You will want to introduce each of these names as you take the animals out from the barn. There are white fence parts that you and your child can put together to make a corral for the animals. Let's see how play would go with this toy.

Single Concept

*"Jesse, do you remember when your class went to the farm to visit? I have a toy farm here that we can play with. Let's see what's **inside**. Look, here are some pigs, a horse, some sheep, and some cows. Which would you like? You like the cow. Here it is. What sound does a cow make? You are right.*

*"Mooooo." I like the way you said that. I am going to build a corral with these fences. Can you put the cow **inside** the fence? That's right, the cow is **inside** the fence. What else should we put **inside** the fence? Oh, you have the sheep. Put the sheep **inside** the fence. How many animals are **inside** the fence? Right—there are two. A cow and a sheep. Are there more animals? I see a pig. Let's put him **inside** the fence too. Now there are three animals **inside** the fence. Listen—can you find the sheep **inside** the fence? Great you found the sheep **inside** the fence. What sound does the sheep make? Baaaaaa. That's great."*

Be sure to introduce all of the farm names: barn, tractor, farmer, pig, sheep, cow, horse, chicken, fence, moo, baa, oink, neigh.

When you are using a toy for teaching language, you will want to put it away after playing with it. This will make it fresh and appealing when you bring it out again later that day or the next. After you have played with it for a while and your child has learned the language you want her to learn, you can leave it out for her to have for free play and time to practice the language she has learned.

Baby Farm Friends Bowling Set™
by International Playthings

Varied repetition is a way of teaching language through a variety of play things using the same language. You have just played with farm animals and now here is a different way of playing using some of the same animals. This bowling set has six animals: cow, sheep, cat, pig, dog, and duck. Each of the animals makes a sound and there are two sets of each sound so you can play a matching sound game. The bowling ball makes a chiming sound that will help children with visual impairments to follow the ball as it rolls towards the animals. These animals and ball are soft and easy for young hands to grasp. Additionally, they stand steadily as your child attempts to knock them down. You will have fun playing with this bowling set. Here's how your language might go.

"This is a bowling game that you and I can play today. Let's see what's in the bag. [Let your child remove the animals one by one.] You have a cow. Listen, can you hear the sound it makes? What else is in there? Oh, wow, a sheep. Let's listen to that sound. Shake it. I hear the sound. Did you find another animal? That's a cat. Can you shake it? That's a different sound. Listen carefully. Does it sound like this? No, it is a different sound. Find another animal. Hooray, a dog. Shake it. What does it sound like? Hmmm, that's a different sound, too. Let's wait until we get them all out and then we can match them. Okay, we have the cow, the sheep, the cat, and the dog. What's left? A pig and a duck.

Now we have all the animals out of the bag. Listen carefully. Let's see if we can match them. Oh, shake the cat. Listen carefully. Now shake the dog. Terrific, they sound the same. We can match them. Now let's try the duck. Listen carefully. That's right. It matches the pig.... Now let's play a bowling game. Watch while I set them up. Here's the cat, now the dog, here's the sheep, and the cow. Now the last two are the duck and the pig. You stand right here and roll the ball. Look at you. You made three of the animals fall down. Can you knock the rest down? Okay, you knocked the cat and the sheep down. Only one more left. Oops, you missed. Let's set them all up again. Now it's my turn to try to knock them down."

Fascination Station™
by Discovery Toys

This toy is a version of a rolling track which is built for small hands. There are sections of track that need to be put together around a tube. A frog goes down the tube and your child pushes a button for the frog to pop out. There are a duck and two balls which roll down and around the track. The objects are large enough that you don't have to worry about a young child swallowing them.

Some of the concepts you can teach through this toy are:

- Names of objects
  - Roundabout slide
  - Blue and yellow track
  - Yellow duck
  - Blue and yellow ball
  - Red and yellow ball
  - Green frog
- Actions
  - Down the slide
  - Around and around
  - Down the tube
  - Push the button

Single Concept

*"Here's the frog. Watch him go **down** the tube. Where is the frog? Is he **down** the tube? Push the button to get froggy out. Can you put him **down** the tube again? There he goes, **down** the tube.*

*Here's the duck. Can you make him go **down** the slide? **Down** he goes. Good job. You made the duck go **down** the slide."*

Continue with the same dialog with the two balls.

Children playing with this toy repeat the actions over and over. You will have plenty of opportunity to practice the language in this toy.

Music Blocks Maestro™
by Neurosmith

Beautiful music in a fun toy for your child to manipulate. What a great toy! There are five different-colored blocks with shapes (squares, circles, triangles, rectangles, stars) on each side. You can choose between Mozart, Beethoven, and Bach on the cartridge that comes with the toy and there are other cartridges that you can buy to add to the fun. When each block is placed in the square place holder, it plays a phrase of the music. When you have placed all of the blocks, you can push the red bar and your entire selection will be played. Children love to dance and twirl to their own musical creations. The shapes are raised on the blocks, so if your child has a visual impairment, she will still be able to figure out the shapes to make them all the same or different as she chooses.

"Here are our music blocks. Let's see if we can put together some music and then we can dance. Tell me the colors you see. There is orange, yellow, red, green, and blue. Listen as we put them in the squares. They

each make a different sound. You can change the sound by turning the blocks around and putting different shapes up. There, you made them all squares. Push the red button and let's see how the music sounds. Great dancing! Let's turn the blocks around and make a different sound. Now push the red bar again and listen to the music. Oh, it is so beautiful. It makes me want to dance and twirl with you."

Homemade Toys

• • • • • • • • • • • • •

Flannel Board   A flannel board is a toy that you will use over and over again. It is very simple to make. You need a backing for the flannel. You can use a piece of plywood, a piece of wallboard, a piece of styrofoam, or even a cardboard box. A cardboard box is nice because it is light and can stand on its own. You can keep your flannel pieces in the box when you're not using it for play.

A word about the "flannel." You do not need to use flannel *per se*. Any material with a nap to it that will allow other pieces to adhere to it will work quite well.

To make the board, all you need to do is cover whatever you have decided to use with your "flannel." If you use wood for the frame, you will need to glue or staple the material to it. With other lighter materials, you can use wide masking tape, glue, or staples.

Once your board is made, you can begin to create materials made out of the same type of fabric—anything with a nap that will stick to it. You can cut out numbers, letters, shapes, just about anything that you would like to teach your child about. If you are not good at drawing, coloring books are a wonderful source of pictures. For example, you can get coloring books that have fairy tales with nice, simply drawn pictures. Trace the picture onto the fabric and cut out the figures. Then you can add the subtle features with magic markers.

Let's assume you're going to do a fairy tale story. You have made all of the story pieces for the story of Goldilocks and the Three Bears. You introduce the story with a book and then take out your characters and you and your child retell the story using the characters you have made. Your child will have great fun remembering the story and imitating the characters. Her retelling may not be exactly as the story goes but she will have great fun acting it out.

The child with partial vision will be able to feel the outline of the shapes, and, with high contrast colors, may be able to see the pieces. Before you tell the story, introduce each of the characters to your child and let her explore the object. Give her the language for what she is seeing and feeling.

. . . .

Shape Lunch*

Isn't it amazing how many shapes our food comes in? If your child eats the string cheese that comes in packages, you will notice that it is a rectangle! Add some Cheerios to her lunch and you have something that is round. Cut her sandwich diagonally, and you have triangles. It can be fun to point out all the shapes that are around us all day. The following is how you might talk to your child during her lunch time.

"What would you like for lunch? Cheese? I will get it for you. Look, the cheese is a rectangle! How about that! What else would you like? Some cereal? Look at these Cheerios—they are shaped like circles. Your cheese is a rectangle and your cereal is shaped like circles. Let's see about this jelly sandwich. I will cut it for you. I can cut it into triangles. Now our sandwich looks like four triangles. Show me the circles. That's right. The cereal is shaped like circles. Show me the triangle. Right—the sandwich is cut into four triangles. Show me the rectangle. Right, the cheese looks like a rectangle."

This conversation at lunch would be a good follow-up activity to playing with the All Shapes and Sizes toy that was discussed above.

---

* Idea suggested by Anna Michelle.

Toy Summary

The following is a list of toys that we have worked with in this developmental year. The asterisk indicates a homemade toy.

Fun Sounds Garage™—Fisher-Price
Little People School Bus™—Fisher-Price
All Shapes and Sizes™—Small World Toys
Farm House and Farm Figures™—Battat
Baby Farm Friends Bowling™—International Playthings
Fascination Station™—Discovery Toys
* Flannel Board
* Shape Lunch

Vocabulary and Concepts

The following list will give you an idea of the vocabulary and concepts that your child should be familiar with by the end of the third developmental year:

- *action words:* walk, run, jump, pull, twist, pour, turn, put, down, eat, erase, open, close, twirl, push
- *animals:* rabbit, elephant, dog, whale, fish, lobster, butterflies, dragonfly, beetle, frog
- *body parts:* eyes, nose, mouth, hair, ears
- *child's name, address, and phone number*
- *colors:* naming and matching
- *expressions:* Please, Thank you
- *farm animals:* sheep, dog, duck, horse, cow, pig
- *farm animal attributes:* tail, fur, ears, udders, snout, webbed feet
- *farm animal sounds:* baa, arf-arf, quack, neigh, moo, oink
- *feelings:* happy, sad, mad, angry
- *mealtime utensils:* spoon, fork, plate, glass, cup, mug
- *nouns:* boat, airplane, car, trucks, road signs, traffic lights, balloon, garage, school bus, wheelchair, tractor, fences
- *numbers:* one through twelve
- *nursery rhymes:* Humpty Dumpty, Jack and Jill, Mary Had a Little Lamb
- *opposites:* up/down; in/out; left/right; fast/slow; inside/outside
- *same/different*
- *prepositions:* on, off, on top of, next to, under, through, round and round
- *questions:* what; what's inside; when; where; who
- *shapes:* square, triangle, circle, star, heart, rectangle
- *traffic signals:* red-stop; green-go; yellow-wait/slow down

Books

During this time, your child will begin to be more interested in her books. Bedtime reading should be a ritual by now. Many stories she will have heard so many times that she may be able to read them to you. Encourage her participation. Let her tell you the story. You'll be amazed at how accurate she can be. Stories that tell about courage—such as *The Little Engine That Could*—and stories involving a problem to be solved—such as *Corduroy*—are easy for your youngster to relate to.

All You Need for a Snowman. Alice Shertle. Illustrated by Barbara Lavallee. Orlando, FL: Harcourt.
> Told in rhyme about making a snowman step by step. It will satisfy a child's dream of building the perfect snowman.

Anno's Counting Book. Mitsumasa Anno. New York: Philomel Books.
> A beautifully illustrated book that teaches the concepts of the numbers one through twelve. Each page unfolds to the changing seasons, offering different things to count on each page.

The Baby's Catalogue. Janet and Allan Ahlberg. Boston: Little, Brown.
> Colorful, detailed drawings point out the numerous objects on each page which tell of the daily lives of young families and their babies. Young children will love looking at the pictures while being introduced to new vocabulary words.

Bearsie Bear and the Surprise Sleepover Party. Bernard Waber. New York: Houghton Mifflin.
> Although the night is cold, Bearsie Bear has a warm fire and a cozy bed. His friends come to join him and all is well until the very end. A wonderful surprise ending.

Brown Bear, Brown Bear, What Do You See? Bill Martin, Jr. Illustrated by Eric Carle. New York: Holt.
> A cumulative rhyme that begins, "Brown bear, brown bear, what do you see? I see a red bird looking at me. Red bird, red bird, what do you see?" After several readings of this book, your child will be joining in on the refrains. A few more readings and your child may be "reading" on her own with the help of the pictures and repetitive texts. A favorite with preschoolers.

Caps for Sale. Esphyr Slobodkina. New York: W.R. Scott.
> Classic tale of a peddler who carries his hats on his head and what happens when he falls asleep under a tree full of mon-

keys. The simple repetitive nature of the story appeals to young children and they shortly know what to say at the right moment giving them a chance to "read" the story too.

Corduroy. Dan Freeman. New York: Viking Press.
An endearing tale that young children have enjoyed for many years. Tells the story of a stuffed bear who searches through the toy store for his lost button, and finds a friend and a home.

Dear Zoo. Rod Campbell. New York: Four Winds.
A lift-the-flap book that shows all of the zoo animals who have arrived in various crates. They are different sizes, shapes, and colors, which gives you plenty of vocabulary to talk about.

Felix Feels Better. Rosemary Wells. Cambridge, MA: Candlewick.
Felix is sick and Mama cannot make him better. So they go to the doctor. Felix is afraid of the doctor and your child may be too. He will enjoy hearing about Felix.

Going to the Potty. Fred Rogers. Photos by Jim Judkis. New York: Putnam.
Your child may be showing interest in using the potty. Mr. Rogers talks with children about using the potty in his usual calm way.

Good Night, Baby Bear. Frank Asch. Orlando, FL: Harcourt Brace.
Children who stall about going to bed will relate to Baby Bear. He wants a snack, a drink, and even the moon. Mama Bear is patient and even delivers the moon. A good bedtime story.

Great Day for Up. Dr. Seuss. New York: Random House.
If you ever wanted to focus on a single vocabulary word, this is the book for "up." The catchy and repetitive rhymes make it fun for children to listen to and join in.

Harry the Dirty Dog. Gene Zion. New York: Harper and Row.
Harry doesn't want to take a bath. He buries his bath brush, runs away, and gets so dirty that when he comes home, no one recognizes him.

Here Comes the Train. Charlotte Voake. Cambridge, MA: Candlewick.
William and his family watch trains go by as they stand on the bridge. Family fun activity with lots of sounds to imitate.

I Can Do It Myself. Illustrated by June Goldsborough. New York: Golden Books.

> Another example of a book that can help a young child going through the stage of wanting to do everything on her own. This book follows a young child throughout her day and shows all the ways in which she can help around the house and do things on her own.

Inside Freight Train. Donald Crews. New York: HarperCollins.

> A bright board book that offers small hands the opportunity to move each colorful freight car to discover hidden things inside.

Is It Hard, Is It Easy? Mary M. Green. Illustrated by Len Gettloman. New York: Young/Scott/Wilson-Wesley.

> During this stage of wanting to do things on their own, some children may become frustrated with things they cannot do very well alone. This little book pictures children doing things that are easy and some that are hard. It shows that we all cannot do things equally.

Little Bunny Follows His Nose. Katherine Howard. Pictures by J.P. Miller. Racine, WI: Western Publishing Co.

> To release the non-toxic fragrance labels in the rose, the strawberry jar, the pine needle, the peach, the dill pickle, and the chocolate mint cookie, scratch vigorously. This book can be used over and over and the fragrances last a long time. Great for extra sensory input for any child who could benefit from the additional stimulation. Especially good for children with visual impairments.

The Little Engine That Could. Watty Piper. Illustrated by George and Doris Houman. New York: Platt and Munk.

> Children enjoy the refrain in this delightful story and get the message that they should continue to try even when they think they can't do the job. This may be especially inspiring for children with special needs who continually need encouragement to try difficult things.

Mouse Mess. Linnea Asplind Riley. New York: Blue Sky Press.

> A clever rhyming story tells the tale of a naughty mouse, a mound of food, and the mess he makes when the people in the house are sleeping.

Mouse Paint. Ellen Stoll Walsh. San Diego: Harcourt Brace.
> Three little white mice discover three jars of paint—red, yellow, and blue. As they jump in and out of each jar, they discover how to make new colors.

My Car. Byron Barton. New York: Greenwillow.
> Sam talks about his car, how he drives it, and where he goes. The story is told in simple words and short sentences. There is a surprise ending.

My First Kwanzaa Book. Deborah M. Newton Chocolate. Illustrated by Cal Massey. New York: Scholastic.
> A young boy and his family celebrate the seven days and principles of this African-American holiday with love and pride.

No Nap. Eve Bunting. New York: Clarion Press.
> It's time for Susie's nap but Susie isn't tired. "No nap," she says. So Dad makes plans to tire Susie out. A fresh and humorous approach to a real-life situation.

On Mother's Lap. Ann Herbert Scott. Illustrated by Glo Coalson. New York: Clarion.
> A very important story that shows older brothers and sisters that Mom will still have room for them in her life after the new baby arrives. Involves a Native American family.

Push Pull, Empty Full. Tana Hoban. New York: Macmillan.
> Black and white photographs showing opposites. A great "talk about" book for naming as well as to introduce the concept of opposites. The concepts shown are: push/pull, empty/full, wet/dry, in/out, up/down, thick/thin, whole/broken, front/back, big/little, first/last, many/few, heavy/light, together/apart, left/right, day/night.

The Snowy Day. Ezra Jack Keats. New York: Viking Press.
> Another fine book with beautiful illustrations and no text about activities to do in the snow. This one ends with a warm bath after the chilling fun day.

Splash. Flora Mc Donnell. New York: Greenwillow.
> The baby elephant splashes in the cool water while her animal friends join her. Lovely sound effects to be imitated.

Talkabout Clothes. Ethel Wingfield. Illustrated by Harry Wingfield. London: Ladybird Books.

> Talks about all different kinds of clothes for all kinds of weather and people. How we make clothes, colors of clothes, repairing clothing. Opportunities for the child to be involved with matching different clothing as well as finding similarities and differences in items of clothing.

Tell Me A Season. Mary McJenna Siddals. Illustrated by Petra Mathers. New York: Clarion.

> Two young children move through the seasons with lovely words and beautiful art.

Vehicle Books: Boats, Cars, Trains, Trucks, Fire Engines, and Big Wheels. Anne Rockwell. New York: E.P. Dutton.

> Simple text and bright illustrations teach preschoolers about all of the vehicles they may see in their world. A rich array of language opportunities in this series.

The Very Quiet Cricket. Eric Carle. New York: Philomel Books.

> A multi-sensory book that tells the story of a very quiet cricket who wants to rub his wings together and make a sound as many other insects do. He finally achieves his wish. Listen for a great surprise at the end of the story! Great self-esteem builder for your child if he is not talking as others his age are at this time.

When Mama Comes Home Tonight. Eileen Spinelli. Illustrated by Jane Dyer. New York: Simon and Schuster.

> Tender illustrations and lyrical rhymes celebrate the end of the day when Mama comes home. Also available as a board book.

Where's Spot? Eric Hill. New York: Putnam.

> A lift-the-flap book that teaches prepositions as Spot's mom looks all over the place to find him.

Summary of Your Child's Third Year (24-36 Months)

LANGUAGE

Developmental Milestones	Date Achieved	NOT YET	PROGRESSING
uses plurals			

uses noun phrases with articles:
    a ball
    an apple
    the door			

uses three-word phrases Mommy bye-bye car			
uses possessive nouns (which ones?)			
uses pronoun "I"			

asks simple questions:
    who?
    what?
    when?
    where?			

adds "ing" to verbs			
uses past tense for verbs			
uses 4-word sentences			
can say whole name			
can respond to questions with choices			

uses social phrases:
    thank you
    please			

sings along with music			
outsiders understand her speech			
knows 800 words			

PHYSICAL

Developmental Milestones	Date Achieved	NOT YET	PROGRESSING
can walk backwards			

can walk up stairs:
   alternating feet
   holding hands or rail			

can run without falling			
can jump; both feet off floor			
can bounce and catch a large ball			
can pedal a tricycle			
can build a tower of blocks (how many?)			
can hold crayon not fisted			
can make snips with scissors			
can hold a glass with one hand			
can hold fork in fist			

COGNITIVE

Developmental Milestones	Date Achieved	NOT YET	PROGRESSING

can point to body parts:
   hair
   tongue
   teeth
   hand
   ears
   feet
   head
   legs
   arms			

can name body parts:
   mouth
   eyes
   nose
   hair			

(COGNITIVE continued)			
Developmental Milestones	**Date Achieved**	**NOT YET**	**PROGRESSING**
hands ears head			
can match colors: orange purple brown black			
can identify colors: give me the red car blue yellow green			
can match shapes: circle square triangle			
can follow directions that include prepositions: put the doll in the box put the doll under the box			
can demonstrate knowledge of opposites: little/big short/long			
can demonstrate knowledge of use of common objects: What do we do with beds? Why do we have coats?			
develops imaginative play more fully			
able to express feelings			
understands math concept of "just one": Give me just one block			

Toy Dialogs for the Fourth Year

You may be relieved to discover that this can be the "calm after the storm" age. The "terrible twos" has ended and magically your child doesn't seem to have tantrums the way he used to. At the developmental age of three, your youngster has graduated from toddlerhood. He is now quite steady on his feet. And he is much more ready to consider other people's points of view, not just his own. All of these things will happen gradually, not overnight.

Now he can look at books for quite a long period of time. Since he may be in a transition time with his daytime naps, you may have some bedtime difficulties. This is an excellent time to reinforce a bedtime routine. A bath after dinner can be followed by a quiet game or toy activity. Then bathroom routines are completed, and you end by reading a story or two to your child, or having him "read" to you. State the number of stories to be read beforehand and then stick to that number. A firm good night with permission to "read" to himself for a few minutes will end your evening with your youngster. Do not be drawn back into the room with pleas of "one more story" or "one more drink of water." Your firmness and consistency are important in order for him to learn limits. Being allowed to "read" for a few minutes gives him the idea that he is in control of when he actually falls asleep. So many of the arguments about bedtime are really "control" kinds of arguments. This compromise solution will avoid many of these arguments.

If your child is not in a preschool program, you might want to consider organizing a play group in your neighborhood so that he can have the opportunity to interact with other children and learn about sharing toys and playing together. You should be within earshot when they are playing together but resist the temptation to step in and solve every problem that comes up. Children need to argue things out. They learn to reason, defend their position, assume leadership, and abandon control through their play at this age.

Your child will have a better idea of the larger world outside his home and may begin to develop some fears. He may be afraid of monsters, or of having you leave him, or of death. Since this is the age when he develops an ability to fantasize, the combination of fantasy and fear can be a potent one. You may have to address some of his fears in your play situations.

Encourage him to share his activities and especially his feelings. You may need to ask questions to spur him on and keep the conversation going. "Then what happened?" "Can you tell me more?" "How did you feel when he said that to you?" Sharing his feelings and his experiences helps him realize that you enjoy listening to him and are eager to discuss things with him.

Now you can begin teaching him how to play games. Waiting for your turn, moving only a certain number of spaces, "reading" the directions, winning and losing are all skills you can teach through games. He'll take great pride in hearing you say, "Daddy likes the way you're sharing your toy with Jodie." If he plays games with other children, keep the number of participants small so that they really have a chance to practice these skills and are not spending a lot of time waiting for their turn.

Board Games

Typically, board games lend themselves to having a winner and a loser. Instead of emphasizing this aspect of the game, encourage playing the game for the fun of it. This way, winning and losing will take on their proper perspective. Once you have taught your child how to play the games and have used them for your language teaching, he will enjoy playing them with friends. In the beginning, it will be helpful for you to be involved in the games to keep things moving along smoothly and to ensure that your language-delayed child has all of the vocabulary that he needs to play the game.

Candyland™ by Milton Bradley

Candyland™ is a classic and your child will love the bright, sturdy, and colorful board, cards, and playing pieces. Allow him to handle the playing pieces freely at first because the game is new and he will want to touch all of the pieces. As he is doing this, name all of the playing pieces for him:

> *"See all the bright cards we need for the game. There are blue, yellow, red, green, purple, and orange. Can you put them all together in a pile? Watch me shuffle*

the cards and mix them all together. This is the board that tells us where to go when we pick a card. We'll move our little marker around the board and match the pictures on the cards we pick. Which color marker would you like? I'll take red. On your mark, get set, go... pick the first card!"

Candyland™ is a wonderful play opportunity to review colors with your child or to introduce them if you have not done so already. Also, you can reinforce the incidental counting that you taught earlier as you two count together the number of squares you must move.

"Let's count how many squares you need to go before you get to the candy cane: one, two, three, four, five... great!"

In addition to teaching colors and counting, Candyland™ helps your child practice the social skills of sharing and taking turns. You may find that he is able to handle sharing and taking turns well when he is playing with you but will be unable to do this yet with friends. Help him by playing with him once or twice and if he cannot share with his friends, then use the game only for teaching times with you.

Fruit Basket™
by Small World Toys
&
Shopping Cart™
by Little Tykes

Your three-year-old will love pretending that he is shopping just like you when you go to the store. This fruit basket contains a strawberry, a watermelon, a pear, a tomato, an onion, a bunch of grapes, a lemon, an apple, an orange, and a pineapple. Most of the foods are split in half and are joined together by Velcro. The pineapple is split in thirds. This gives you a great opportunity to talk about a variety of foods and for your child to

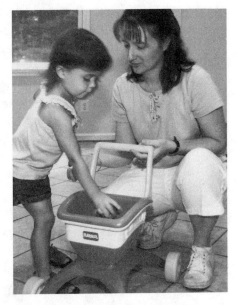

pretend to go shopping. Children this age just love pushing objects around. The shopping cart is excellent for this fun. Your child, at this age, is a little too young to fully understand about halves and thirds but there is no reason why you can't talk about it as you play. Remember that a child must have a receptive bank of language before he can actually use that language. It is fun for your child to pull the food apart and then fit the pieces back together again as you talk about halves and thirds.

"Hi, Debra. What are you playing with? Oh, you have your fruits and vegetables. Are you going shopping? Where is your shopping cart? You can put your purchases in the cart. Let's see if you remember all these names. Hmm, you have a red fruit with speckles on it. That's a strawberry. Pull it apart. Now you have two halves. See—one, two. Put them back together and now it is a whole strawberry. What else have you got in your cart? Yum, delicious. I see a bunch of grapes. What color are the grapes? Right, they are purple. Can you pull them apart? That's right. Now you have two halves. Put them back and the bunch of grapes is whole again."

You will get the opportunity to talk about halves and whole throughout this play time.

. . . .
Madeline and Genevieve™
by Learning Curve

Most little girls love the story of Madeline. Because the story is told in rhyme, many young children learn to recite it by heart at a very young age. If your child has been fascinated by the Madeline stories and videos, she will love to play with this dressable Madeline and her faithful dog, Genevieve.

"Oh, Jamie. That was fun reading the story of Madeline. Genevieve saved her when she fell into the water. I have a surprise for you. Look what I have. This is a Madeline doll and her favorite friend, Genevieve. Look, Genevieve has her own carrier and little bed. Would you like to play with her? Let's pretend to tell the story with Genevieve and Madeline. 'In an old house in _____. Paris, that's right. Lived twelve little_____.' Girls, good."

Then continue with the rest of the story, pausing so your child can fill in the blanks. Children love to tell this story over and over.

You can play with the doll and the dog and have your child act out the story. The doll itself is dressed in a plaid dress and a blue overcoat just like the Madeline in the story. The coat has large buttons that may be fairly easy for your child to unbutton and the dress is fastened with Velcro, which also makes it easy to take off. You may have to help with dressing the doll again after all the clothes are off.

There are videos and DVDs of all the Madeline stories and you can watch them with your child as she enjoys seeing the books in action. Try to limit your viewing time to one video at a sitting. It is too much to have children sit for long periods of time watching videos or TV.

Thomas and Friends Wooden Railway™
by Learning Curve

This set includes one Thomas the Tank Engine, one box car, one caboose, a tree, a crossing gate, a stop sign, a gentleman rider, a conductor at the gatehouse, a bridge and tunnel piece, and enough track to make a figure 8. This is a set that you can continually add pieces to as your child's abilities and creativity expand. It is very well constructed and durable. Your child should get a lot of play time with this toy.

"Let's play with our railway today, Miguel. You take out the track and I will get the cars. Do you need some help putting the track together? I can help you with that. You hold the piece and I will push the other track onto it. There we go. Two pieces of track are together. Can you get some more track? Now we have four pieces of track. You put that together very well.

Where's the bridge? We can attach it right here. Only a few more pieces and then our track will be put together. Great job. Now we have finished our track. Where are the trains? Do you remember what this is called? Yes, that is Thomas the Tank Engine. This car is called a boxcar. Sometimes it carries animals and

other times it carries things we might buy in the store. And this last car is called the caboose. Okay, let's put them on the track. That's right. The engine goes first. Then the boxcar and finally the caboose. Who is this guy over here? He is the conductor. He raises and lowers the crossing gate. If the gate is down the train has to stop. Okay, you push the train around the track and I will be the conductor. Here comes the train. You can go right through and go over the bridge. Now you are going round and round the track. Now let's change jobs. You be the conductor and I will drive the train. Here I come."

Children this age love to pretend and this is a wonderful toy for them to learn new language and new play options. Learning to take turns is also a skill your child will begin to learn at this age. With you as a playmate, he can learn these skills and then practice them when he is in his preschool or play group.

. . . .

Bear Blocks™

by Discovery Toys

This early learning game requires no reading skills. There are four blocks, each side showing a bear with a different accessory. For example, one bear may have a blue vest, another one a yellow tie, and yet another a red hat. This is a great game for reviewing colors and distinguishing critical elements.

You play the game by stacking all of the bear cards in a pile. Then each player gets three bear cards. You place the cards in front of you with the bear side up. Each player gets a chance to roll all four blocks. Your child looks at his cards to see if he has a bear that matches any of the bears that are face up on the blocks. If he has a match, he turns that card over. The first person to turn over all three cards wins.

If your child has a hearing loss, you can use this game for listening practice. You can give your child three cards, cover your mouth, and say, "Where is the bear with a blue tie?" "Where is the bear with a red hat?" This will be a fun listening game for your child.

After your child has had some fun listening with only three cards, you can add more, which makes the listening game more challenging.

Single Concept

*"Show me the bear with the blue **vest**. Where is the bear with the green **vest**? Can you find the bear with the yellow **vest**? I see the bear with the red **vest**."*

Take turns being the "teacher" here and let your child ask *you* for different bears. This is a great game to play with your child.

You can also practice speech reading in the same way. That is, have your child watch you as you say the sentence without voice and then choose the correct card.

If you are teaching your child a new concept such as "vest," you can play by asking only for the blue, yellow, red, or green vest. This gives him practice with a single concept. You have the opportunity to review the word "vest" over and over again using vocabulary that your child does know such as the colors.

Unit Blocks™ by Small World Toys We have played with blocks from the earliest ages in all kinds of forms. These are more sophisticated blocks and should lead your child into new building skills he will use for the next few years. The blocks are called Unit Blocks because two small unit blocks equal one large unit block. There are columns, pillars, triangles, half circles, arches, and large and small unit blocks. Your child will be learning the elements of geometry as he plays with these blocks. You can introduce the vocabulary as you play alongside of him. Let him lead the play. Don't interject your own ideas. Try and see what he is doing and ask lots of questions so you can get the language from your child.

"Hey, Tracy, what are you building? [A house.] Wow, look at that. Are those the windows over here? Yes, I see you made windows out of the arches. Now you are building the roof. I see the flat unit blocks are for the roof. What's that on the side? Oh, you used a column for the chimney. Do you want to get some of your "Little People"™ and play inside the house you built? Here's Maggie and Sarah. Who else is here? Ah, there is Eddie and Freddy. And over here is Michael and Sonya. You can play house with your friends and I will go in and start dinner. I will be right in the kitchen if you need me."

Village Vet Set™
by International Playthings

If you have a pet, your child has probably been to see the veterinarian with you and your pet. He will enjoy pretending to be the vet and helping the animals that come to the clinic. In this set, there is the animal clinic, a veterinarian, a nurse, a dog, a bunny, an older woman with a cat, a young girl with a mouse, and a man with a parrot. When you enter the clinic, a bell rings at the threshold to tell the veterinarian that you are in the clinic. When you place your animal on the examination table, you hear the sounds of dogs and cats. Veterinarian may be a hard word for your child to pronounce. Remember to accept what he says and model the correct pronunciation when you say the word back to him.

"Max, do you remember when we took Tyler to the veterinarian yesterday? Tyler was not feeling well so we had to take him to the doctor. When you don't feel well, we take you to your doctor too. Here is a play set that we can use to talk about our trip to the veterinarian. Here's the clinic. Listen, it plays a sound when we enter the building. Here's a dog. Let's pretend this is Tyler. Okay, let's take Tyler to the vet. The doctor will examine Tyler. She will listen to his heart and feel his stomach. Maybe she will draw some blood from him. Show me how the vet listens to Tyler's heart. Good. Now show me how she feels his stomach. Now we can draw some blood from him. The doctor will check the blood and see if she can find out why Tyler doesn't feel well. What do you think is wrong with Tyler? Oh, maybe so. Maybe he ate too much dinner last night. Look, in this play set. There is a little girl and she is carrying her pet mouse. She will bring her mouse to the veterinarian for a check up. Bring her into the clinic. Listen, the bell rang again. The mouse is so tiny. Put it on the table for the vet to check it out. Oh, listen. I hear cats and dogs. They must be in the cages in the back. Well, the veterinarian says that the mouse is okay so the little girl can go home now."

Rescue Fire Truck™
by Fisher-Price

Many young children love to play with fire trucks and other rescue equipment. A fun trip for you and your child would be to visit a fire station. You should call ahead of time to make sure that the time you would like to come is okay with the fire personnel at the station. Some areas also have an Open House at the fire station where you are welcome to visit the station, touch all of the equipment, and see some fire demonstrations.

Your child will enjoy pretending to be a fire fighter with this rescue fire truck.

"Dong, dong, dong. I hear the fire bell ringing. There must be a fire somewhere. Let's get our fire truck and see if we can help. Turn the siren on. Listen to the siren. Let's drive to the building [let your child drive the fire truck around]. Look, I see flames leaping out of that building. Get your ladder out and climb to the top window. Can you help that lady out of the burning building? Hurry. You got her. Now climb back down the ladder. See these water barrels. You can shoot them into the building. The water will help to put the fire out. One, two. Shoot those barrels of water. Hooray, the fire is out. Let's drive back to the station."

Homemade Toys

Playdough

Another classic toy that you can make easily at home is playdough. There are many recipes for this mixture. A few are included below.

Nonedible Playdough (nontoxic)
Ingredients:

1½ cups flour
½ cup salt
½ cup water
¼ cup vegetable oil
liquid food colors

Mix the food color with the water before adding to the flour mixture. The color will be more even this way. You will want to talk about the colors as you decide which color to make the playdough. When your child is four or five, you can talk about how you can mix colors together to make different colors. For example, red and blue mixed together make purple, and blue and yellow mixed together make green.

Mix flour and salt together. Add water and oil and knead the dough well. If you leave your finished product out in the air, it will harden. If you do not want your dough to harden, put it in the refrigerator in a covered jar and it can be used again.

Baker's Clay

Ingredients:

4 cups flour	1-2 cups salt
1½ cups water	

Mix dry ingredients, then add the water slowly. Knead for five minutes. (You will have to take turns with your child because he will not want to continue this for long.) Then cut or mold shapes or objects and bake at 350 degrees for 45-60 minutes. Decorate with paint or markers. If you think you will want to put a string through your creation to make a necklace, make a hole in it before you bake it.

Peanut Butter Playdough

Ingredients:

> 2 cups peanut butter
> 2 cups powdered milk
> 1 cup honey

Mix all of the ingredients together. Add more powdered milk to make it less sticky. You can roll and form this playdough like any playdough, but you would not want to make too much or keep it too long. Once you have played with it and eaten as much as you both want, put it in the refrigerator to keep it cool.

You can keep it in covered containers for several days without it spoiling.

Making playdough together with your child is a wonderful time to introduce measuring concepts. He can help you measure, pour, and mix.

"Oh, it's raining out today and we won't be able to go to the park. I have an idea. Would you like to help me make some playdough? Let's see if we have what we need. Let's look in the cupboard. We need flour. Do you see the flour? Right, there it is. Okay, can you find salt? Good! We need salt also. Now where is the oil? Oh, I see it—way in the back. Can you carry the salt? Good! Bring it to the table. Up you go—come on up where you can see and help.

"I'll measure the flour and you can dump it in the bowl. Good job! Now we need the salt. I'll measure the salt. Can you dump that in the bowl? Now you can mix it up with this big spoon. Good. Now we're ready to add the liquids. We need water and oil. What color should we make the playdough? [Your child probably can tell you the names of the colors at this developmental age.]

"Okay, let's make yellow playdough today. Yellow is a good color for today because the sun is not shining and we can still make it a sunshiny day. What a good idea you had. Now we can pour the water into this small bowl. Then we can add the oil. You did that very well. Do you want to squeeze the yellow food color? Oops, that's a lot of yellow in there! Okay, we will have a very bright playdough. Now we can add the liquid to the flour and then mix up our playdough....."

There is no limit to what you can do with playdough. Most children enjoy the squooshing and squeezing of the dough. Do not interfere with this fun, but you can have your own plan in mind for what you are going to make with yours. I have always enjoyed making balls out of the playdough and rolling them across the table to the child to roll back to me. Another favorite activity that encourages new language concepts is rolling out looooooong snakes and short snakes.

"Would you like to make something with your playdough now? Can you get it from the shelf? Here's some for you and I'll play with some....."

It's important that you follow your child's lead here and be ready to comment on whatever he's making without making him do what you are doing. Comment on what he is doing and then add comments about what you are making.

"You like to squeeze the playdough. It feels so good when you are squeezing it between your fingers. I'm going to roll my playdough. Oh, look, I made a long rope. Now I can make a short one. This one is long and this one is short. Did you make a short rope too? Good work. Let's see what else we can make. I made a small ball. Shall I roll the ball to you?"

Anticipate when your child is tiring of playing with playdough, so that you can leave enough time for him to participate in clean-up with you.

Another time, you may want to use a rolling pin and cookie cutters to make different shapes to discuss and perhaps even create a story about. You can match the cookie cutters to whatever vocabulary you want to work on. For example, there are cookie cutters in animal, toy, and holiday shapes. Let your imagination run wild with this wonderful, expandable toy.

Crayon Rock   This activity combines two things children love, crayons and music. In this activity, your child will learn about the concepts of fast and slow.

Put on some slow music and have your youngster use his crayons on paper to the rhythm of the music. You can have your own piece of paper so you can model how this should be.

Single Concept

*"Listen to the music, Jake. Do you hear how **slow** it is? Color on your paper to show how **slow** sounds. **Slowly.** The music is **slow.** Watch, I will show you. **Slow**— the music is **slow.** I am coloring **slowly.** That's right. The music is **slow** and you are coloring **slowly.**"*

*"I am going to change the CD now. I am going to put on some music that is **fast.** Listen. Can you hear how **fast** it is? Show me how **fast** looks on your paper. Color **fast.** That's right. You are coloring **fast.** I am going to color **fast,** too. Watch me. We are coloring **fast.** The music is **fast.** Good job.*

Toy Summary

The following is a list of toys that we have worked with in this developmental year. The asterisk indicates a homemade toy.

Village Vet Set™—International Plaything
Thomas and Friends Wooden Railway™—Learning Curve
Fruit Basket™—Small World Toys
Shopping Cart™—Little Tykes
Unit Blocks™—Small World Toys
Madeline and Genevieve™—Learning Curve
Bear Blocks™—Discovery Toy
Rescue Fire Truck™—Fisher-Price
* Playdough
* Crayon Rock

Vocabulary and Concepts

The following list will give you an idea of the vocabulary and concepts your child should be familiar with by the end of the fourth developmental year.

- *action words:* mix, match, spin, pick, color, stack, squeeze, roll, go, stop, take turns, pull, push, dial,
- *body parts:* hands, fingers, knees, toes, feet
- *colors:* blue, yellow, red, green, purple, orange
- *directions:* straight ahead, left, right, round and round
- *emergency number:* 911
- *fairy tales*
- *feelings:* angry, happy, worried, afraid
- *foods:* strawberry, grapes, pineapple, orange, lemon, apple
- *matching:* same/different; bigger/smaller
- *math words:* halves, thirds, whole, part
- *measuring words:* cups, half, quarter
- *negatives:* don't, won't, can't
- *nouns:* flour, salt, oil, rain, sun, boxcar, engine, caboose, crossing gate, stop sign, bridge, conductor, fire truck, fire, water, ladder, vest, tie, hat, windows, roof, chimney
- *numbers:* zero through twelve
- *opposites:* long/short; forward/backward; day/night; light/heavy; first/last; fast/slow
- *ordinal numbers:* first, second, third
- *people names:* mommy, daddy, little boy, little girl, grandma, firefighter, grandpa, nurse, doctor, police officer, fire chief, veterinarian

- *questions:* how many, who, what, when, where, how much, why
- *shapes:* pillars, triangles, arches, half circles
- *tenses:* past, present, future
- *time words:* today, tomorrow, tonight, yesterday, last night
- *weather words:* sunny, rainy, cloudy, cool, hot, cold, warm
- *zoo animals:* hippopotamus, giraffe, elephant, zebra, lion, kangaroo

Books

There are many wonderful books that help teach preschoolers such invaluable skills as counting, recognizing shapes and letters, and distinguishing colors.

Alvie Eats Soup. Ross Collins. New York: Scholastic.
Although Alvie's little sister eats everything, Alvie only eats soup. Granny who is a chef is coming to visit and there is a surprise ending for everyone. Great book for those fussy eaters.

Animal Friends. Maya Ajmera and John Ivanko. Watertown, MA: Charlesbridge.
Children from all over the world are featured in full color photographs with animals from around the world. The story compares the physical traits of the animals and the love that binds the animals to those who care for them.

At the Edge of the Woods. Cynthia Cotton. Illustrated by Reg Cartwright. New York: Holt.
Woodland animals are made out of cut paper and are easy to count.

Bears in the Night. Stan and Jan Berenstain. New York: Random House.
A story of the adventure of little bears that uses very few words on each page. The emphasis is on prepositions. The prepositions are: in, out, to, at, down, over, under, around, between, through, up.

Bob. Tracey Campbell Pearson. New York: Farrar, Straus, and Giroux.
Bob, the rooster, does not know how to crow. Each of the animals teaches Bob to make their sound but it is not until Bob meets another rooster that he learns to crow.

Brown Angels: An Album of Pictures and Verse. Walter Dean Myers. New York: Harper Collins.

> Shows the author's collection of over 30 pictures of African-American children with original poems that celebrate the life and pride that shines out of their faces.

The Carrot Seed. Ruth Kraus. Illustrated by Crockett Johnson. New York: Harper.

> Simple pictures show a little boy's faith in the carrot seed that he plants. No one else believes that it will grow. What a surprise for the grown-ups.

Cat in the Hat. Dr. Seuss. New York: Random House.

> A well-loved favorite for many years. The children's mother goes out on a rainy day. The Cat in the Hat moves in, makes all kinds of messes, but nearly cleans up before Mom walks in the door. A fun story to tell and retell.

Close Your Eyes. Kate Banks and Georg Hallensleben. New York: Frances Foster.

> A scared tiger doesn't want to go to sleep. Mama Tiger assures him that she will be there when he wakes up. A great bedtime story.

Count and See. Tana Hoban. New York: Macmillan.

> This photographic study of objects focuses on numbers. The numbers one through fifteen are represented and then the numbers are by tens to fifty and from fifty to one hundred. The highest numbers may be too difficult for this age, but this is a good age for exposure to the idea.

Cowboy Baby. Sue Heap. Cambridge, MA: Candlewick Press.

> The cowboy baby cannot go to sleep without his Texas Ted, Denver Dog, and Hank the Horse. A nice bedtime story.

Curious George. H.A. Rey. New York: Houghton Mifflin.

> Curious George is like a child in a fur suit. He is always getting into scary situations and being rescued by his protector—the man in the yellow suit. Children enjoy all of the books in the series which involve this little monkey.

The Daddy Book. Todd Parr. New York: Little, Brown.

> This lovely book about dads talks about and celebrates the differences in dads. There is a companion book about moms.

Dahlia. Barbara McClintock. New York: Farrar, Straus and Giroux.
Charlotte gets a delicate doll from her Aunt Edme. But Charlotte is not the delicate doll type. As it turns out, Dahlia, the fancy doll, turns out to be a mud-pie-making and tree-climbing kind of doll.

Do Like a Duck Does. Judy Hindley. Illustrated by Ivan Bates. Cambridge, MA: Candlewick.
While Mama Duck is taking her ducklings for a walk, they imitate everything that Mama Duck does. A fox enters the scene and Mama makes him imitate what the ducks are doing.

Frances Series. Russell Hoban. Illustrated by Lillian Hoban. New York: Harper and Row.
This series features Frances, a bear who experiences many of the situations that children of this age experience. In *Bedtime for Frances* we see her posing all of the protests that young children make when faced with bedtime. Her parents handle it in a very calm way and Frances learns. In *Bread and Jam for Frances*, Frances will only eat what she wants, which happens to be bread and jam. Her mother and father give her that for every meal of the day until, of course, she gets sick of it and begins to see that variety is more fun when it comes to food.
These stories are amusing to young children and also show them in a nice way that these problems can be handled and that other children feel the same way they do.

Freight Train. Donald Crews. New York: Greenwillow Press.
A train moves along next to the highway, going through tunnels, crossing different railroad tracks, and going in both the dark and in the light. Each component of the train is shown and then linked together to show the entire train. Beautiful pictures. Excellent vocabulary.

Golden Sound Story Books™. Golden Books. Racine, WI: Western Publishing Co., Inc.
Electronic story books which talk, play music, and create sounds. Replaceable long-life batteries are included. Your child can follow the story, press the matching sound picture, and hear the sound. Look for popular titles such as: *Aladdin, Bambi, Beauty and the Beast, Dumbo, 101 Dalmations, Peter Pan, Pinnochio, Snow White and the Seven Dwarfs,* and *Winnie the Pooh and Tigger Too.*

Hands Are Not for Hitting. Martha Agassi. Illustrated by Marieka Heinlen. Minneapolis, MN: Free Spirit Publishing.

> This book illustrates gently that words are to be used and that hands are not for hitting. Gets the message across.

Hey, Look At Me, I Can Be. Merry Thomasson. Illustrated by Valerie Poole. Charlottesville, VA: Merrybooks.

> Children will be delighted as they become everything they ever wanted to be through the magic of "Look at Me Windows."

If You Give a Mouse a Cookie. Laura Joffe Numeroff. Illustrated by Felicie Bond. New York: Harper and Row.

> Relating the cycle of requests a mouse is likely to make after you give him a cookie takes the reader through a young boy's day.

Is It Red, Is It Yellow, Is It Blue? Tana Hoban. New York: Greenwillow Books.

> Another excellent photo essay, this time emphasizing colors. These concept books are an excellent addition to a child's book shelf.

It's My Body. Lory Freeman. Illustrated by Carol Deach. Seattle, WA: Parenting Press.

> This book will help young children learn how to communicate their feelings about their bodies.

Jamberry. Bruce Degen. New York: Harper and Row.

> A bear and a young boy are joined by a variety of farm animals as they ramble down streams, through fields, and into a village, picking mouth-watering berries of all kinds along the way. The story is written in a lively verse.

Loving Touches. Lory Freeman. Illustrated by Carol Deach. Seattle, WA: Parenting Press.

> A book that teaches children the difference between loving touches and those that make them feel uncomfortable. It is a reminder that loving touch is necessary to a productive life.

Madeline Series. Ludwig Bemelmans. New York: Viking Press.

> A classic in children's literature. These lovely stories written in captivating rhyme have charmed children and adults for many years. Madeline is the smallest of twelve orphans under the care of Miss Clavell, and each story tells of the mischief that Madeline gets into. A delightful series.

McDuff Moves In. Rosemary Wells. Illustrated by Susan Jeffers. New York: Hyperion.

>A West Highland Terrier is rounded up by the dog catcher and after several frightening encounters finds just the right people to rescue him.

My Five Senses. Aliki. New York: Crowell.

>This book helps children become more aware of how they learn through all five of their senses. Particularly important for children who are delayed in one of these areas. It makes them aware that the area exists.

My Friend Isabelle. Eliza Woloson. Illustrated by Bryan Gough. Bethesda, MD: Woodbine House.

>A beautifully told story of two friends who share many of the same likes and dislikes even though one has Down syndrome. A wonderful story to introduce individual differences in children.

The Napping House. Audrey Wood. Illustrated by Don Wood. San Diego: Harcourt, Brace, Jovanovich.

>A cumulative story of a sleepy grandmother, grandson, dog, cat, and mouse, who pile on a cozy bed to nap on a rainy day. What happens when a wakeful flea joins them is startling and hilarious.

One Fish, Two Fish, Red Fish, Blue Fish. Dr. Seuss. New York: Random House.

>Always a favorite with children, this book emphasizes counting and color with Dr. Seuss's usual delightful rhythm and rhyme. This is one you will read and read again many times.

1 2 3 Follow Me. Phillipe Dupasquier. Cambridge, MA: Candlewick.

>Flip the pages of this book to find a small drama unfold, as an ever-increasing number of creatures chase each other. From one to nine, the line grows longer until a small surprise turns everyone around at ten.

Over, Under, and Through. Tana Hoban. New York: Macmillan.

>A photo essay showing children illustrating all of these prepositions. A very nice conversation starter and perhaps an encouragement to have your child imitate actions.

Peter's Chair. Ezra Jack Keats. New York: Harper and Row.
> Peter is upset when he sees all of his things being refinished
> for the new baby. So far, his special chair has not been
> touched, so he takes it and a few other priceless possessions
> and runs away to the outside of his house. He finds that he is
> too big for the chair and when his mother convinces him to
> come inside and join his parents at the table in a grown up
> chair, he decides that he really is grown up now.

The Polar Express. Chris Van Allsburg. Boston: Houghton, Mifflin, and Co.
> A magical Christmas Eve train ride takes a little boy to the
> North Pole to receive a special gift from Santa Claus.

The Red Balloon. A. Lamorisse. New York: Doubleday.
> No words in this elegant picture story. Tells the story of a lonely
> little boy who is teased by his friends, but finds a friend in a red
> balloon who is always around to help the little boy and take him
> on beautiful rides high above Paris. Photographs are excellent.

Rolling Along with Goldilocks and the Three Bears. Cindy Meyers. Illustrated by Carol Morgan. Bethesda, MD: Woodbine House.
> This is a classic tale with a special needs twist, as Baby Bear is
> in a wheelchair and goes to physical therapy. Ultimately he
> makes friends with Goldilocks.

The Rose in My Garden. Arnold Lobel. Illustrated by Anita Lobel. New York: Greenwillow Press.
> Written in a pleasant rhythm, making it an ideal read aloud
> book, this tale tells a cumulative story starting with a single
> rose in the garden. The young listener will soon be adding the
> words that he has learned by listening to this story.

The Runaway Bunny. Margaret Wise Brown. Illustrated by Clement Hurd. New York: HarperCollins.
> A little bunny imagines all kinds of ways to run away but his
> mother assures him that she will follow him. The mother bunny's
> calm and steadfast love gives children a feeling of safety and
> security. Also available in board book form for younger readers.

Sammy Spider's First Hanukkah. Sylvia Rouss. Illustrated by Katherine Janus Kahn. Rockville, MD: KAR-BEN Copies.
> Sammy watches longingly as a little boy lights another candle
> and gets a new dreidel every night of Hanukkah. On the last
> night of the holiday, Sammy gets his own spinning surprise.

School Bus. Donald Crews. New York: Greenwillow Press.
> An excellent book to introduce the school bus to your child. This may be the first year that he is going to ride the school bus and you can begin his adventure for him with this wonderfully illustrated book.

Seven Candles for Kwanzaa. Andrea Davis Pinkney. Illustrated by Brian Pinkney. New York: Dial Press for Young Readers.
> Follows the sequence of Kwanzaa week, describing the symbols and their meanings. A realistic look at the way many African-American families today celebrate Kwanzaa.

Sheila Rae's Peppermint Stick. Kevin Henkes. New York: Greenwillow Press.
> Mouse sisters Sheila Rae and Louise show young readers how to share.

Snow Bears. Martin Wadell. Illustrated by Sarah Fox-Davies. Cambridge, MA: Candlewick.
> Three little bears go out to play in the snow. When Mama comes out, the little bears pretend to be snow bears not baby bears. Children of this age love pretend play and will enjoy this story.

Starting School. Janet and Allan Ahlberg. New York: Viking Kestrel.
> Warm and humorous book about a preschooler just starting to school. Should help to reassure your child about being away from Mom and Dad.

Tale of Peter Rabbit. Beatrix Potter. New York: Warner.
> One of the first books ever to use animals acting like little children. The story is well known and the drawings are exquisite. Should be added to your child's personal bookshelf.

Ten Nine Eight. Molly Bang. New York: Greenwillow Books.
> A different slant on counting and a lovely way to say goodnight. Pictures are charming. Counting backwards from ten little toes to one big girl who is ready for bed. A sleepytime favorite.

Ten Seeds. Ruth Brown. New York: Knopf.
> A counting backwards book as ten sunflower seeds fall to a mole, cat , boy, puppy, etc. Children this age are fascinated by counting backwards, as they have learned to count forward.

This and That. Illustrated by Tanya Linch. New York: Farrar, Straus and Giroux.

> This is a cumulative tale of a cat gathering items from various farmyard friends. The ending is not so surprising.

Too Many Tamales. Gary Soto. Illustrated by Ed Martinez. New York: Putnam.

> Maria tries on her mother's ring while her hands are sticky with the "masa" she is kneading to make tamales. Panic ensues when she discovers the ring is missing. A look into a tender and funny Mexican-American celebration.

Trashy Town. Andrea Zimmerman and David Clemesha. Illustrated by Dan Yaccarino. New York: HarperCollins.

> Mr. Gilly collects trash in his big blue truck while listeners join in the often repeated refrain of, "Dump it in, smash it down, drive around the trashy town."

Truck. Donald Crews. New York: Greenwillow Press.

> As the truck winds through town, it goes over, under, across and through. Additionally, many traffic signs familiar to young children, such as "STOP," "ONE WAY," "ENTER," are shown. Other vehicles are pictured as well.

A Turn for Noah. Susan Remick Topek. Illustrated by Sally Springer. Rockville, MD: KAR-BEN Copies.

> Things have been going wrong for Noah all week in nursery school. Soon the holiday of Hanukkah will be over. When will it be his turn? There is a series of Noah stories for several holidays, including *A Taste for Noah* and *A Holiday for Noah*.

We Can Do It! Laura Dwight. New York: Checkerboard Press.

> Five special children show what they can do—and they can do just about anything. Fun and inspiring, children will love the words and beautiful photographs.

Whistle for Willie. Ezra Jack Keats. New York: Harper and Row.

> Peter wants very much to learn to whistle so that his dog will come to his very special whistle. With much practice and persistence, Willie is successful. A wonderful boost to children with special needs who have to work a little harder and practice a little harder to get some things done.

William's Doll. Charlotte Zolotow. Illustrated by William Pene du Bois. New York: Harper and Row.

>   William loves all of his "boy" toys but he also wants a doll. Finally his grandmother helps to explain to William's parents why he should have a doll so that he can learn to take care of the baby when he is a Daddy.

You're My Nikki. Phyllis Rose Eisenberg. Illustrated by Jill Kastner. New York: Dial Books for Young Readers.

>   A beautiful story that reassures children that love has no boundaries. Particularly good for young children whose mothers may be just starting to work away from home.

Summary of Your Child's Fourth Year (36-48 Months)

LANGUAGE

Developmental Milestones	Date Achieved	NOT YET	PROGRESSING

uses negation:
   don't
   won't
   can't			

uses plurals			
asks questions			
can tell of experiences in sequence			
can say age and sex			
uses 5-word sentences			
can deliver a simple message			
can respond to conversation of others			
knows some songs			
knows 1800 words			

PHYSICAL

Developmental Milestones	Date Achieved	NOT YET	PROGRESSING
can walk downstairs alternating feet			
can climb low ladder			
can run smoothly			
can jump several times in a row (how many times?)			
can hop (how many times?)			
can catch a large ball bounced by someone else			
can bounce a large ball two or three times			
can wind up a toy			
can build a tower of blocks (how many?)			
can do puzzles of 3-5 pieces			
can put on clothing			
can pull a wagon			

COGNITIVE			
Developmental Milestones	**Date Achieved**	**NOT YET**	**PROGRESSING**

can point to body parts:
    fingers
    thumb
    toes
    neck
    stomach
    chest
    back
    knee
    chin
    fingernails			

can name body parts:
    legs
    arms
    fingers
    thumb
    toes
    neck
    stomach
    chest
    back			

can match colors:
    pink
    gray
    white			

can show colors when asked:
    orange
    purple
    brown
    black			

can name colors:
    red
    yellow
    green
    blue			

(COGNITIVE continued on next page)

(COGNITIVE continued)

Developmental Milestones	Date Achieved	NOT YET	PROGRESSING
can show shapes when asked: circle square triangle			
can match shapes: hexagon rectangle star			
understands time concepts: today tonight last night			
can point to opposites: tall/short slow/fast over/under far/near			
can sort objects by color			
can sort objects by shape			
can count to 4			
understands ordinal numbers who goes first? whose turn is second?			
can tell about the use of household objects what do we use a stove for? what are dishes for? why do we need houses?			
can tell what part of the day is for certain activities when do we eat breakfast? when do we go to sleep?			
plays with friends own age			
can express feelings			
develops more fantasy play			
can match letters			

Toy Dialogs for the Fifth Year

As you look back over the earlier developmental stages, it is hard to believe how far your infant has come. From total helplessness, she has emerged as a sturdy individual capable of carrying on long conversations with you. If she has no physical disabilities, she should be able to walk up and down stairs alternating feet on the steps even while carrying things in her hands. She may be able to ride a bike with or without training wheels. She will enjoy coloring and can often draw simple round objects such as balls or apples after you show her how. She will be interested in letters and may be able to trace them and perhaps write some on her own. We have included some school-oriented toys in this category because she may be going to nursery school during this time. If she has older brothers or sisters, she will enjoy doing "homework" while they are doing theirs.

As you have been for the last four years, you are still your child's model and her teacher. Continue to build her receptive language and give her new and wondrous words for everyday things. She can learn that "huge," "gigantic," and "humongous" are fancy words for "big." Children this age just love to play around with multi-syllabic words. Their love for dinosaurs at this age surely is largely because they get to say neat words like "Diplodocus" and "Tyrannosaurus Rex." Continue to talk about all of your daily activities when you are together. Building an enriched vocabulary will pay major dividends as your child moves along in school and reads and writes. Her knowledge of language will be a valuable asset for her.

While you are continuing to bolster her receptive language skills, you may want to add some idiomatic expressions. Examples of these are "It's raining cats and dogs today"; "My eyes are bigger than my stomach"; "You look as cool as a cucumber." Your child will enjoy learning about these different ways to use and understand words.

I do not recommend a lot of high pressure teaching at home, but you can begin getting your child interested in school types of activities. Having lots of paper, crayons, and other art materials around will help her develop the fine motor skills for beginning writing next year in kindergarten. Be sure to provide plenty of large paper and let her choose whether to color within the lines. My favorite coloring paper is a huge roll of white shelf paper from the grocery store. It is inexpensive and lends itself to borderless pictures that can become wall murals or paintings that can be added to over a period of time.

Your play with your child can include some basic concepts related to numbers, letters, and prepositions, which will be fun for her to learn. Resist having her "recite" her letters and numbers for friends and family, however. She doesn't need the stress of performing at this age.

Magnetic Sketch Board™
by Battat

Do you remember the sketch pads that had a special pencil and after you wrote on the pad, you lifted up a clear plastic sheet to clear it? Sketch pads have come a long way since then. This magnetic sketch board offers hours and hours of play for your child. It comes with a writing instrument that is attached so it cannot easily be lost. It has five small metal shapes that can be used on the board: a flower, a square, a circle, a heart, and a car. These are fun for children to "stamp" on the board to make the shape. They can add to the stamped design using the metal-tipped writing instrument.

First you will want to make sure your child understands the vocabulary related to this toy. Naming each of the parts is a start. She may want you to do the drawing. This is okay when you are first using the sketch board. Then you want to gradually ask her to add a part to the drawing that you made so that she will gain confidence that she can draw also. The "eraser" is a red bar that you pull down and then let go. It gradually slides up the sketch board, effectively erasing what you just drew. Sometimes when children are in preschool, they begin to work with drawing circles and lines. This sketch board is a great place to practice those skills.

One word of caution. It is easy to lose the five shapes that are in the board. If your child turns it upside down when she is carrying it, they might easily fall out. You might want to put a piece of Velcro on the bottoms of these five shapes. It will prolong the play value of the toy.

> *"Evan, let's play with this magnetic sketch board. Look at these pieces along the top. Do you know their names? Right, this is a flower, this is a square, this one is a circle, this one is a heart, and this one is shaped like a car. You know all the names. Which one do you want to use first? The car. Okay. Let me show you how to stamp the shape of a car. Now you try it. Great, that is a good car shape. Do you want to use the pen to draw a road? No, I'll watch. You draw it. Okay, I will start the road for you, then you can finish it. Do you want to stamp more cars on your road? Wow, let's count how many cars you drew. One, two, three, four. You stamped four cars. You will need more roads for them. Now you know how to draw them. Very good. That looks like an excellent road."*

> *"See what else we can do. I can make a circle. Let's see you make a circle. Excellent! That is a great circle. Now let's do some lines. Top to bottom. Wonderful. Those are good lines that you made. Let's do some more circles. Wow, you are good at circles. That is terrific."*

Art Materials Your child has been enjoying and experimenting with basic arts and crafts materials for some time now. When she is four, you will probably begin to see a vast improvement in her fine motor skills, and she will have the desire to create all sorts of exciting pictures and designs with her newfound skills.

Children at this age have vivid imaginations that you can encourage and stimulate by providing the right materials and asking the right questions. At this age, offer oversized paper so your child can draw and print freely. She's still working on improving her fine motor skills! Because large muscles develop first, it is easier to draw on large surfaces. Your child will still appreciate being allowed to outline shapes with stencils and to trace pictures with tracing paper. She now can take a great deal of time to work on an artistic masterpiece and will feel a great sense of pride on its completion.

Tremendous language can be pulled from your child's experimentation with art supplies. Listed are the "basics" that are recommended to have in your household as well as a list of language concepts that can be introduced.

I recommend that with any of these toys, you let your child create the ideas for the pictures and designs. Rather than asking, "Can you make a happy face?" ask, "What can you think of to draw?" If she "draws a blank," which happens to even the finest artists from time to time, then offer a few ideas for her to choose from. Once she begins to draw, paint, or create a three-dimensional object, begin to stimulate her imagination even further.

> *"What will you make today? A puppy...what a good idea. What color will you make him? I see your puppy has ears, legs, and a tail. Where does your puppy live? At your house? Can you draw a picture of yourself next to your puppy? Will you decorate your picture with a lot of colors?"*

If your child is not ready to create pictures, encourage her to experiment with the basic properties of each of the materials and create designs.

> *"What will you use to make a collage today? You need paper, pictures from the magazines you cut out, and glue. Would you like to make a collage about animals?"*

For a child with a visual impairment, make collages using materials that provide a tactual experience—dried beans, corn, pasta, old puzzle pieces, sandpaper of varying coarseness, ribbons, string, and items from nature such as leaves, pinecones, shells, pebbles, and so on. Let your imagination soar.

Handling art materials involves using fine motor skills of hands and fingers and coordinate their movements with what you see. For a child who may not be able to hold a crayon well, try inserting the crayon through a small Styrofoam ball two and a half inches in diameter. The easy-to-grasp Styrofoam ball (which can be purchased in craft stores) now becomes the handle. This inexpensive adaptation makes it less frustrating for your child to hold the crayon and also allows her to concentrate on the large motor skill involved rather than the finer motor skills she may not yet have.

Your child can refine these perceptual-motor skills by drawing, painting, molding clay, and cutting with scissors. Painting pictures, coloring within lines, tracing, and copying shapes and designs are all precursors to writing and reading, the developmental milestones your child is working on. If your child has a visual impairment, you can use Elmer's™ glue on an outline of a drawing. When the glue dries, there will be a raised edge that will help her stay within the lines when she is coloring. If your child has partial vision, use colored glue or dark markers to make the outline.

While using art materials such as crayons, markers, or paints, you can help your child learn about working from left to right, top to bottom, and making straight and curvy lines. Moreover, the strokes she makes in her art work will provide practice for making the same basic strokes that form letters and numbers.

If you haven't offered your child an opportunity to create a masterpiece on your driveway or front sidewalk with colored chalk, we recommend this highly. We bet you'll start a new trend with the neighborhood children in no time flat. Thick, one-half-inch to one-inch sticks of chalk are recommended when drawing on sidewalks or driveways as they will not break as easily as thinner pieces. Offer your child several colors and suggest that she draw a welcome home picture for Daddy on the front sidewalk of the house. Rest assured, your child's picture will eventually wash off in the rain.

Art Materials List

• brushes	• stickers	• clay
• crayons	• colored pencils	• tracing paper
• construction paper	• magic markers	• scissors
• tissue paper	• chalk	• chalkboard
• eraser	• stapler	• string
• yarn	• stencils	• paper
• plates and cups	• toilet paper rolls	• paper towel rolls
• pastels	• old greeting cards	• magazines to cut up
• glue/paste	• tape	• paint

• • • • • • • • • • • • • •

Clown Bop Bag™ **by Small World Toys**

Have you noticed that your child is sometimes frustrated and doesn't know what to do with her anger or disappointment? A Bop Bag is the perfect solution. She can bang away at this clown and it always comes back ready for another bop. Your child can do this regardless of her disabilities because the clown stays where it is and is ready for your child to hit again.

Some parents worry that punching these kinds of toys may actually make children more hostile. This has not been found to be the case. Most children, and often those who have a challenge in their lives, will experience these feelings of frustration. Truth be told, it is really fun to bop this clown and you don't have to be working out any frustrations at all. It is just fun to do.

"Jackie, do you remember yesterday when you were feeling a little angry? We talked about those feelings

and you didn't know what to do. Dad found this clown bop bag for you and you can punch it all you want when you feel like it. Watch, I will show you how it works. Look, I will punch it and it will bounce right back. I want to do it again. Would you like to try? That's right. Just punch it and it will bounce right back. When you are feeling angry and just want to punch something, this clown bop bag is the perfect thing for you. Try it again. Isn't this fun? Be sure you don't punch a real person. That person doesn't want to get punched but the clown doesn't mind at all."

Power Transport™ by Small World Toys

Many children enjoy playing with cars. Boys and girls alike enjoy this play especially if you play with them. The Power Transport™ features a large car carrier that has two racing cars that can be used to race each other. When you push the car carrier, it makes a sound like it is changing gears. The smaller racing cars drive up the ramp to be carried to the next race.

"Are you taking the cars to a race? Can I play with you? I like to race cars too. Where shall we have this race? In the hall. That's a good idea because they can race fast on the tile floor. Let's go. Which car do you want, the yellow or the white one? Okay, I'll take the white. Line them up. Good, you made a starting line with your blocks. Okay, are we ready? Ready, set, gooooooo! Ah, you won. You crossed the finish line first. Listen, I hear the doorbell. Let's see who it is. Hi, John. It's your friend, John. Now you can play race cars with him. I'll be in the living room if you need me."

Once you have given her the language related to this toy, she will be able to play with her friends and understand the vocabulary that her friends are using. Leaving them alone but staying close by is a good idea in case intervention is needed.

Felt Kids—
Zoo Trip™
by Learning
Curve

Earlier, I suggested that you make a flannel board for your child. You can use the one you made and buy the story kits that Learning Curve makes, or, if you didn't get around to making a board or would rather have a commercial product, you can buy the felt board from them as well. Learning Curve offers many different Felt Kits. Some of the sets offered are: Down on the Farm, Prima Ballerina, Time for School, Cinderella, Wizard of Oz, and many more. For this book, I've chosen to highlight the Zoo Trip set. The kit has a monkey, a giraffe, a bear, a wolf, an elephant, a zebra, an alligator, a lion, and some pieces to make a fence. This kit would make a great activity for before and after a trip to the zoo. Before the trip, you can talk about what you will see and after the trip you can talk about what you saw. This is great practice for future and past tenses.

Before the Trip:

> *Guess what, Will! Tomorrow Mom and I are taking you to the zoo. We haven't been to the zoo in a long time. What do you think you will see at the zoo? Do you remember any of the animals? Hmm, let's see. Yes, I think we will see a zebra. Which one of these animals is the zebra? Right, the one with stripes. What else will we see? A bear! Right, we will see a bear. Can you think of any other animals that we will see? Yes, a monkey. We will see some monkeys….etc.*

Continue in this way until your child has named all the animals she can think of. As you name each one, put the appropriate felt animal up on the board.

After the Trip:

> *"What a wonderful time we had at the zoo. What did you like best? Ha ha, you liked the ice cream the best! Which animals did we see? Let's look at the flannel board animals we played with yesterday. Ah, there's the*

lion. We saw three lions at the zoo. What else? Yes, we saw some monkeys. Oh, they were very funny. We laughed and laughed. What else did we see? Yes, we saw the alligators. Really? You were scared of the alligators? Well, they are behind a tall fence so they can't hurt you. I remember the elephants. They were huge and drinking a lot of water. We saw people feeding them peanuts. You know the zookeeper does not really want us to feed the animals because they get special food. What else do you remember? That's right, we saw the zebras. What color are their stripes? Black, that's right."

Continue for as long as your child maintains interest. Don't push her too far but remember that you can always pull out the flannel board and play again later.

Magnetic Dress Up with Storage Closet™
by Battat

What a fun way to learn the names of occupations as well as clothes that are worn for those occupations! This neat toy has a storage box to keep all the clothes and accessories in. The top of the box is magnetic and shows a girl's and a boy's closet. The boy's closet includes outfits for an astronaut, a football player, a police officer, a chef, and a doctor. The girl's closet includes outfits for a tennis player, a ballerina, an artist, a businesswoman, and a firefighter. The clothes are interchangeable so that either the boy or the girl figures can wear any of the outfits. This is all wonderful language for your child to learn. Here's a sample of how your play might go:

"Here's a dress-up game we can play. Open the closet doors. Shall we dress the girl or the boy? Okay, let's dress the boy. Take out all of his outfits. Let's see what

we have. Here's an outfit for an astronaut and here's one for a police officer. I see an outfit for a football player and another one for a chef. There's one more outfit. Do you know what that is? It's to dress him as a doctor. Which one do you want to do first? Okay, let's dress him as an astronaut. Where's his head? Great. Put that on the front of the boy where his head is. Terrific. Now find the top of

*the astronaut suit. Super. Put that on under the boy's
head. Now where are his pants? There they are. Put
them under the top of the suit. Finally, there's his
shoes. Put them where his feet are. Oh look, there is
an astronaut helmet too. Put that next to him. He will
put it on when he goes into his spaceship. Have you
seen an astronaut on television? He gets in his spaceship and then—zoom, up to the moon! An astronaut
has to be very strong and brave. Maybe one day you
will be an astronaut. Would you like that?"*

If your child remains interested in this toy, you can continue with
the rest of the outfits and talk about parts of the outfits and what
people in those occupations do. This is excellent language for your
child at this developmental stage.

**Puzzle
Rhymes™
by International
Playthings**

Your child may be starting to match words with pictures and even
"read" some stories that she knows very well. If so, this will be a fun
game to play with your child alone or with friends or brothers or
sisters. There are sixteen puzzles with pictures and simple rhymes to

match. The puzzle pieces are not interchangeable and only fit together
in the right puzzle. It is hard for your
child to make a mistake.

Start with the three-piece puzzles.
There are four of them: an ape eating
a grape; a bee on a ski; a fish making
a wish; a lizard who's a wizard. See if
your child can do the three-piece
puzzles before moving on to the four-,
five-, and six-piece puzzles. Take the
first piece of each of the groups and
deal them out to you and your child.
Then turn the other pieces face down
on the table. In turn, each of you picks a piece from the table and sees
if it matches your puzzle. Each of you will only have two puzzle pieces
in your hand so it will be easy to see which matches.

*"Meghan, I have some puzzles for us to play with
today. I will give you two pieces and I will have two
pieces. Then I will put the rest of the pieces on the
table. I will go first to show you how to play. Watch. I
will pick up one of the pieces. Let's see—does it match*

one of my puzzles? Yes, so I will keep it. Now it's your turn. Pick up one of the pieces from the table. Does it match your puzzle? No, okay put it back on the table. You can have another turn after me."

Continue picking up and matching pieces until all four puzzles are finished. Then practice reading them. The pictures are helpful. You will be amazed when you play this game a few times that your child begins to "read" the puzzles. It is a great reading readiness game. The rhyming is fun for children this age because they like to play around with sounds and words.

Opposite Pairs™

by Discovery Toys

This is another language puzzle toy. With these puzzles there are only two pieces to each puzzle. They are easy to solve and provide a great way to talk about opposites. You have been using this language for a long time but your child will see it in a new way as you introduce the idea of words having opposites.

The language that will be learned with this toy follows:

over and under	frogs and toadstools
front and back	bunnies
in front and behind	cows
awake and asleep	tigers
happy and sad	cats
empty and full	fishbowl
dirty and clean	pigs
together and apart	bears
day and night	owls
big and little	fish
hot and cold	birds
old and young	rooster and chicks
shut and open	crocodiles
dry and wet	hippos
out and in	mice

Once you have played with the puzzles and learned the language involved, you can put the opposites into sentences. "One fish is big and the other fish is little. Show me the big fish. Right, that is the big fish. Tell me that in a nice sentence. That's right. Now it's your turn. Ask me about one of the other puzzles."

You can have your child act out these puzzles. Have her pick one of the puzzles and pretend to be the animal on the puzzle and act out the opposite concepts. Your conversation might sound like this:

"Which animal would you like to pretend to be? Oh, you like the tiger. What is this tiger doing? Show me. [Child pretends to be asleep.] Good for you. Now what does the other half of the puzzle show? Right, now you are awake. You did a good job with that. Let's pick another pair and pretend again."

Pets Mini Puzzle™ by International Playthings This is a set of mini blocks that have parts of pictures on each block. When you manipulate the blocks, you can make pictures of six pets. The pets are shown on the accompanying paper so your child can follow the picture when she is putting the blocks together. The pets featured are a puppy, a kitten, a hamster, a pony (not many people have a pony for a pet), a goldfish, and a bunny. The blocks fit neatly into a small carrying case. Encourage your child to put them back in the case when she is finished playing with them.

"Look at these blocks, Natalie. What animals do you see? A puppy, a kitten, a hamster, a pony, a goldfish, and a bunny. Wow. Which one should we try to make? Okay, let's try the kitten. See if you can find one part of the kitten. The kitten picture has a pink border. Let's look for all the pink borders. Great, now we have all the parts of the kitten picture. Let's put it together. There's the head of the kitten but it only has one ear. Let's find the block with the other ear. Here it is. Those are his back feet and his tail. You finish it. Oh, you did it all by yourself. Wonderful job. See this word over here. The word says

kitten. That's a ball of yarn. Kittens like to roll around and play with yarn. They think it is fun. Pick out another picture and we'll mix the blocks up and see if we can make another picture."

Continue this way until you have made all of the pictures and have talked about the language of all six pets.

. . . .

Puppy Play Card Game™
by International Playthings

This may be the first game your child will play that has a spinner and cards to hold! There are fifty puppy cards in five sets of ten. The cards feature a puppy and a number from one to ten. There are also eight cat cards.

There are five different games to play with these cards. The easiest game to play at this age involves matching the cards. Start with only 20 cards and lay them face down on the table. The first player spins the spinner and then can turn over as many cards as the number on the spinner. She can keep all the cards that show a puppy. If she turns over a cat card, her turn is over! The person with the most cards at the end of the game is the winner. If your child is able to understand this game with only twenty cards, gradually increase the number of cards laid out by ten. Her job is to remember where the cat cards are and avoid picking them up.

"Say, Catherine, look at this nifty card game. There are numbers and a cute puppy on some of the cards and cats on the rest of them. Let's practice with the numbers. I will turn them over and you tell me the number. Wow, you are doing a good job. You only had trouble with number seven. I can help you with that while we play the game. You go first and spin the spinner. Okay, it landed on number four. You can turn over four cards, but be careful not to turn over a cat card. Okay, go ahead. Wonderful. You have four cards and no cat cards. My turn. I spun a number eight. I will turn over eight cards. One, two, three, four, uh oh—that's a cat card. My turn is over. Let's see how many cards you

have. One, two, three, four. Let's see how many I have.
One, two, three, four. We have the same amount of
cards. Great, let's spin again. It's your turn."

Continue until all the cards are picked up except the cat cards. Try not to make a big deal about who won and who lost. Children at this age are beginning to accept the idea of a winner and a loser but it is still difficult for them.

As your child gets closer to the developmental age of five, she should be able to play some of the more challenging games in this set. Be sure to include her friends or brothers and sisters to make the game more exciting.

The Fabulous Book of Paper Dolls™
by Julie Collings
(Klutz)

In this creative fold-out book are six pop-out paper dolls of different ethnic colorings, six backdrops from beaches to ballrooms, and hundreds of double-sided clothes and accessories. (The clothes stay on with restickable tape shapes.) There is a closet to hold the clothes once they are punched out but I suggest that you keep the clothes and the dolls in a zip lock bag. They will stay more usable that way. The outfits that are included for the girls are a princess, a queen, a ball gown, everyday play clothes, a cheerleader, a summer outfit, a sun dress, a bathing suit, an overalls outfit, a witch costume, a white long dress, and a cowgirl outfit. The outfits for the boys are: a camouflage

outfit, a bathing suit, a man's shirt and pants, a soccer player, a grandfatherly looking person, a scuba diver, pajamas, a baseball outfit, and a Robin Hood costume. There are hats and accessories and enough language to keep both of you busy for a long time with this toy. There are also three babies and their clothes and accessories, as well as a couple of paper pets.

"Check out this new paper dolls game I got for you,
Jill. It has six paper doll people. Which do you want to
play with? Okay, you chose the little girl. Look at all
these outfits she can put on. Which would you like?
Okay, the bathing suit. It is a two-piece bathing suit.
Some people call it a bikini. Let's put the top part on
first. You have to use these little pieces of sticky tape. I

will help you peel it off. It's a little bit hard. Now you put it on the back of the top of the bathing suit. Wonderful. Let's find the bottom. You've got it. Can you do the tape now yourself? She has some beach shoes too. Do you see them? Super. Now we have to decide on the hair for her. You want dark hair. Good, can you put it on top of her head? And look, there's a little bucket for her hand. Which scene should we put her in? Yes, the beach scene. Shall we put her under the beach umbrella? Remember when we were at the beach and you had to be careful about the sun? Let's put her under the beach umbrella so she won't get too much sun. Somebody built a sandcastle on the beach. We did that this summer when we went to the beach, too. Look, I see a crab and two starfish. Let's leave her here and find another doll to dress."

Homemade Toys

. . . .

Packing Peanuts Play Did you save the packing peanuts from your last delivery? Do you need a small break time for yourself? Give your child some of the packing peanuts and some washable markers. She will spend a long time coloring each of these peanuts. Spread out some newspaper so the marker won't get on the table. Even if it does, it is washable! After your break, come back and admire her work. Then help her glue them on to some stiff cardboard for a wonderful colorful picture she can show grandma and grandpa when they visit the next time.*

 Safety note: Do not let your child do this activity, unless she is no longer putting things in her mouth. Be especially careful if you are going to leave her alone for a while.

"Oh, Devon. You colored those peanuts so well. They are beautiful and colorful. Here, I have some card-board. Do you want to glue some peanuts on to make a picture? OK, just a drop of glue. Right there. Put one of your colorful peanuts right there. What color is that? Right, it's blue. Let's do some more. You pick a color and I will put the glue down. Show me where you want the glue. What color is that one? Purple. Right. This is going to be a very colorful picture. We

---

* Idea suggested by Sara Jossy.

will show Grandma and Grandpa when they come over later. Let's finish up with some more colors."

. . . .

Roller Ball Get a long piece of PVC pipe from your local hardware store. Make sure it is wide enough for some of your child's toy cars or balls to fit through. The idea is to experiment with rolling the balls and cars through the pipe. Here is an idea of how you can use this homemade toy to talk about the opposites top and bottom. The toy also lends itself well to talking about fast and slow.

Single Concept

*"Get your cars, Charles, and we can play with this piece of pipe. Put your car at the **top** and let it go. Down, down, down it goes, all the way to the bottom. Put another car at the **top**. Let it go down to the **bottom**. Down it goes, all the way to the **bottom**. Do you have another car to put at the **top**? Let it roll to the **bottom**. What else can we roll? How about this ball? Will it fit through the pipe? Put the ball at the **top** of the pipe. Now let it roll down. Super, it went to the **bottom**. Try another ball. Excellent. Put it at the **top**. Down it goes, all the way to the **bottom**. I like this game. Let's find more things to roll through the pipe."*

Toy Summary

Clown Bop Bag™—Small World Toys
FeltKids Zoo Trip™—Learning Curve
Power Transport™—Small World Toys
Rescue Fire Truck™—Fisher-Price Toys
Magnetic Sketch Board™—Fisher-Price Toys
Magnetic Dress Up with Storage Closet™—Battat Toys
Puppy Play™ card game—International Playthings
Pets Mini Block Puzzles™—International Playthings
The Fabulous Book of Paper Dolls™—Klutz
Time to Rhyme™—International Playthings
Opposite Pairs™—Discovery Toys
* Packing Peanuts Play
* Roller Ball

Vocabulary and Concepts

The following list will give you an idea of the vocabulary and concepts that your child should be familiar with:

- *actions:* draw, color, punch, race, "Ready, set, go"
- *adjectives:* huge, gigantic, tiny, humongous
- *art materials:* markers, pastels, tissue paper, construction paper
- *children's songs*
- *clothing outfits:* princess, queen, ball gown, play clothes, cheerleader, shorts, overalls, sun dress, bathing suit, cowgirl outfit, camouflage suit, shirt, pants, soccer outfit, scuba diver, pajamas, baseball outfit, Robin Hood costume.
- *counting 1-20*
- *dinosaur names:* Diplodocus, Tyrannosaurus Rex, Stegosaurus, Triceratops, etc.
- *fairy tales*
- *feelings:* anger, disappointment
- *health care and community helpers:* doctors, nurses, audiologists, speech pathologist, physical therapist, teacher, dentist
- *idioms:* It's raining cats and dogs
- *last week*
- *letters and sounds of the alphabet*
- *occupations:* astronaut, police officer, football player, chef, tennis player, ballerina, artist, businesswoman/man, firefighter
- *opposites:* old/young; shut/open; dry/wet; over/under; front/back; in front/behind; awake/asleep; happy/sad; empty/full; dirty/clean; together/apart; day/night; big/little; out/in; higher/lower; more/less

- *prepositions:* above/below; behind/in front of; by the; beside; top/bottom
- *rhyming words:* e.g., ape/grape; bee/ski; fish/wish; lizard/wizard
- *safety rules:* never talk to strangers, children don't touch matches, look both ways before crossing the street
- *things in space:* stars, planets, space suit
- *transportation vehicles:* cement truck, dump truck, steam shovel, jeep, taxi, race car
- *zoo animals:* monkey, giraffe, bear, wolf, elephant, zebra, alligator, lion

Books

Books that focus on special interest areas are fun for children of this age. They are interested in a variety of topics and can get heavily into books about dinosaurs, rocks, or trucks.

Airport. Byron Barton. New York: T. Crowell.
    Clear, beautiful pictures tell what happens on an airplane trip, from arriving at the airport to the take-off of the plane. A great prelude or follow-up to an actual visit.

Apollo. Caroline Grefoire. La Jolla, CA: Kane/Miller.
    A fun way to learn basic concepts. A little dog can be viewed from above, below, front, back, vertically, horizontally, diagonally. A delightful and fun book.

Countdown to Kindergarten. Alison McGhee. Illustrated by Harry Bliss. Orlando, FL: Harcourt.
    The little girl is getting ready to start kindergarten and is pleased with all the things she can do but worried that she cannot tie her shoelaces. Children will feel comfortable with this story knowing that everyone cannot do everything.

Dig, Dig Digging. Margaret Mayo. Illustrated by Alex Ayliffe. New York: Holt.
    Trucks, tractors, helicopters, fire engines are featured in this book that explains the work these vehicles do. Great illustrations.

Each Peach, Each Pear, Each Plum. New York: Viking Press.
    Familiar nursery figures such as Jack and Jill and Mother Hubbard are hidden in the pages of this book. The rhyming words continue from page to page. A fun book for learning to look for clues and details.

Epossumondas. Coleen Salley. Illustrated by Janet Stevens. New York: Harcourt.
This is the retelling of an old tale. The hero of the story makes many mistakes but the reader can see what the hero doesn't. A fun story with great humor.

Fire, Fire. Gail Gibbons. New York: T. Crowell.
A nice book to precede and follow a trip to the station. Talks about how firemen handle fires in the city, country, forest, and waterfront. Lots of new vocabulary and opportunities for discussion about fire as a safety issue.

The First Thing My Mama Told Me. Susan M. Swanson. Illustrated by Christine Dacenier. Orlando, FL: Harcourt.
The first thing Lucy learns is her name and we watch her enjoy it as she grows and learns to say it, then write it and even write it in the snow. Charming book to celebrate our names.

Fox and Fluff. Shutta Crum. Illustrated by John Bendall-Brunello. Morton Grove, IL: Albert Whitman.
When Fluff hatches the first thing he sees is Fox. Fox tries to get rid of the little chick and eventually the chick wins his heart.

Hello Arctic. Theodore Taylor. Illustrated by Margaret Chodos-Irvine. Orlando, FL: Harcourt.
Describes the cycle of the arctic year with few words and beautiful art.

Hello Hello. Miriam Schlein. Illustrated by Daniel Kirk. New York: Simon and Schuster.
An unusual discussion of how animals other than the usual farm animals greet and make contact with each other. A fascinating book to children of this age.

The Jolly Postman or Other People's Letters. Janet and Allan Ahlberg. Boston: Little, Brown and Co.
Open this book, take out the letters, each from its own envelope, and you'll discover what well-known fairy tale characters have written to each other.

The Kettles Get New Clothes. Dayle Ann Dodds. Illustrated by Jill McElmurry. Cambridge, MA: Candlewick.
A variety of textures and names of fabrics are introduced in this fine book about clothing and choices. Words such as stripes, plaids, polka dots, checks, and paisley are discussed. Great vocabulary for language building.

Leo The Late Bloomer. Robert Kraus. Illustrated by Jose Aruego. New York: Windmill Press.
> Leo, a tiger, is slow to talk, read, write, and draw but when he is ready, he does learn. An excellent story for a child who may be a little slower than her friends in learning new things.

Little Toot. Hardie Gramatky. New York: Putnam Books.
> A classic tale of a playful tugboat who didn't like to work until he was faced with a dangerous situation.

Mike Mulligan and His Steam Shovel. Virginia Lee Burton. New York: Houghton Mifflin.
> Another story similar to *The Little Engine That Could* and *Little Toot* of a smaller and less able steam shovel beating the more modern fancy equipment. An excellent example for children who may have to work a little harder to achieve their best.

New York's Bravest. Mary Pope Osbourne. Illustrated by Steve Johnson and Lou Fancher. New York: Knopf.
> A legendary tale about a firefighter who can do extraordinary things. A tall tale, once, but now a tribute to New York's bravest and finest firefighters.

Rain. Peter Spier. New York: Doubleday.
> No words in this lovely story of two children exploring the rain.

Shelley, The Hyperactive Turtle. Deborah Moss. Illustrated by Carol Schwartz. Bethesda, MD: Woodbine House.
> After a visit to the doctor, Shelley begins to understand why he feel so wiggly inside. He has AD/HD. His doctor helps him with medication and his family helps him with love.

The Story about Ping. Marjorie Flack. New York: Penguin Books,
> The little duck, Ping, does not hear the call from Mother to come home and when he finally realizes it, everyone else has left. Afraid of being spanked, he hides and ends up in many frightening adventures. After being caught and almost cooked for dinner, he is set free and finds his way home again, happy to be safe and secure.

Swimmy. Leo Lionni. New York: Pantheon.
> A story with beautiful pictures that tell a tale of a little fish who is different from the others. He is the one to save his friends in the story. Nice for children who may feel different from their friends.

The True Book of the Mars Landing. Leila Boyle Gemme. New York: Children's Press.
> Full-page photos of the planet Mars taken by the spacecrafts Mariner and Viking. There is a clear and simple text for youngsters who are interested in space.

Walt Disney Series. New York: Random House.
> This series is comprised of stories and adventures and special adaptations of the Disney Classics. Donald Duck, Mickey Mouse, Dumbo, Peter Pan, and all of the other Disney favorites will be along to assist every youngster in exploring the wonderful world of reading. Some examples of titles are: *Peter Pan and Wendy*; *Cinderella*; *The Sorcerer's Apprentice*; *Lady and the Tramp.*

When Sophie Gets Angry— Really Really Angry. Molly Bang. New York: Scholastic.
> Shows a child how to work through anger that is bound to happen.

Where's Waldo? Martin Hanford. Boston: Little Brown and Company.
> Follow Waldo in this series of detailed picture books as he travels through the world and takes on various roles. Requires clear attention to little details.

The following books can be used for "problem solving" discussions with your child:

A Birthday for Frances. Russell Hoban. New York: Harper and Row.
> One of the hardest things for young children is to be the person not having the birthday. This book helps a young child to understand those feelings.

My Mama Says There Aren't Any Zombies, Ghosts, Vampires, Creatures, Demons, Monsters, Fiends, Goblins, or Things. Judith Viorst. New York: Atheneum.
> Explores some of the fears of night creatures that some children have.

When I Have a Little Girl. Charlotte Zolotow. New York: Harper and Row.
> It is difficult to understand why there have to be so many rules when you are young. This book helps with those feelings.

Summary of Your Child's Fifth Year (48-60 Months)

LANGUAGE

Developmental Milestones	Date Achieved	NOT YET	PROGRESSING
asks for definition of words			
can define more common words and tell how used: book, shoe, table			
almost complete use of correct grammar			
uses 6-8 word sentences			
knows town or city			
knows street address			
uses social phrases (excuse me)			
can carry on a conversation			

PHYSICAL

Developmental Milestones	Date Achieved	NOT YET	PROGRESSING
can walk down stairs carrying object			
can skip, alternating feet			
can do a broad jump (how far?)			
can hop (how far?)			
can throw a ball (how far?)			
can play rhythm instruments in time to music			
can ride small bike with training wheels			
can do puzzles that are not single pieces (how many pieces?)			
can hold a pencil in proper position			
can color within lines			
can cut with scissors			
can use knife for spreading			

COGNITIVE

Developmental Milestones	Date Achieved	NOT YET	PROGRESSING
can identify all body parts			
can name all body parts			
can name all colors			
can name all shapes			
understands directions			

uses prepositions:
    by the
    beside
    below
    behind
    above
    in front of			

understands time concepts:
    yesterday
    tomorrow
    tomorrow night			

understands opposites:
    bottom/top
    go/stop
    low/high
    off/on
    inside/outside
    closed/open			

Toy Dialogs for the Sixth Year

Five-year-olds step out into the world! At this age, your child's world expands far beyond your house and neighborhood into school. It is most likely that your child has been in a day care setting, a play group, a nursery school, or a special-needs placement by this time, but regardless of his early exposure, age five is his introduction to the formal world of school. He no longer is "a preschooler" but is "school age." In many states, he is required by law to attend school.

Going to school with age-appropriate peers and curricular expectations presents new opportunities and places new demands on your child. If his developmental delay has been mild, this may be when you start to see differences in your child compared to others his age. If you have been working on his developmental needs for some time, you may find he has "caught up" with his peers at this point.

By the end of this year, your child should have a full command of the English language with very few errors of articulation or grammar. If he does not, and you have not done so to date, you will want to have his speech and language evaluated by a speech-language pathologist. The Resource Guide at the end of this book lists some references that may help you. A general guide to follow is that if your child is easily understood by the end of his sixth year by adult friends, new acquaintances, and friends of his own, then a visit to the specialist is probably unnecessary.

During this year, it is a good time to help your child's language continue to become more precise and specific. Instead of saying, "Look at the beautiful flowers you drew," say, "Those look like long-stemmed roses!" Remember to use language at, or slightly beyond, your child's level of comprehension.

Pre-reading and Reading Skills

Compared to a four-year-old, the five-year-old expresses a much keener interest in learning letters and words. The written word has taken on a real personal meaning and the child now conceptualizes that the written word is a symbol for the receptive and expressive language he has mastered so far.

The five- to six-year-old often resembles a "kid in a candy shop"—a word candy shop, that is. Your child suddenly begins to notice, and be fascinated by, words all around him: "EXIT" signs, 35 mph signs, McDonald's logos, street signs, tee shirt logos, words in TV commercials. The five-year-old can't seem to get enough of them, and constantly tries to sample as many new words as possible. Pointing to a restaurant logo, he will ask, "Does it say McDonald's?" And then of course, "Can we stop here?" Children at this age are attracted to these things because they are now developmentally ready to take on mastery of the written word.

For a child with a language delay, the interest in learning letters and words may be just starting to blossom. Remember, the rate at which your child develops language is not as critical as the fact that he is moving steadily along in learning more complex skills. Many five-year-olds begin to relate the written word to their experiences, and need lots of repetitions to remember and retain new information. For example, the word m-o-m stands for the object, mom or mother. The red sign on the street corner stands for the action to stop, and so on.

There is a direct correlation between the five- to six-year-old's developing fine motor skills and developing cognitive skills. Along with his increasing ability to identify and copy shapes accurately (a circle, a square, a diagonal, and a cross) comes his interest in the written word. You could say that for most, age five is when the spoken word meets the written word. Cognitively, five is the age when children can developmentally start to understand this relationship. Why does this happen at this age?

As you may remember, all children go through fairly predictable, hierarchical stages of development—with each more advanced skill building on the previous skill. Now that speaking (signing, cueing) skills are developing, many five-year-olds are ready for the next complex skill: developing readiness skills in reading and writing. By five and a half, some children will recognize all upper and lower case letters of the alphabet. A wide range of pre-reading and reading skills can be seen at this age. There is such variation because every child is a wonderful and unique individual.

Most parents of five-year-olds tend to compare their child's reading ability or lack thereof with others the same age. This is a bad trap to fall into. Remind yourself that learning to read is a developmental process. It takes time and practice. You, as parents, can help by providing play activities that will enrich your child's language development and your child will learn to read when he is ready.

Parents ask whether their child's language development can be accelerated. The answer is yes! An enriched language and experiential environment can increase the rate at which your child learns to read and write. We, as parents and teachers, *do* have the ability to influence our children's development. Research shows us that toy play can contribute to the development of reading/writing readiness skills.

Children with a developmental lag need more time and more experience to develop more complex language. A larger vocabulary (spoken, signed, cued, or pointed to with the use of a communication board) as well as longer and more complex sentences must be developed before any sort of formal reading readiness program is attempted.

The key to helping your child develop necessary tools for reading and writing is to help him associate the written word with meaningful experiences he has in his life. In effect, you're helping to make the printed word come alive for him. We therefore recommend a language experience approach to teaching reading in which all language (listening, speaking, writing, and reading) is woven into your child's personal experiences. For example, if you take a trip to the zoo and visit the Panda bears, you may want to come home and write a little story about the trip. Have your child give you the language as you write it down. Then he can illustrate the story with his own pictures. This makes the written word much more meaningful to him.

The toys and activities in this chapter provide a language experience approach to helping your five-year-old learn necessary skills to read and write. Simultaneously, they will also help your child improve his receptive and expressive language. You will see that all of these activities are fun for your child. He can learn and practice new language concepts in a way that will sustain his interest and challenge him to a higher level of thinking.

Remember to use the simple language dialogs as a guide. Use your playtime to challenge your child and always try to stay one step ahead. Introduce new words. ("Would you like to *borrow* a book from the library? If we go there, you can get a library card and they will *lend* you a book for free. After you've *borrowed* it for three weeks, you'll have to return it.")

Motor Skills and Sports

Besides making great strides in language skills, children between the ages of five and six also take off in other areas. Usually there is a rapid and tremendous increase in muscle and bone growth. Typically, children look suddenly slimmer, taller, and stronger by the time they turn six! All large motor abilities such as walking, hopping, running, throwing, catching, and jumping are done with much greater ease and precision compared to one year ago. Five-year-olds are a constant whirlwind of motion. Children with no physical delay love to jump and run and are extremely flexible.

Fine motor skills such as eye-hand coordination also improve greatly during this year. Five-year-olds can grasp and release objects more easily and more accurately and aim at a target more precisely compared to when they were four. That's why any type of ball play is enjoyed more. This is a great time to provide space and an opportunity to practice motor skills.

As a precursor to organized team sports, solo physical activities such as running, climbing, throwing, catching, bicycling, roller skating, and jumping rope all help build physical strength and endurance and are just plain fun for the five- to six-year-old. The child who is in good physical condition will more likely want to play sports on a team because he will be a better team player and enjoy being part of a social group.

As mentioned before, a big difference between age four and five is that the latter begins to take a big step away from family and into the larger community. This can be seen many ways. Strong friendships outside the immediate family circle begin to intensify at this age because children at this age become more interested in cooperative play. For the first time, parents may notice that their child's friends and shared activities may take on as great a significance as those relationships within the family, and are tied to the child's sense of self-esteem.

Child development research indicates that there is a strong relationship between motor skills and competence among peers. Starting at age five with the onset of formal education in kindergarten and with participation in organized sports, five-year-olds are beginning to be cooperative and helpful members of a social group.

One way to help many language-delayed children foster friendships with peers is through organized games and sports. We have seen many children increase their self-esteem and develop friends by enrolling in extracurricular sports beginning at this age. The language delay that separates the child from his peers fades in importance as he shares his love and abilities in physical activities with the other children. For children with mental, visual, or physical disabilities who are not comfortable participating with their typically developing peers, I recommend the Special Olympics or other community sports programs designed for children with these special challenges. Consider starting your own group if none are available, as specialized sports teams such as these give every child a chance to excel. Look for the reference for Special Olympics in the Resource Section.

It is no secret why sports and organized games such as soccer and basketball are offered in school and in the community for children this age. Such activities tie together the emerging physical, cognitive, and social interests of five-year-olds in physical activities, organized games and rules, and peers.

Cognitively, your child is much more advanced than he was at age four. Your child's attention span lengthens and it may be easier for him to memorize and retain rules necessary for playing cooperative games. In fact, the five-year-old loves rules. They are the standards that govern his play.

Socially, the five-year-old is able to play much more cooperatively, compared to a year before. Five-year-olds play together quite well when they have a common goal in mind. They can understand and even relish the notion of teamwork. They can really dig their heels in and accomplish the learned tasks of sharing and taking turns. It is not uncommon for a leader to emerge who gains the respect of his peers and who assigns the rules of the game to the others.

As teachers and parents, we feel it is far more valuable to stress the cooperation aspect of team sports than the competitive aspect. Children benefit a great deal more from feeling that they are a valuable and contributing member of the team than they do from worrying about whether they are winning.

To introduce sports-related vocabulary words and rules of the games, picture books are helpful. For example, *The Young Soccer Pl*ayer by Wayne Holder presents all the rules and vocabulary of the game in simple words and pictures. This is especially helpful for language-delayed children who need the extra clarification and repetition an introductory sports book can offer.

Stencils and Pencils™
by Discovery Toys

This activity consists of thirty stencils and seven colored pencils to help your young child let his imagination run wild. The stencils help you to review vocabulary and add new words as your child draws and traces. The stencils are:

- chicken
- hen
- rabbit
- bunny
- cow
- cat
- pig
- birds
- house
- dog
- butterfly
- duck
- turtle
- frog
- trees
- star
- moon
- flowers
- house
- barn
- clouds
- train
- boat
- tractor
- airplane
- car
- train cars
- sun
- cloud & rainbow
- boy with a kite
- boy & girl playing with a ball

You can structure the play with this toy by only putting one category of stencils in the box. For example, if you wanted to review animal names, you could remove all of the other stencils and concentrate only on those with animal names. And you could do the same with the other vocabulary words. Let's see how that play would go.

"Let's play with the Stencils today. Which pencil would you like? Let's see, we have yellow, red, purple, black, blue, orange, and green. Which color would you like to start with? Red? Okay, and which animal will you make red? Good, you picked the hen. Sometimes hens are red. Can you trace around the hen? You did that well. Now you can color the hen. What's this one? A baby chick. The hen is the chick's momma. What color will you choose for the chick? Purple? OK, that's an interesting color for a baby chick. What shall we pick next? You want me to choose? Okay, here's a horse. How about making him black? The Black Stallion is a black horse. Do you remember that story?"

Continue in this way making a large picture with all of the stencils and going over the names of colors and animals. Allow your child the freedom to make the animals any color he likes. It doesn't matter which color he picks. He is having fun. This fine motor skill of tracing will help your child when he is learning to write his letters. The toy is engaging and will entertain and teach your child for a long time.

If your child has a visual impairment, he will be able to feel around the stencils and keep his finger close to the pencil and be able to trace the objects. You could also put the textures that you have taught him earlier on each of the pencils so that he can identify the colors. Keeping the textures consistent will help him learn.

Magnifying Lens™ by Small World Toys

Children are fascinated by the world we live in. They love to explore around them as you take them on walks in the neighborhood or nearby gardens. As they explore, they can use this magnifying lens to see things in a whole new perspective. You will need to show your young scientist how to observe through a magnifying lens and then help him with the language of seeing things this way.

The following is an example of how your dialog might sound with your youngster as you present this new toy.

"I have something neat to show you. Look, do you know what this is? It's called a magnifying lens. It lets you see little things very big. You want to see? Isn't that cool? Let's go outside and explore some things. What did you find? A leaf. Wow, tell me how it looks. Right, it looks big under the magnifying glass. Can you see the lines in the leaf? Those are called the 'veins' of the leaf. What else did you find? Oh, I see you have a bug—be careful not to squash it. What can you see? Those are his antennae—they act like his nose and his ears. They tell him how to get around. With the magnifying lens, you can see tiny things like that. Let's go find some more!"

Remember to be sure to give your child time to speak and share what he sees while you are giving him new words to expand the language he already knows.

If your child has a visual impairment, he might already be using a magnifying lens to help him see things in his environment. Using this as a toy will make it fun for him. Gather a couple of neighborhood children so they can explore together.

Money Money™
by Discovery Toys

Your child will probably begin to be interested in money at this age. Perhaps you even give him some pocket money of his own every week. You could assign him some chores that he can get paid for. However you choose to do this, your child will be fascinated by money.

This game helps him learn the value of the coins and bills as he plays the game with you. You may want to involve a sibling or have a friend of his come by so the three of you can play. As you go along the play board doing chores and running errands, you accumulate money. Your child can practice addition and subtraction as well as learning the names of the coins.

"Zachary, do you want to show Ryan our new money game? It is so much fun. I think Ryan will like it. Here we are. Let's put the money over here. Now you choose

which player you will be. Put your player at the starting point. Ryan is our guest. Let him roll the dice first. Oh, he got a three. Move your player three spaces. Let's see what it says. Aha, you lost a tooth and the tooth fairy gave you a quarter. Do you see the quarter, Ryan? You can take the quarter. That is the same as twenty-five cents. Zach, it's your turn now. You rolled a two. Move your player two spaces. You can vacuum the rug and get 55 cents. What will you take? You need two quarters and a nickel. Here, I will help you. One quarter is 25 cents and one more makes 50 cents. Then you will need a nickel, which is five cents. Now you have 55 cents. Good job. My turn now."

Calculating Cash Register™
by Battat

A fun way to continue practicing and learning about money is with this Calculating Cash Register. It is fully operational. It has a scanner that bleeps as it passes over objects, play money, and a credit card that can be scanned. The cash register itself is a calculator. This is great practice for your child as he pretends to be a cashier or just enjoys manipulating the toy. You can play with him after a visit to the store and act out what he saw the cashier do.

"Turn on the cash register, Tyler. See that number up there? It is a zero. That means we have nothing put into the cash register. Why don't you put some numbers in and let's see what it can add up to. You can use the scanner to scan my purchases. Listen, can you hear that sound? That means it is scanning my purchases and figuring out how much they cost. Can you push the number one? Great, now add in number three. Push the plus sign. Right here. That's right. Now the total number up there is four. Open the cash register. This button says 'open.' I will

give you four coins to put in the cash register. Now the sale is finished. Oh, wait, maybe I will use my credit card. See, this is where you scan the credit card. Hear that sound? The voice says, 'credit approved.' That means it's OK to use my credit card instead of money."

Foam Paddles and Balls™
by Small World Toys

When your children need to let off steam and it's too cold or too hot to be outdoors, it's a great time for indoor paddle ball. The racquets and balls are made of foam and cannot hurt the children or the furniture. You can also play paddle ball outdoors and at the beach. It is a safe toy to use around younger children.

Language concepts to be learned during play:

- Paddles
- Balls
- Foam
- Hit the ball
- Again
- Hard
- Softly
- Over here
- Over there
- Far
- Near

Single Concept

*"Let's play with our paddle ball set. Which color do you want? Oh, you chose the red one. I'll take yellow. Here's a ball. Can you hit the ball? Wonderful, you hit the ball **hard**. I'll try to hit the ball **hard** also. Wow, it went far. Can you hit it back? Let's see. I'm going to hit it **softly**. Oh so **softly**. Can you hit the ball **softly**? You did! You hit it **softly**. You know, it is easier to hit it **softly** than **hard**.*

"Softly" and "hard" are adverbs that tell how the ball is hit. Adverbs are hard to teach so it is best to use them naturally in your play. Try to think of other activities where you can use these and other adverbs.

What Time Is It?™
by International Playthings

In this game box, there are fourteen self-correcting puzzle pieces that show a time on the clock and an activity associated with that time. When introducing the game, you could use only half of the pieces starting with the AM times and increase as your child gets more familiar with the time concepts. By the end of this developmental period,

he should be getting the idea of the times during the day when certain activities occur.

For play, separate and scramble the seven puzzles that you are going to start with. Use the clock that comes with the game. Ask your child to put the time hands at a certain time. He may need help with this in the beginning. Let's say he chooses 8 AM. Together you look for the puzzle pieces that represent 8 AM. The clock shows the hands that will match the hands on the play clock and the picture shows two children waiting for the school bus. Let your child put the pieces together. Talk about the time shown on the clock and on the puzzle piece. Continue until you have matched all seven of your time puzzles.

> *"Look at this clock. You can move the hands around to show different times. What time do you usually get up in the morning? Oh, about 7 AM. Make the hands show that time. Watch, I can help you. Now the hands on the clock say 7 AM. Do you think we can find a puzzle piece that says 7 AM? Is it that one? No. Is it this one? Yes, this is it. Now let's find what activity we do at 7 AM. What do you do at 7 AM? Right, you wake up. Is there a picture showing someone waking up? Good, you found it. Can you put them together? Let's use a sentence here. 'I wake up at 7 AM.' Now you can make another time on the clock and we will find the right puzzle for it."*

As your child gets more comfortable with these concepts, you can add other puzzle pieces and time designations. When you introduce this game, stay with the time concepts that show "on the hour," then move to the half hour, and finally the quarter hour.

- - - - - - - - - - - - - - -

Get Up and Go Games™ by International Playthings   This is a great game to play when there are only two of you or when you have a group of friends over. There are eight different active games including: Super Simon Says, Leap Frog Relay, Hot Potato Parade, Twist, Turn and Twirl, Backwards Toss, Three Legged Race, Betcha Can't Balance, and Challenging Chin Pass. The Super Simon Says has a spinner board that tells players which pose to assume. It is similar to

Flying Statues. One player spins the arrow and "reads" out what the direction is. There are pictures that show the positions. The one who is left not doing the activity or moving during it is out. It is best to have an adult on hand to help make these determinations.

"It's your turn to spin, Ginny. Let's see, where did it stop? Can you read what it says? I will help you. It says, 'sit with arms and legs out.' Quick, who can do that first? George, you did a great job but you moved just then so you are out. You can be the next spinner. Spin the arrow. What does it tell you to do? 'Balance on tippy toes.' Okay who's the fastest? Keep balancing. Keep still. Great, Samantha, you did a good job and now it's your turn to spin."

If your child or one of your guests has a physical disability that makes the games a challenge, alter the rules a little and see who tries the hardest. Or do the activities just for the fun of it, without declaring winners or losers.

After you and your child have had an opportunity to play these games several times so that he is familiar with them, you may want to play some of them at his next birthday party.

• • • • • • • • • • • • •

Croquet Set™
by Small World Toys

This is a fun activity to play outdoors or on a large surface in your house. The pieces are made out of foam, which makes it safe to play indoors. When we played this game on the grass, we found that it was difficult to keep the wickets upright on the uneven grass. A slicker surface such as a wood floor or the driveway works better. It is not necessary to play this game competitively. It is just as much fun for each child to proceed at his own pace. An important skill reinforced in playing this game is to wait for your turn. Your child can play this game even if he is in a wheelchair. He can just roll up to the side of the ball and slam it through the wicket.

"Michael, would you like to play croquet with your friends today? Let's set it up on the driveway. I think it is easier to hit the ball there. John, help me set up the wickets. Space them out around the driveway. Here's

the start pole and over here will be the finish pole. Who wants to go first? Sophie, you can go first. You have a purple croquet ball and your mallet. Okay, try to hit your ball through that wicket. Yes! You did it. Now it is still your turn. Try the next one. Oops, missed that one. Now, John, it is your turn. Put your ball at the first wicket and try to hit it through. That's it. Now you are up with Sophie. Try and hit it through the second wicket. You did it! Now on to the third. Oops, missed that one. Now it is Michael's turn. Michael, roll your wheelchair just next to the ball. There you go. Now hit the ball with your mallet. Great, you made it through. Roll over to the next one. Oops, you missed. Now it's Sophie's turn again. You will get another turn. It's okay."

Baseball Card Game™
by International Playthings

Spring is here and baseball fever is in the air. Baseball is America's national sport, so of course you want your children to have the language associated with the game. This is a fun card game, which will teach your child the language of our national sport. This game includes: nine inning cards, twenty field cards, three strike cards, four ball cards, three out cards, and one "who's up" card. There are three red and three blue hats that represent the players, four cards to make the baseball diamond, and one trophy for the winning team. There is also a spinner.

Before you begin to play, set up the four baseball diamond cards on the floor or the table to represent the field. Give one player the three red hats and the other player the three blue hats. These are your players. To see which team goes first, throw the "who's up" card in the air. If it lands on the blue side, they are up first. Flip over the first inning card and you are ready to play. As you spin the spinner, you collect ball cards or strike cards and keep them to keep track of where you are batting. There are slots in the box to keep your score. Then you play the game just the way the real game is played.

"Ah, Maya, baseball season has started! Who's your favorite team? The Baltimore Orioles? Yeah, I like them too. Let's play this game of baseball and we'll see which team wins. We have the red team and the blue team. Which do you want to be the Orioles? Okay, the red team it is. Here goes. You spin the spinner. Uh oh, a strike. That is strike one for you. Do you know how many strikes make an out? Yes, three strikes make an out. You get another turn to spin. A double. That means you get to run two bases. Hooray. Now it's my turn to spin. I got a ball. So I will take a ball card and put it over here. Now it is still my turn. Oh, man, ball again. Now I have two balls. Do you know how many balls it will take until I can walk to first base? Right, it is four. So now I have to spin again. Strike. Uh oh! Two balls and one strike. My turn again. Strike. Now I have two strikes and two balls. I need to spin carefully. Wow, a single. Now I'm on base. You're on second base and I'm on first. It's your turn again."

Perhaps your child is not physically able to get out and play tee ball or softball with the other kids. This game is a great way for him to get in the spirit of the season and the game. For children with visual impairments, there are games that use a beeping ball so the child can follow the sound when it is pitched toward him. There are many ways to include your child in the language of our national sport. Enjoy the play with him.

Stethoscope
by Battat

Your child may have to make many visits to doctors for a variety of reasons associated with his delaying condition. You can help to prepare him for these visits by letting him play doctor. Most children this age enjoy this activity. You can use this realistic stethoscope and have him pretend to listen to your lungs and heart. He will enjoy being in control.

"Tomorrow we are going to see Dr. McElrath. She will listen to your heart and your lungs with a stethoscope. Can you say stethoscope? Boy, that is a big word. You did a good job saying that huge word. Do you remember how she puts these two ends in her ears and then listens? You try it. Can you hear my heart? Boompa, boompa, boompa. It's beating in there. It means I am healthy. Listen to your own heart. Boompa, boompa, boompa. You are healthy too. Dr. McElrath will be pleased that you are feeling so well. Now let's listen to your lungs. Whoosh, I can hear you breathing. Listen to mine. Whoosh, I am breathing well, too. We should have a good checkup at the doctor tomorrow."

Homemade Toys

Pretend Restaurant The typical five-year-old loves to act out the social roles of adults he sees. A highly popular play-acting scene for five-year-olds is creating a restaurant. Pretending to prepare food or to be a waiter, waitress, or customer at a favorite restaurant are all popular games. It is important to encourage this sort of play. It provides a tremendous opportunity for teaching language—spoken, signed, pointed to, written, or read—meaning that all aspects of a language experience approach are inherently built into this play activity. Did you know that many fast food restaurants today have pictures on their cash registers so developmentally delayed adults can work and order there? A few small props will enable your child to carry out his playacting to its fullest:

- a cash register (you can use the Calculating Cash Register by Battat here);
- toy money (coins and bills);
- basic drawing materials (paper, markers, or crayons) for writing items on menus or signs;
- plastic fruits, vegetables, or other foods;
- a kitchen area and eating area.

The following are some great reading readiness activities:
- Write out food prices on items to sell.
- Label food items for sale with their names printed on a 3 x 5 card next to the item.
- Advertise the restaurant and daily specials on poster or storefront.
- Write out menus with pictures or words.
- Add up food items purchased in the restaurant.

- Describe the food served to the customers.
- Take food orders.

In the beginning, you'll need to help your child. Eventually, he will do this writing on his own using invented or made-up spellings by sounding out the words.

> *"Roberto, would you and Alexa like to play restaurant? I'll get some big pieces of poster board and markers so you can make a sign for the front of your restaurant. What will you call your restaurant? Would you like help spelling the name of it so you can write it on your sign? How about writing the time of day that your restaurant is open so your customers know what time they can come in to order a meal? There are many other signs you could make, too. Roberto, while you're working on the restaurant sign, Alexa can start making another sign advertising the daily specials at your restaurant. Alexa, you can even draw pictures of the foods you'll be serving. Why not think of some of your favorite foods, like pizza or spaghetti or tacos, and draw those for starters. Try to sound out the words and label your pictures with the names of the foods on them. I'll be happy to help you if you'd like."*

> *"Is everyone having fun? Roberto, you're finished with your sign? That looks terrific. I'm sure a lot of customers will want to come in your restaurant when they see your bright sign. Let's hang it up at the entrance of your restaurant so everyone passing by will notice it. Now you can get started on making the menus for your customers...."*

This play incorporates a thematic curriculum of social and cognitive skills. It is a perfect opportunity to test out new skills in math and language (oral skills, reading, and writing). The goal here is to help your child associate words and their meaning with experiences he has in his life. Remember: children relate words to their experiences and need lots of varied repetition to test out all the words they are learning.

Playacting using a restaurant theme naturally lends itself to your child developing what's called a sight vocabulary: recognizing printed words and their meaning without necessarily being able to sound them out by their letters. Help your child label in clear print on a 3 x 5 card the word associated with the item he's using in his play scene. Cards such as "cash register," "restaurant," "kitchen," "menu," "fruit," or "vegetables," etc. can be taped to play items. With frequent exposure, your child will begin to associate the written word with the actual item. This way, written words take on a real personal meaning and will therefore be recognized and retained more easily by your child. Your child can clearly see that writing is speech (sign or cues) written down and that the two are integrally related.

Yet another way you can use this playacting scenario to enrich your child's language is to focus on mathematical concepts. Encouraging your child to establish his own prices, to buy and sell his own foods at his restaurant, and to make change for customers are all fun ways to help improve language skills.

> "Alexa, Roberto, I think your customers need help figuring out the prices of the dinners you're serving tonight. Why don't you go over the different costs of each of the entrees on the menu? Spaghetti is $3.00 and comes with salad and garlic bread. Soda is fifty cents extra. You say you have $5.00 to spend? That will be plenty! You'll even have plenty of money left over to give the waiters a tip. . . ."

Sandpaper Numbers and Letters

Your child will likely be interested in numbers and letters at this developmental stage. This activity will let him engage a variety of his senses when playing with letters and numbers. You will need:

- numbers cut out of sandpaper,
- stiff cardboard,
- a glue stick,
- objects to count,
- crayons,
- blank paper.

After you have cut out the numbers, glue them to the stiff cardboard, one letter or number to each piece of cardboard. Help your child trace over the sandpaper number or letter with his fingers. Talk about the feel of the sandpaper and the number or letter it represents. Take a piece of blank paper and a crayon and rub over the sandpaper letter or number. Here's what your play might sound like:

> "Let's glue this number on the cardboard. Hmm, what number is it? It's a number two. Can you feel it with your fingers? It feels so scratchy. It feels rough. That's the number two. Let's make a picture of the number. What color crayon do you want? Great—

you made a green number two. Can you find two
clothespins [or whatever object you are using]. Let's
count them: one, two. There are two clothespins. The
same number as the sandpaper number. Which
number shall we do next?"

Be aware that children with sensory issues such as autism or sensory integration disorders may be sensitive to the touch of sandpaper. You can also do this activity with glue. You make the number with glue, allow it to dry, and then have your child move his finger over it.

Toy Summary

The following is a list of toys that we have worked with in this developmental period. The asterisk indicates a homemade toy.

Stencils and Pencils™—Discovery Toys
Magnifying Lens™—Small World Toys
Money Money™—Discovery Toys
What Time Is It?™—International Playthings
Baseball Card Game™—International Playthings
Get Up and Go Games™—International Playthings
Calculating Cash Register™—Battat
Stethoscope—Battat
Croquet Set™—Small World Toys
Foam Paddles and Balls™—Small World Toys
* Pretend Restaurant
* Sandpaper numbers and letters

Vocabulary and Concepts

There will be further improvement in many of the skills introduced in your child's fifth year:

- *action words:* divide, add, subtract, catch, explore, investigate, compare, decide, scan, buy, purchase, sell, etc.
- *adjectives:* tremendous, fastest, slowest, hard, soft, far, near, etc.
- *bugs and insects*
- *calendar concepts:* week, month, year, last week, this week, next week, last year, this year, next year
- *computer skills and terminology:* monitor, keyboard, hardware, software, computer, disk, printer
- *counting skills:* 1-100; first, second, third, etc.
- *fantasy play—role playing*
- *letters of the alphabet:* letter recognition improves; handwriting improves; phonetic skills improve, although invented spelling dominates
- *money:* names and value of coins, saving, spending, borrowing, sorting, collecting
- *moral issues:* following the rules, telling the truth, learning to say, "I'm sorry," using words to explain feelings
- *safety rules:* never talk to strangers, look both ways before crossing the street, wear your seatbelt, use the sidewalk for walking, wear your bicycle safety helmet

- *school terminology and concepts:* riding the bus, bus driver, respecting the teacher and school principal, and fellow classmates, learning is fun, homework
- *self-esteem:* finding a skill or area of interest your child enjoys and feels good about himself when doing
- *social skills:* sharing, taking turns, taking another's point of view, cooperation
- *sports vocabulary:* swing, step up to the plate, keep your eye on the ball, all for one and one for all, team spirit, equipment names, rules of the games, playing fair, wicket, mallet, strikes, balls, out, bases, homerun, inning, etc.
- *taking initiative and responsibility:* being a valuable member of a team at home, in school, or in the community
- *telling time skills*

Books

Books that focus on special areas of interest continue to appeal to the five-year-old. So, too, do books presenting moral issues, issues about school experiences, and self-concept books about your child's special needs.

Alexander and the Terrible, Horrible, No Good, Very Bad Day. Judith Viorst. Illustrated by Ray Cruz. New York: Atheneum/Aladdin.
> This is a story every child can relate to, but particularly the child with special needs who has more challenges and, perhaps, frustrations than most others. It is an amusing story and comforting to know that this experience happens to other people as well.

All About Hanukkah. Judye Groner and Madeline Wikler. Illustrated by Rosalyn Schanzer. Rockville, MD: KAR-BEN Copies.
> A highly praised retelling of the Hanukkah story with full-color illustrations. Candle lighting blessings, games, recipes, and songs. Everything you need for a happy Hanukkah.

All the Better to See You With. Margaret Wild. Morton Grove, IL: Albert Whitman and Co.
> This is a clear, well-written introduction to the concept of the child with a visual impairment. Recommended reading for your child with a visual impairment or if your child has a family member or friend with a visual impairment.

Berenstain Bears Series. Jan and Stan Berenstain. New York: Random House.

> Your child will love to start collecting this series of books that tell the story of the popular bears and their family tales. Children learn great morals from these stories and can apply them directly to their own lives and similar situations. Especially recommended are *Trouble at School, Go Out for the Team, Trouble with Money, Go to the Doctor,* and *Trouble with Friends,* but each and every book is valuable and recommended.

Harry, the Dirty Dog. Gene Zion. New York: Harper.

> Harry gets so dirty his own family no longer recognizes him. Look for other books in this series which will entertain and lighten your spirit.

He's My Brother. Joe Lasker. Morton Grove, Illinois: Albert Whitman and Co.

> This well-told story introduces the concept of the invisible handicap, the learning disability. Clearly and compassionately told, it will give your child a great introduction to children with this special need.

Hillel Builds a House. Shosana Lepon. Illustrated by Marilynn Barr. Rockville, MD: KAR-BEN Copies.

> Hillel loves to build houses—tree houses, pillow forts, and closet hideaways. But he can't seem to find the right time to celebrate in one of his houses until fall comes, bringing the holiday of Sukkot. A fanciful trip through the Jewish year.

Howie Helps Himself. Joan Fassler. Morton Grove, IL: Albert Whitman and Co.

> This terrific, clearly illustrated book features a boy in a wheelchair. It is a book that will foster independence and a positive self-image.

If You Made a Million. David M. Schwartz. Illustrated by Steven Kellogg. New York: Lothrop, Lee, and Shepard Books.

> This outstanding book introduces coins, dollar bills, and how to count, spend, and save them. The story is presented by a magical wizard who will enchant you and your child.

I'm Deaf and It's Okay. Lorraine Aseltine. Morton Grove, IL: Albert Whitman and Co.

> The authors portray this boy's special needs realistically and compassionately. This is a great book for opening up a discussion with your child about his or her deafness.

The Lucky Sovereign. Stewart Lees. Watertown, MA: Charlesbridge.

> Sam and his Dad set sail for the new land with enough money to buy land and one special gold sovereign that a friend gave them for luck. They are robbed and Sam comes through in the end.

Matthew's Dream. Leo Lionni. New York: Knopf.

> A young mouse visits an art museum and is encouraged by this experience to become a great painter.

The Mitten. Alvin Tresselt. New York: Lothrop.

> In this Ukranian folk tale, the mitten becomes a warm, cozy home for many forest animals. Incredible illustrations and story that will mesmerize you and your child.

Opera Cat. Tess Weaver. Illustrated by Andre Wesson. Boston: Clarion.

> When the opera lead gets laryngitis, her cat sings all of her songs for her.

The Rainbow Fish. Marcus Pfister. Translated by J. Alison James. New York: North-South Books.

> The Rainbow Fish with his shimmering scales is the most beautiful fish in the ocean. But until he learns to share his most prized possession, he cannot learn the value of friendship.

The Real Tooth Fairy. Marilyn Kaye. Illustrated by Helen Cogancherry. New York: Harcourt, Brace, Jovanovich.

> Alice loses a tooth and discovers the magic of the real tooth fairy in this magnificently illustrated book.

Russ and the Apple Tree Surprise. Janet Elizabeth Rickert. Photographs by Pete McGahan. Bethesda, MD: Woodbine House.

> Russ desperately wants a swing in his backyard but all he has is apple trees. When Grandma and Grandpa come to visit, Russ helps to make an apple pie and then gets a huge surprise. A wonderful story to help with the concept of sequencing. Reading could be followed up by baking an apple pie.

Russ and the Firehouse. Janet Elizabeth Rickert. Photographs by Pete McGahan. Bethesda, MD: Woodbine House.

> All children love to visit the firehouse. Russ's uncle works at the firehouse so Russ gets to go there whenever he wants. Wonderful photographs show how Russ helps out his uncle and the other firefighters. Every child's dream.

Shelley, the Hyperactive Turtle. Deborah Moss. Illustrated by Carol Schwartz. Bethesda, MD: Woodbine House.

> The author provides clear information about the physical and emotional aspects of hyperactivity in an upbeat, positive tone. Your child will grasp the concept of what hyperactivity means and will feel better about himself, just like Shelley in the story.

The Story of Babar. Jane De Brunhoff. New York: Random House.

> Introduce your child to this classic story, as well as others in the Babar series. Magnificently illustrated, deeply told stories of issues involving family matters with moral lessons to be learned.

Where's Chimpy? Berniece Rabe. Photos by Diane Schmidt. Morton Grove, IL: Albert Whitman and Co.

> This delightful story, recommended for children ages three to seven, follows a little girl with Down syndrome as she searches for her missing stuffed animal.

Why Am I Different? Norma Simon. Illustrated by Dora Leder. Morton Grove, IL: Albert Whitman and Co.

> This is a book that will help the very young child develop a realistic self-image. The text and lively pictures help explore the theme of individualism, and that it's okay to be different.

Conclusion

We have traveled an interesting journey from the first sound of the birth cry to complicated thoughts of diplodoci and fungi. Your patterns of communication with your child should last throughout your lifetime together. You may be amazed that your teenager will share his thoughts with you because he knows that you have always been there to listen to him. In teaching him language skills, you have not only opened up a world of communication but also helped him gain the confidence he needs in order to participate fully in the adult world. Because your child has special needs for learning language, this road to language development may be challenging for you, but spending time with him now, giving him the gift of language, will bring rewards later.

Teaching Language Throughout the Day

The emphasis in this book is on enriching your child's language by using specific toys, activities, and books. There are many other toys, activities, and books that you can use as successfully as the ones that have been described. There are also many other ways for you to teach language to your child. Basically, if you are paying attention to your child when you are with her, you will be teaching all of the time. A beautiful way for her to learn is for you to simply talk to her in short, understandable phrases about things that she is interested in. You can discuss what you are doing, try to imagine what Grandma is doing, or show her the variety of colors in the world around her. Anything will work for you if you go about it correctly.

Going on Outings

Going for a walk on a beautiful day can be an incredible language learning time if you are willing to walk at your child's pace and stop for the things she wants to explore. A caterpillar crawling on the ground, a fallen leaf, a crack in the sidewalk are all new and fascinating for her. Take your time; stroll along and let her explore and ask questions about all of the wonders that she sees.

> "Look at that beautiful red leaf. Can you find which
> tree it fell from? I think you're right, I think it fell
> from that maple tree over there. Look at all the red
> leaves on that maple tree. Soon they will all fall to the
> ground. In the summer those leaves are green. But it is
> fall, so the leaves are turning red. They are getting
> ready for winter. In the winter all the leaves fall to the

ground and next spring what happens? Right, they
will bud again on the trees...."

A trip to the grocery store can be a wonderful language learning experience if you do a little planning ahead of time. Have her participate with you in the kitchen before you go to the store. The two of you look through the pantry and the refrigerator to decide what you need to buy. As you stand in front of the refrigerator, ask her if you need to get more milk. Look at the milk container and determine if it is full, empty, or almost empty.

Whenever you can, give your child a list that she can shop for. Use the ads in the paper to clip out pictures of items and paste them on index cards. When you make your list, choose the cards that you'll need and give them to her for her list. Since many items are the same from week to week, you can re-use your index cards each week. She may be so busy looking for her list on each aisle that you will not run into the problem of screaming for candy. If she is big enough to be out of the cart and walking around, let her take the items off the shelf herself and put them in the cart. If your child has a visual impairment and cannot see the index cards, you might verbally give her a list of two things to remember and guide her with verbal language as to where she might find them. For example, you might say, "Today we need to get some ice cream and some frozen orange juice. They are both in the frozen food section. You can tell when you are there because the air will feel colder. Will you remind me when we get to the frozen food section that we need ice cream and orange juice?"

For other children your conversation might be like this:

"Can you help me find the pictures of things in the
paper that we need to get at the store? Let's look at this
page. We need milk. Good. Let's cut out that picture and
paste it on an index card. Now we also need some
apples. Do you see any apples on this page? That's
right, those are apples. Let's cut that out and put it on a
card. What color apples do you want to get at the
store? Should we get red ones or green ones? I like
green ones too. We'll look for green ones when we get to
the store. What else do you see that we should get?"

Continue in this way until she has a group of cards of items that she can look for when you get to the store.

Another learning opportunity is visiting friends. This often starts out as a good idea that quickly changes into a scene of screaming and fighting because your child is not properly prepared for a new environment. Planning ahead can eliminate this conflict, as well as provide an opportunity for language learning. We suggest that you have a calendar for your child's activities. Let's say that you are going to visit Barry and his family today. Take your child to the calendar and help her find the correct day. Then take Barry's photo (which you took before) and put it on the day of the calendar. Talk about going to Barry's house this morning and the toys that you remember that Barry has. Suggest that your child take one of her toys that Barry may not have so that they can share their toys. If the worst does happen and no one wants to share, then your child will have her own toy and Barry can have his. Keep your visit short and geared to the attention span of your child.

> *"Look at the calendar. What do we have that is special for today? Right! We are going to Barry's house. Do you remember Barry? He has a lot of cars that you like to play with. What do you have that you think Barry might like to play with? Do you want to take your dump truck? Maybe you can build a road and play with the cars and the truck. It's always fun to share your toys with your friends. . . ."*

At Home

During the course of any ordinary day, there are numerous times for pouring language into your child. Keep her near and talk to her as much as possible about your everyday activities. You may think that this sounds like a lot of trouble, but when you stop and think how short a time it really is and the value of what you are doing, you will agree that the long-term payoffs are great. Just think of all the things you do that you can turn into learning experiences. We have given you a few examples and you will be able to think of many more things during your day at home. Be sure to involve all of your child's senses as you talk about things—her sense of touch, sound, smell, and sight. This helps her to learn through every avenue.

Washing Dishes

> *"Let's wash the dishes. We need soap and water to get the dishes clean. Look at all the bubbles. Let's get the sponge and wash the dishes clean. We can even sing a song while we wash the dishes. This is the way we wash the dishes, wash the dishes, This is the way we wash the dishes so early in the morning...."*

Cooking

While cooking, state out loud each of the steps you're taking to put together the ingredients for the recipe.

"Let's cook some rice for dinner. You love rice. That's one of your favorite foods. We need a pot with a lid to cook the rice. Can you help me look in the cabinet for a pot? Here's one. Now we need to fill the pot with water, exactly up to here. That's two cups of water...."

Vacuuming

"Time to vacuum the carpet. Do you want to be my helper? We can vacuum the carpet, and surprise Grandma and Grandpa when they come to visit. Everything will be so clean. The vacuum will be very loud after we plug it into the wall. We can take turns as we vacuum...."

Doing and Folding the Laundry

"Ali, can you help me sort the laundry? Can you find all the clothes that are white? Excellent, let's put all the white things in the washer. Here's the detergent. Pour it in. OK, let me change the water temperature to warm. Thank you for your help. Shall we go and play now while the clothes are washing?"

Washing the Car

"Would you like to help me wash the car? We need to do that because the car is very dirty. It doesn't get a bath every night like you do. What do we need to wash the car? Right. We need a bucket of water, some soap, and a sponge. Can you help me find the bucket? We are going to make the car look shiny again...."

Driving in the Car

As a parent, you probably spend many hours driving in the car with your child. Driving to your child's school, to the store, to the doctor, dentist or speech therapist, to visit with friends . . . the list is endless. Why not make the most of this time together by building your child's language skills? Talk, point, gesture, cue, or sign about any number of different language enriching experiences. For example, if you are on your way to see your child's therapist, you can discuss with her where you are going and whom you will see:

"In a few minutes, we have to get ready to see Dr. Fields. Remember, we drive past the supermarket on the way. Let's count how many red cars we pass on the way. I see a red car over there. Look! I wonder how many more red cars we'll see? There's another red car ahead of us. He's making a left turn. We keep going straight to the doctor's office."

Sometimes your child will just want to listen to music or stories in the car. You do not have to be talking all the time. She can learn language from the CDs or tapes that you play. Each child has her favorite CD that she would like to hear over and over again. Repetition is a good way to learn the language from the tapes or CDs.

Other Activities

There are any number of other daily activities that can be turned into fun learning experiences, including:

- Ironing
- Cleaning the refrigerator
- Making beds
- Mowing the lawn
- Raking the leaves
- Washing the dog
- Feeding the dog or cat
- Scrubbing the bathtub
- Getting dressed
- Putting toys away

Enjoy the time with your children. You are their first and best language teacher. The relationship you establish now will last a lifetime.

Computer Technology and Language Learning

In the last edition of *The New Language of Toys,* this chapter was introduced by saying, "It is September 1, 2005 and you are getting your child ready for the first day of school. New shoes, new backpack, new lunchbox, and don't forget the laptop computer." Well, here we are in the year 2004 and most children do not take their own laptops to school yet. However, in many schools, children have their own computer to use or at least go to the computer lab several times a week. Your children may be able to do more with a computer than you can!

Computer technology has opened a whole new world to children with special needs. It has enabled mute children to "talk," children with physical disabilities to "move," blind children to "read," and deaf children to "hear." It has also made it easier and more entertaining for children with a variety of disabilities to learn needed skills and concepts. Your child's life will be so much easier because of computer technology.

How does this relate to the subject of this book? Is the computer a toy? Yes and no. Can computer technology be used to teach language? Most definitely yes. In the sections below, we will explain some of the ways that computers and toys that utilize computer technology can be used to teach and reinforce important concepts and language skills.

Electronic Toys

In previous chapters, I have recommended many electronic toys. Many of these computer-based toys help your child understand the very important concept of cause and effect. When your child pushes a button, flips a switch, or otherwise interacts with the toy, something happens—cause and effect. We see this with the toy that we talk about in the first year, the Sunshine Symphony™ by Neurosmith. All your baby needs to do is touch the face of this toy and it will produce music. Imagine an infant interacting with a computer!

Almost every toy made today has a computer chip in it. Most infant toys have computer chips that activate as the child plays with the toys and plays melodies that young children enjoy. Fisher Price has put music that is activated by your child as he plays with the toy into many of its infant toys. The Ocean Wonders aquarium that is discussed in the first year offers wonderful sights and sounds to help your young one drift off into sleep or simply enjoy the music as he lies in his crib.

Throughout the book, it is up to you to play with your child and expand on the vocabulary offered through these electronic toys in order to enrich his language development. Remember: it is fine for him to have time alone with the toy but he should also have ample opportunity to play with you.

When you are choosing electronic toys, listen to them before you buy them. Most of the toys on the market today have exceptionally fine quality due to computer chips but there are still some that are difficult to understand and have an "electronic" quality to them. You want your child to be listening to the finest sound that is possible to find.

Computers and Software

When you actually introduce a computer to your children is a matter of your own preference and lifestyle. In some homes, a computer is standard equipment and one or both parents are familiar with how it operates. The computer can be set up so that both parents and children can use it at different times yet not interfere with each other's work. There are programs that allow each member of the family to access his own part of the computer. These packages can both be used on either a personal computer or an Apple product. This will help alleviate fears parents may have of their child using the adult computer and inadvertently erasing very important documents!

When you decide to purchase a computer, get a large-capacity hard drive to be sure that your computer will run the software you want; and get a CD-ROM (read only memory stored on a compact disc) to open up many avenues of interactive computing for your young child. If the cost is not prohibitive, you will want to get a sound card and speakers also. A used computer is okay, but don't compromise on desirable features for the sake of cost alone. Computers have come down so much in cost that it is possible to get a high functioning machine for a relatively low cost.

Would you believe that some children as young as two show an interest in the computer and become quite adept at using the computer mouse to interact with the software on the screen! These children definitely need adult supervision and interaction to benefit the most from computer use. However, most software is recommended for children starting at age three. Again, you know your child best and you know what will and won't work for him. Use your best judgment.

For children with limited physical ability, there are many adaptations for the computer keyboard. A children's catalog called *Sensational Beginnings* shows a keyboard made by a French company, Berchet, which fits over a standard keyboard. Big color-coded keys make it easy for children to interact with the screen. Included are three CD-ROMs that are packed with games geared to the young child. The age range suggested is 12-36 months. You need to judge whether your child is at this developmental stage and is ready for this kind of interaction. Remember, it is very important for you to be there and hold your child on your lap as you talk about the experience that he is having with the computer. In the same catalog there is a small mouse designed for tiny hands. (See pages 207-208 for information about this catalog and these products.)

There is also a keyboard called Intellikeys made by Intellitools, which is a flat keyboard that is used in place of a regular keyboard. This flat keyboard can be programmed to use an overlay of a keyboard or any overlay you want to create. For example, if your child is able to choose between two objects, you can make an overlay with two shapes on it—a circle and a square. When your child hits the circle, he gets a response on the screen, and when he hits the square, he gets a different response on the screen. You can program this keyboard for any language that you are trying to teach your child. Another keyboard made by Li'l Hands Gadgets and Gizmos is color coded: vowels are purple; consonants are green; punctuation is yellow; numbers are red; functions are blue. One keyboard is called the Learning Board and another keyboard that has the same color coding but is 60 percent larger is called My Board. You might want to investigate any of these keyboards that might fit your child's special needs.

When it comes to selecting software, it can be difficult to stay abreast of what is available. New software programs are being created daily and new editions of old software pop up regularly. One good way to find out what is out there is to subscribe to a magazine called *Scholastic*. It reviews the latest in software packages on disk and CDs for both personal computers and Macintosh computers. The listing for this magazine is in the Appendix. Another option is *Children's Software Revue*, which is both a magazine and a linked website: *www.childrenssoftware.com*. There are some free websites that review kids' software, too, including:

- SuperKids Educational Software Review at *www.superkids.com*
- Kids and Computers at *www.kidsandcomputers.com*
- Reviews of software and sites at *www.worldvillage.com*
- Tested educational software at *www.creativekids.com*
- A site for games, software, and tutoring at *www.cyberkids.com*
- A site for demonstrations of software and projects for kids at *www.theconnectedfamily.com*

In her book, *Kids and Computers* (which is currently out of print but available used at www.amazon.com), Judy Salpeter gives some ideas to help parents choose developmentally appropriate software for preschool children. She says, "Developmentally appropriate software is:

- **Open ended and exploratory.** It doesn't focus on right and wrong answers but allows children to investigate and discover for themselves.
- **Easy for a young child to use independently.** It does not require reading, has easy to understand directions, and only expects children to find a limited number of keys on the keyboard. Furthermore, it is flexible about input devices, allowing a child to use a mouse, the keyboard, or an alternate device—whichever is easiest for that child.
- **Focused on a broad range of skills and concepts.** It works on more than just the numbers, letters, colors, and shapes so often identified as preschool skills. In addition (or instead), it encourages children to classify, to experiment using trial and error, to create and, in general, to think.
- **Technically sophisticated.** It appeals to a child's multi-sensory learning style, offering attractive graphics, appealing animations, and outstanding sound. It loads quickly and does not have long delays between screens (during which time a young child can become bored).
- **Age-appropriate.** It doesn't push the child to master skills for which he's not yet ready. The images and examples it uses are from real life or are at least understandable to the young child (within his realm of experience).
- **Play and fun.** It encourages children to imagine, might involve fantasy play, and is definitely enjoyable. Furthermore, the fun is derived from the activity itself, not from some extrinsic reward given if the child succeeds at a given task.
- **Encouraging.** Children experience success when using this software; it helps build their self-esteem." (Judy Salpeter, *Kids and Computers: A Parent's Handbook*. Englewood Cliffs, NJ: Alpha Books - A Division of Simon & Schuster, 1991, p. 43.)

Computers and Special Needs

During the last few decades, a great deal of exciting new computer technology has evolved, opening a world of possibilities for children with special needs. There are now computers that respond to voice commands, touch screens, speech synthesizers that talk for the user, and switches that allow the computer to be accessed by a head movement, a puff of air, or a wink of an eye.

Computers have connected the deaf to others through TTYs (see next section), chat rooms, listserves, and FAX machines. The deaf are getting better use of hearing aids that are digital and can be matched to their individual hearing losses. There are cochlear implant devices that are surgically implanted in the child's inner ear and are programmed for the individual who is profoundly deaf to be able to respond to speech as well as environmental sounds.

For individuals with learning disabilities, there are word processing programs with spelling and grammar checkers, as well as a number of programs designed to help teach reading as well as other subjects. For the blind there are visual scanners that can "read" any book out loud for the listener. There are portable Braillers as well as devices with the capability of converting printed letters to tactile codes. The computer has the ability to display large print and output large print hard copy. For those with physical disabilities, the computer has opened the world to environmental control through electronic wheelchairs, and technology that can perform such tasks as opening and closing curtains and opening and closing the front door. Computers with Internet access can also enable people with limited mobility to shop, inquire for information, and manage banking from their homes.

Making your child comfortable with computer technology is becoming more and more of a

Watch Out for Computer-Related Vision Problems

Although this discussion has focused on the benefits that can be had from accessing computer programs, it is necessary to pause and put in a word about how computers may affect vision. In an article by Dr. Sanford Cohen, O.D., F.O.V.D., he states that "Children—especially those with developmental delays—often do not know the difference between normal and abnormal visual experiences. They may not complain of any discomfort. Therefore, parents and teachers must watch for computer-related symptoms including:

- blurred or double vision
- headaches, back and neck aches
- frequent eye rubbing
- squinting
- head turns or other unusual postures
- trouble seeing the chalkboard and words in books."

("Computers and Children," *Developmental Disabilities Research*, Vol. 5. No.4, p. 146.)

need as we progress in the 21st century. Teaching your infant to reach and touch to control a computer switch and access a touch talker will have far-reaching benefits for him. Teaching your child words such as disk, hard drive, and mouse is important for him to maximize the use of computer technology.

TTY (Telephone Typewriter)

As said earlier, the concept of "speech written down" is becoming more and more appealing to your five- to six-year-old. Additionally, he has a strong developing desire to communicate with family and friends across the telephone wires. This need to communicate is inherent in each of us. (Thank you, Alexander Graham Bell, for inventing the telephone.)

If your child has difficulty hearing on the telephone or his speech delay inhibits phone usage, he can still participate in a telephone conversation with family and friends by using a device called a TTY (Telephone Typewriter). (This is also sometimes referred to as a Telephone Device for the Deaf or TDD.) This device was originally designed for use by the deaf in 1963 by Dr. Robert H. Weitbrecht. It can also be used by people whose speech impairment prevents them from being understood on the telephone. A TTY converts the acoustic message from the telephone into a printed format. Its basic function operates like that of a typewriter. If your child cannot use a telephone in the conventional way, he can use a TTY to read and write his telephone conversation.

There are two ways to make a TTY call. First, the two people on either end of the telephone line can have a TTY attached to their telephones. In this case, the caller dials the other person's number and when the phone is answered, he types his message onto his TTY keyboard, which resembles a typewriter or computer keyboard. The receiver reads the printed message on the display panel on his TTY.

Calls may also be placed using a TTY if only one of the people involved in the telephone conversation has a TTY. This is accomplished through a telephone relay operator. This service is offered through the telephone company in each state. When using this type of service, there are two ways to go about it. The caller may type his printed message on a TTY to a relay operator, who then transmits the message to the receiver by way of voice. Or, the caller may give a spoken message to the relay operator, who then converts it into a printed message for the receiver to read on his TTY.

If your child is just beginning to read, a parent or another adult will have to sit with him to help him pick out letters on the TTY keyboard and to help with spelling of words. An adult will also have to be available to help your child read the printed words displayed on the TTY screen. However, this is a really *fun* form of beginning reading and writing for children. They enjoy the practice of the activity itself, as well as the built-in pleasure of easy communication with a friend. Don't be surprised if this develops into one of your child's favorite language building activities. With practice, you will see his writing, or, in this case, his typing skills as well as his reading skills, begin to grow quickly.

Even if you have no access to a TTY, your five- to six-year-old will love practicing writing on a typewriter or computer keyboard. An old discarded typewriter can be brought out especially for this purpose.

To purchase a TTY, check your local yellow pages directory to find a store that sells items related to deafness. If you have Internet access, go to www.google.com or another search engine and enter "telephone typewriter for the deaf."

Resources

The following resources will help you access the newest technology in hardware and software. Make use of them. Get on the mailing lists, so as new devices are developed, you will be among the first to know. Enjoy exploring these new avenues with your child. Although computer technology will ease the daily living needs of your child, you are still a very important component. You must be a part of this learning experience with him.

Books Healy, Jane. *Failure to Connect: How Computers Affect Our Children's Minds—And What We Can Do about It.* New York, NY: Touchstone, 1998.

Lindsey, Jimmy D., ed. *Computers and Exceptional Individuals.* Austin, TX: PRO-ED, 1992.

Salpeter, Judy. *A Parent's Handbook: Kids and Computers.* Englewood Cliffs, NJ: Alpha Books - A Division of Simon & Schuster, 1991.

Webb, Colin et al. *Computers and Kids: A Parent's Guide.* New York, NY: Harper Collins,1996.

Wolock, Ellen L. et al. *Young Kids and Computers: A Parent's Survival Guide.* Flemington, NJ: Children's Software Revue, 1998.

Websites Abledata
www.abledata.com
Has a database of 20,000 assistive technology products with information about where they can be purchased.

Center for Applied Special Technology

www.cast.org

> CAST is a nonprofit organization that uses technology to expand opportunities for all people especially those with disabilities.

Children's Software Revue

www.Childrenssoftware.com

> A website that introduces you to the quarterly magazine that reviews children's software.

Common Sense Media

www.commonsensemedia.org

> A website devoted to helping parents choose appropriate television shows, videos, and computer games.

Entertainment Software Rating Board

www.esrb.org

> The Entertainment Software Rating Board is a group established by the video game industry to give parents a better idea of the suitability of products for their children.

FCC Parents' Place

www.fcc.gov/parents

> This website is sponsored by the Federal Communications Commission and offers information about TV programming, rating systems, and channel blocking systems.

Kid Defender

www.actiontec.com

> Kid Defender software allows you to remotely watch your computer's activity in real time.

National Institute on Media and the Family

www.mediafamily.org

> This organization has developed a ratings system that includes input from media specialists as well as parents and has created a guide for television shows and video games.

Net Nanny

www.netnanny.com

> Net Nanny 5 software keeps logs on your computer of sites that are accessed.

Netgear Wireless
www.netgear.com
> Netgear Wireless allows you to filter any computer by typing in sites you wish to block. Works on wireless modems.

Symantec
www.symantec.com
> Symantec sells the Norton Internet Security 2004 software, which keeps logs on selected computers (among other things).

Catalogs

Apple Computer-Disability Solutions Group. 20525 Mariani Ave., MS 36SE., Cupertino, CA 95014. 408-974-7910; 408-974-7911 (TTY). *www.apple.com/disability*
> Solutions for accessing Mac computers for special needs

Don Johnston Developmental Equipment, Inc. 26799 West Commerce Dr., Volo, IL 60073. 800-999-4660. *www.donjohnston.com*
> Catalog of assistive technology such as switches, adapted keyboards, and touch windows, as well as appropriate software for children with special needs.

Edmark. A Division of Riverdeep. Riverdeep, Inc., 500 Redwood Blvd., Novaato, CA 94947. 415-763-4700. *www.riverdeep.net*
> Early Learning Software as well as programs for all major educational areas: art, music, social studies, reading, science, mathematics.

Educational Resources. 1550 Executive Drive, P.O. Box 1900, Elgin, IL 60123. 800-624-2926. *www.edresources.com*
> Multi-media resources. Has some Pre-K programs.

Intellitools, 1720 Corporate Circle, Petaluma, CA 94954. 800-899-6687. *www.intellitools.com*
> Source of the Intellikeys keyboard described above, as well as educational software.

Learning How. 8895 McCaw Rd., Columbia, MD 21227. 410-381-0828. *www.learninghow.com*
> Educational software packages.

Li'l Hands Gadgets and Gizmos. 1926 Como Lake Ave., Ste. 203, Coquitlam, BC V3J 7X8 Canada. 604-468-9577. *www.lilhands.ca*
> Keyboards and mice sized for children's hands.

RJ Cooper and Associates. 24843 Del Prado, #283, Dana Point, CA 92629. 714-240-1912. *www.rjcooper.com*
> Carries software packages and keyboards for people with special needs, switch-adapted mouse, touch windows.

Scholastic. 557 Broadway, New York, NY 10012. 212-343-6100. *www.scholastic.com*
> A source for books as well as software. Operates a software club newsletter.

Sensational Beginnings. 987 Stewart Rd., Monroe, MI. 48162. 800-444-6058. *www.sensationalbeginnings.com*
> Toys and equipment for young children. Has the oversized keyboard for the computer.

Sunburst/Wings for Learning. 101 Castleton Street, P.O. Box 100, Pleasantville, NY 10570-0100. 800-338-3457; 914-747-4109. Email: wain@nysunburst.com
> Source for software, CD-ROMs, Videos, Videodiscs.

Tom Snyder Productions. 80 Coolidge Hill Road, Watertown, MA 02472-5003. 800-342-0236. *www.tomsnyder.com*
> Offers a selection of software and workbooks of current products.

Videotapes, DVDs, and Television

The video and DVD market for home televisions is a soaring industry. Almost every movie that has ever played in the theater is available for home TV and can be rented or bought. Through this medium, parents can bring quality entertainment into their homes and help to minimize the amount of violence that children see on commercial television. A cool summer evening or a cozy winter evening spent watching videos can help bring families together after hectic weeks of running from day care to work and home again. It is a pleasant interlude. A family does not have to worry about taking small children to a theater, where they may be disruptive, or about incurring the expense of a babysitter to go out for the evening.

Take the time to enjoy a video with your child from time to time. Do not, however, get into the easy habit of using the video as an electronic babysitter and leave your child unattended for long periods of time. If you do, you will be wasting valuable opportunities to bond with your child, as well as to teach language, reading, and other important life skills. While you are watching the video, engage your child actively by pointing out certain people or actions that are going on and asking questions to see if she understands what she is watching.

Bear in mind that it is not necessary to view any video or DVD in its entirety in one sitting. Your child may want to watch a while, then play outside, then nap, and watch again later on. She will let you know when enough is enough.

Buying videos can be expensive, especially since children's interests can change so quickly. Your local library is a good source to borrow videos. Remember to exchange with friends as you do with your toys.

Captioning

Most movies and TV programs today are closed captioned, which makes them very accessible for the deaf and language delayed child. Look on your video or DVD carton or in the TV guide for the symbol "cc," which stands for closed captioned.

Captioned television, DVDs, and videotapes are not just for the deaf. Caption decoders, first marketed in 1980, are an exciting breakthrough for all children learning to read, with or without a language delay. TV watching is *fun* for your child. Captioned TV, DVDs, and videos are especially suited for helping your child develop good reading readiness skills. Captioning makes it clear to your child that reading is speech or signs or cues written down. (In fact, some speakers of other languages use a caption decoder to help them learn to read and speak English.) In the last decade, captioned TV has increasingly been used to assist deaf and hearing children with learning disabilities develop better reading skills.

Studies conducted in Maryland public schools and at the University of Maryland found that comprehension and motivation to read also improved with captioning. Children not only learned more words, but retained more words over time. One interesting result which came out of the studies was that some students learning to read benefited greatly from being able to comprehend the story line first as a precursor to attacking the sight reading words on the TV screen. In other words, learning to read captions with an accompanying visual display and contextual study was easier than just learning to read individual letters or words with no accompanying visual display.

There are two types of captions, **open** and **closed.**

Open captions can be read without the need for a decoder. Open captions sometimes appear on your television set to alert the viewing audience about weather or government emergencies, etc. They are "open" to everyone watching the TV set.

Closed captions are similar to subtitles you read on foreign films. They can be viewed only if you have a specially equipped TV or a caption decoder. A caption decoder can be purchased through stores or catalogs that feature assistive listening devices for people with special needs. Captioners generally cost under $200.

Captioned TV helps your child develop the visual discrimination skills she needs before she can learn to read. These skills include being able to recognize and name upper and lower case letters, distinguishing left from right, up from down, following a progression of words from left to right, and being able to pick out the figure from the background.

Captioned TV also provides yet another way for your child to develop good sight reading skills to correspond with the words she hears and sees. For example, we have seen the success of *Sesame Street,* which uses a visual input system of letters, words, and numbers on the screen in a fun and interesting way. Through repetition, the child sees the letters, numbers, and simple words over and over and begins to integrate them into easily recognizable words wherever she sees them. We have seen this in families where there are deaf adults and the children, both deaf and hearing, are exposed to captioned movies and TV. No one knows at exactly what point the child makes the connection between the words that are captioned and those that are spoken but we do know that early exposure to the printed word results in better reading ability later on. This is true for books as well as captioned TV or movies.

Captioned TV is also great for helping your child develop sound-symbol correspondence skills, or phonetics. It can help her begin recognizing the names of letters, as well as the sounds they represent. She learns at this stage that C is called "see" and stands for the sound "kuh" at the beginning of the word "cat." Your child will start to understand that the sounds of letters blend together to form a word that she sees on the TV screen.

It is recommended that you consider using captioned TV and films on a regular basis at home to help your child develop her reading vocabulary. Your child will think she's got the most fun reading toy of all the kids in the neighborhood.

Videos for Children with Visual Impairments

If your child has a visual impairment, you will want to investigate videos, DVDs, and television programs with descriptive video—a spoken, pre-recorded description of actions on the screen that can be heard through a special simultaneous radio broadcast or directly from video. Descriptive video is becoming more available for television shows (especially on public television) and movies. Your television set may well already have the capability to decode descriptive video. If not, check for this feature when you buy your next TV.

If your child uses sign language, you should be aware that videos and computer CDs in sign language are available. Because sign language is a visual language, children who know the system can enjoy some of their favorite stories told through this medium.

The Washington Post newspaper (October 29, 2003) recently published an article describing a recent survey for the Kaiser Foundation. This article reported that "25 percent of children under the age of two have a television is his/her room. Nearly a third of children under age 3 have used a computer. Nine percent play computer games daily for about 49 minutes and about 12 percent of parents surveyed said that computer products mostly help children's learning."

Children today are learning more from electronic media than from books. It is important to find a balance here. All electronic media are not bad and all books are not good. This leaves a burden on parents to screen out the programs that will not be beneficial to their children and to bring more books into the home.

Toy Safety

Protecting children from unsafe toys is everyone's responsibility. Careful toy selection and proper supervision of children at play is still the best way to protect children from toy-related injuries.

Safety has been discussed throughout this book as specific toys in each of the age categories are presented. In this section suggestions are offered about toy safety in general. This information was obtained from the U.S. Consumer Product Safety Commission in Washington, D.C. Under the Federal Hazardous Substances Act and The Consumer Product Safety Act, the Commission has set safety regulations for certain toys and other children's articles. Manufacturers must design and manufacture their products to meet these regulations so that hazardous products are not sold.

If you have further questions, you can call a Toll Free Hotline at 800-638-CPSC or 800-638-2772 or go to the website, www.cpsc.gov. You are encouraged to call these numbers and report any dangerous conditions that you find in any toys. This office is very interested in having up-to-date information about toy safety.

When Buying Toys

Choose toys with care. Keep in mind your child's age, interests, and skill level. Look for quality design and construction in all toys for all ages.

Make sure that all directions or instructions are clear to you, and, when appropriate, to your child. Plastic wrappings on toys should be discarded at once before they become deadly playthings.

Be a label reader. Look for, and heed, age recommendations such as "Not recommended for children under three." Look for other safety labels, including: "Flame retardant/Flame resistant" on fabric products and "Washable/hygienic materials" on stuffed toys and dolls.

When Maintaining Toys

Check all toys periodically for breakage and potential hazards. A damaged or dangerous toy should be thrown away or repaired immediately.

Edges on wooden toys that might have become sharp or surfaces covered with splinters should be sanded smooth. Paint is regulated for lead content by the Consumer Product Safety Commission. Examine all outdoor toys regularly for weak parts that could become hazardous.

Hazards to Avoid

Sharp Edges and Points. A Consumer Products Safety Commission regulation prohibits sharp points in new toys and other articles intended for use by children under eight years of age. With use, however, older toys may break, exposing cutting edges. Broken toys may have dangerous points or prongs. Stuffed toys may have wires inside the toy that could cut or stab your child if exposed.

Small Parts. Older toys can break to reveal parts small enough to be swallowed or to become lodged in your child's windpipe, ears, or nose. There is a small tube that can be obtained from the Consumer Products Safety Commission or through toy stores that can help you decide how safe a small piece is. The tube is the size of a child's windpipe and any toy or part that can fit into it is not safe for a child under three.

The law bans small parts in new toys intended for children under three. This includes removable small eyes and noses on stuffed toys and dolls and small, removable squeakers on squeeze toys. Double check that infant toys, such as rattles, squeeze toys, and teethers, are large enough so that they cannot enter and become lodged in your infant's throat.

Loud Noises. Toy caps, noisemaking guns, and other toys can produce sounds at noise levels that can damage hearing. The law requires the following label on boxes of caps producing noise above a certain level; "Warning—Do not fire closer than one foot to the ear. Do not use indoors." Caps producing noise that can injure a child's hearing are banned. On many of today's electronic or musical toys there are volume controls that you can adjust.

Cords and Strings. Toys with long strings or cords may be dangerous for infants and very young children. The cords may become wrapped around an infant's neck, causing strangulation. Never hang toys with long strings, cords, loops, or ribbons in cribs or playpens where children can become entangled.

Remove crib gyms from the crib when your child can pull himself up on his hands and knees; some children have strangled when they fell across crib gyms stretched across the crib.

Propelled Objects. Your child's flying toys can be turned into weapons and cause serious injuries. Children should never be permitted to play with adult lawn darts or other hobby or sporting equipment with sharp points. Arrows or darts used by children should have soft cork tips, rubber suction cups, or other protective tips intended to prevent injury. Check to be sure the tips are secure. Avoid those dart guns or other toys that might be capable of firing articles not intended for use in the toys such as pencils or nails.

Electric Toys. Electric toys that are improperly constructed, wired, or misused can shock or burn your child. Electric toys must meet mandatory requirements for maximum surface temperatures, electrical construction, and prominent warning labels. Electric toys with heating elements are recommended only for children over eight years old. Children should be taught to use electric toys properly, cautiously, and under adult supervision. Equally important is to make sure that battery-operated toys have safe storage compartments so that young children cannot gain access to the batteries.

When Storing Toys

Teach children to put their toys safely away on shelves or in a toy chest.

Toy chests, too, should be checked for safety. Use a toy chest that has a lid that will stay open in any position to which it is raised and will not fall on your child. For extra safety, be sure there are ventilation holes for fresh air. Watch for sharp edges that could cut and hinges that could pinch or squeeze.

See that toys used outdoors are stored after play. Rain or dew can damage a variety of toys and toy parts, creating hazards.

All Toys Are Not for All Children
Keep toys designed for older children out of the hands of little ones. Follow labels that give age recommendations—some toys are recommended for older children because they may be hazardous in the hands of a younger child. Teach your older children to keep their toys away from their younger brothers and sisters.

Even balloons when uninflated or broken can choke or suffocate your child if he tries to swallow them. More children have suffocated on uninflated balloons than on any other type of toy.

Street Smarts

By the time your child is five, safety issues expand to toys used outside the home. Riding a bicycle, dribbling a basketball, playing tee ball, or jumping rope outside near the street must be done with caution.

As you allow your child increased independence, you must continue to stress safety. He must be taught to look both ways a number of times before crossing the street, and not to dart in the street to chase after a ball. When using a bicycle, skateboard, scooter, or roller blades, your child should wear a safety helmet. In fact, in many states, it is now against the law to allow your child to bicycle even down a public sidewalk without an approved safety helmet.

Consider kneepads and elbowpads for rollerblading or scooters or even for the five-year-old learning to ride a two-wheel bicycle without training wheels. Protective gear such as this will soften your child's falls.

Conclusion

Most children's toys for sale today are well constructed and safe *for their intended age group*. Still, accidents can happen. But if you choose toys carefully and supervise your child at play, you will greatly diminish the chances that your child will be injured.

Alternate Sources of Toys

For many parents, the cost of continually buying new and stimulating toys for their children can be prohibitive. Fortunately, there are several low-cost alternatives to buying brand new toys. Sometimes small groups of friends swap toys for their children for short or indefinite periods of time. This, of course, instantly increases the number of toys you and your child have to work with when doing the language development dialogues. Imagine if you were to arrange to borrow or exchange a few selected toys from one friend, a few toys from a second friend, and a few more toys from yet a third friend. You would have managed to accumulate close to a dozen different toys for you and your child to play with.

On a similar, but slightly larger scale, we have seen neighborhood groups of parents organize a toy-sharing cooperative. This can be organized on its own or as part of an already existing neighborhood organization or a community play group. Each child brings in a different toy to exchange with another child for a period of a week or two. This way, the novelty of getting a new toy never quite has time to wear off. One new toy is continually replaced by another new toy. A child's dream come true! Again, the cost of buying new toys is drastically reduced and parents have an opportunity to see which toys their child enjoys the most before purchasing them.

Now that you have the idea of this type of alternative to buying brand-new toys in the department stores, you can see why some neighborhood preschools, special education programs, and local libraries provide this service or take it even one step further. Either for free or for a very small rental fee, you and your child can choose to borrow a toy for a designated period of time. Next time you go to your local library, find out if they have such a service. You may be surprised to find a toy lending library already in your area. Another source may be your local Arc (formerly Association for Retarded Citizens), Easter Seals, or other special-needs organizations.

Be on the lookout for garage sales and consignment shops in your area. These are two other good places to locate children's toys, often for greatly reduced prices. In these cases, the toys are often out of their boxes, which gives you a chance to look them over thoroughly. You can see how interested your child is in the toy before you buy it.

Another alternative is Ebay (www.ebay.com), an online site where anyone can post descriptions of anything they would like to sell. On Ebay, many toys can be found inexpensively, some still in the box. Ebay can also be a good source of older toys that are no longer available in stores. Someone somewhere may have that toy for sale.

One final option is to contact the National Lekotek Center at 1-800-366-PLAY. Lekotek centers offer individualized assistance in selecting appropriate toys and play materials for children with disabilities, and may also have toys available for loan. The national office can tell you the location of the Lekotek center nearest you.

With all borrowed or secondhand toys, it is recommended that you take special safety precautions before letting your child play with them. Wash the toys thoroughly with soap and water. Run your hand over them, looking for sharp or broken edges. Make sure there are no small parts that may present a danger to your child.

Appendix **B**

Materials List

Many of the materials you need to make homemade toys may already be in your cupboards, recycling bin, rag bag, or basement. To help you recognize these valuable materials before you throw them in the trash, this section lists common items useful in making your own toys. Also listed are stores and other sources of free or low-cost materials.

Materials for Homemade Toys

- *Arts and Crafts necessities:* tape, paper clips, string, paper fasteners, pipe cleaners, wire, rope, string, staples, paste glue, tempera paint, crayons, markers, scissors, paper in various sizes and colors, stickers, paper towels, etc.
- *Barrels:* fruit and vegetable crates
- *Baskets*
- *Boxes:* all types; match boxes, gift boxes, jewelry boxes, candy boxes, etc.
- *Cardboard Tubing:* paper towel tubing, toilet paper rolls, aluminum foil and plastic wrap tubing, etc.
- *Food Items:* macaroni noodles, kidney beans, dried peas, cereal bits, etc.
- *Kitchen Utensils:* pots, pans, measuring utensils, sifters, bowls, cooking pans, wooden spoons, spatulas, etc.
- *Miscellaneous Items:* rubber bands, Popsicle sticks, sponges, clothespins, cotton balls, cork, leaves, pine cones, small stones and shells, straws, pipe cleaners, etc.
- *Paper and Cardboard Items:* aluminum foil, waxed paper, wallpaper scraps, contact paper scraps, newspaper, shirt cardboards, vegetable cartons and trays, oatmeal containers, old magazines, greeting cards, gift wrapping paper, etc.

- *Plastic Bottles:* milk bottles, dish soap dispensers, hand lotion dispensers, ketchup bottles, etc.
- *Plastic Containers:* egg cartons, ice cream cartons, butter containers, cheese containers, microwave dinners
- *Sewing Notions:* yarn, decorative tape, buttons, zippers, beads, ribbons, thread, empty spools, cloth in different colors and textures, clasps, belt buckles, etc.
- *Styrofoam:* Styrofoam packing, fruit trays, etc.

Materials for Dramatic Play

- *Baskets, grocery carts, bags*—to go "shopping."
- *Boxes*—to represent the stove, refrigerator, a spaceship, playhouse, etc.
- *Broom, dustpan*—to play clean up.
- *Crates and boxes*—for doll or stuffed animal beds.
- *Empty food storage cans and boxes*—for the pretend kitchen.
- *Hats, hats, and more hats*—kids love them.
- *Miscellaneous*—glasses, aprons, pocketbooks, wallets, mittens, etc.
- *Old clothes*—dresses, skirts, blouses, pants, slips, hats, coats, scarves, gloves. Discarded nylon nightgowns make great formal wear for kids.
- *Old jewelry*—bracelets, belts, necklaces, earrings, etc.
- *Play money, boxes*—to play cashier.
- *Pots, pans, dishes, cups, eating utensils, paper plates and cups*— for restaurant play, pretending to be Mommy and Daddy, etc.
- *Telephones*—a great way to practice language!
- *White coats or shirts*—to pretend to be a doctor, dentist, etc.

Places to Find Materials

- *Carpet Stores:* carpet samples and scraps
- *Fabric Stores:* sewing notions, remnants, patches
- *Garage Sales:* an infinite variety of objects
- *Grocery Stores:* boxes, plastic and cardboard cartons, food items
- *Lumber Yards:* wood scraps, cinder blocks, etc. Check out construction sites also for end pieces of wood and other materials you might be able to use.
- *Newspaper Companies:* newsprint end-of-rolls and scraps
- *Paint Stores:* paint color cards
- *Paper Companies:* paper samples, damaged sheets of paper
- *Produce Markets:* vegetable and fruit crates, barrels
- *Tile Companies:* scraps of mosaic, ceramic, or vinyl tile
- *Wallpaper Stores:* out-of-date sample books, swatches

Sources for Information about Children's Books

Amazon.com
www.amazon.com
   Site includes book reviews from journals and consumers.

Baby's First Book Club
2931 McCarty St.
Jefferson City, MO 65101
877-667-4420 (toll free)

Barnes and Noble
www.barnesandnoble.com
   Site includes book reviews from journals and consumers.

Children's Book Council, Inc.
12 W. 37th St.
New York, NY 10018
212-966-1990
www.cbcbooks.org

Children's Books in Print
(revised annually; available for use in most libraries and bookstores)
R.R. Bowker
LLC P.O. Box 32
New Providence, NJ 07974
800-521-8110

Exceptional Parent Magazine
P.O. Box 3000, Dept. EP

Denville, NJ 07834-9919

800-247-8080

www.eparent.com

Horn Book Magazine

11 Beacon St., Suite 1000

Boston, MA 02108

www.hbook.com

Highlights for Children

P.O. Box 182167

Columbus, OH 43218-2167

www.highlights.com

Seedlings Books

Twin Vision Books (books in print and Braille)

P.O. Box 51924

14151 Farmington Rd.

Livonia, MI 14154800-777-8552

www.seedlings.org

Sesame Street Magazine

Children's Television Workshop

One Lincoln Plaza

New York, NY 10023

800-678-0613

www.NetMagazines.com

Appendix **D**

Resource Guide

Included in this section are national organizations that provide support and information for children with disabilities and their families. For specific information about the goals and services of any organization, call or write and request an information packet.

General

Council for Exceptional Children
1110 N. Glebe Rd., Suite 300
Arlington, VA 22201-5704
888-232-7733
TTY 703-264-9446
www.cec.sped.org

Developmental Delay Resources
4401 East West Highway
Bethesda, MD 20814
www.devdelay.org

Division of Early Childhood (DEC)
634 Eddy Ave.
Missoula, MT 59812
406-243-5898
www.dec-sped.org

Family Resource Center on Disability
20 E. Jackson Blvd., Rm. 900
Chicago, IL 60604
312-939-3513
www.fred.org

National Information Center for Children and Youth with Disabilities (NICHCY)
P.O. Box 1492
Washington, DC 20013
202-884-8200; 800-695-0285
www.nichcy.org

National Lekotek Center
3204 Armitage Ave.
Chicago, IL 60647
773-276-5164
800-366-PLAY
www.lekotek.org
   (Information on toys and play for children with disabilities)

National Safe Kids Campaign
1301 Pennsylvania Ave. NW
Washington, DC 20004
202-662-0600
www.safekids.org

Special Olympics International
1325 G St. NW, Suite 500
Washington, DC 20005
202-628-3630
www.specialolympics.org

TASH
29 W. Susquehanna Ave., Ste. 210
Baltimore, MD 21204
410-828-8274
TTY 410-828-1486
www.tash.org

• • • • • • • • • • • • •
Autism Spectrum Disorders

Asperger Syndrome Coalition of the United States
P.O. Box 351268
Jacksonville, FL 32235-1268
866-4-ASPRGR
www.asperger.org

Autism Society of America
7910 Woodmont Ave.
Bethesda, MD 20814

800-3AUTISM
www.autism-society.org

Online Asperger Syndrome Information and Support
www.aspergersyndrome.org

● ● ● ● ● ● ● ● ● ● ● ● ●
Deaf Blind DB-Link: The National Information Clearinghouse on Children
Who Are Deaf-Blind
c/o Teaching Research
Western Oregon University
345 North Monmouth Ave.
Monmouth, OR 97361
800-438-9376
TTY 800-854-7013
www.dblink.org

Helen Keller National Center for Deaf Blind Youths and Adults
111 Middle Neck Rd.
Sands Point, NY 11050
516-944-8900
www.HKUC.org

● ● ● ● ● ● ● ● ● ● ● ● ●
Deaf and Alexander Graham Bell Association for the Deaf
Hard of 3417 Volta Place NW
Hearing Washington, DC 20007
202-337-5220
www.agbell.org

American Society for Deaf Children
P.O. Box 3355
Gettysburg, PA 17325
800-942-2732
www.deafchildren.org

International Parents' Organization
c/o Alexander Graham Bell Association for the Deaf
3417 Volta Place NW
Washington DC 20007
202-337-5220
www.agbell.org

National Association of the Deaf
814 Thayer Ave., Suite 250
Silver Spring, MD 20910
301-587-1788
www.nad.org

National Cued Speech Association
23970 Hermitage Rd.
Shaker Heights, OH 44122
800-459-3529
www.cuedspeech.org

Self Help for Hard of Hearing People
7910 Woodmont Ave., Suite 1200
Bethesda, MD 20814
301-657-2248
www.hearingloss.org

• • • • • • • • • • • • •
Down Syndrome

National Down Syndrome Congress
1605 Chantilly Rd.
Atlanta, GA 30324
800-232-NDSC
www.ndsccenter.org

National Down Syndrome Society
666 Broadway
New York, NY 10012
212-460-9330; 800-221-4602
www.ndss.org

• • • • • • • • • • • • •
Epilepsy

Epilepsy Foundation of America
4351 Garden City Dr.
Landover, MD 20785
301-459-3700; 800-EFA-1000
www.epilepsyfoundation.org

• • • • • • • • • • • • •
Facial Differences

FACES—National Association for the Craniofacially Handicapped
P.O. Box 11082
Chattanooga, TN 37401
423-266-1632; 800-332-2373
www.faces-cranio.org

• • • • • • • • • • • • •
Fetal Alcohol Syndrome

National Organization on FAS
900 17th St., NW, Suite 910
Washington, DC 20006
800-66NOFAS
www.nofas.org

• • • • • • • • • • • • •
Fragile X Syndrome

National Fragile X Foundation
P.O. Box 190488
San Francisco, CA 94119
800-688-8765; 925-938-9300
www.nfxf.org

• • • • • • • • • • • • •
Learning Disabilities

Council for Learning Disabilities
P.O. Box 40303
Overland Park, KS 66204
571-258-1010
cldinternational.org

International Dyslexia Association
Chester Building, Suite 382
8600 La Salle Rd.
Baltimore, MD 21286-2044
410-296-0232
800-ABCD123
www.interdys.org

LDOnline
www.ldonline.com

Learning Disabilities Association of America
4156 Library Rd.
Pittsburgh, PA 15234
412-341-1515
www.ldaamerica.org

The National Center for Learning Disabilities
381 Park Ave. South, Ste. 1420
New York, NY 10016
212-545-7510
www.ld.org

Nonverbal Learning Disorders Association
2446 Albany Ave.
West Hartford, CT 06117
860-570-0217
www.nlda.org

• • • • • • • • • • • • • •
Mental Retardation

The Arc
1010 Wayne Ave., Ste. 650
Silver Spring, MD 20910
301-565-3842
www.thearc.org

Division on Mental Retardation
c/o Council for Exceptional Children
1110 Glebe Rd., Suite 300
Arlington, VA 22201
703-620-3660
www.cec.sped.org

• • • • • • • • • • • • •
Physical Disabilities

Division for Physically Handicapped
c/o Council for Exceptional Children
1110 N. Glebe Rd., Suite 300
Arlington, VA 22201
703-620-3660
www.cec.sped.org

Muscular Dystrophy Association
3300 E. Sunrise Drive
Tucson, AZ 85718
602-529-2000
mdausa.org

Spina Bifida Association of America
4590 MacArthur Blvd., NW, Suite 250
Washington, DC 20007-4226
202-944-3285; 800-621-3141
www.sbaa.org

United Cerebral Palsy Associations
1660 L St. NW, Ste. 700
Washington, DC 20036
202-776-0406; 800-872-5827
www.ucp.org

· · · · · · · · · · · · ·
Speech and Language Disabilities

American Speech Language Hearing Association
10801 Rockville Pike
Rockville, MD 20852
301-897-5700; 800-638-8255
www.asha.org

National Association for Hearing and Speech Action
10801 Rockville Pike
Rockville, MD 20852
301-897-8682; 800-638-8255

National Center for Stuttering
200 E. 33rd St.
New York, NY 10016
212-532-1460
800-221-2483
www.stuttering.com

National Institute on Deafness and Other Communication Disorders
National Institutes of Health
31 Center Dr., MSC 2320
Bethesda, MD 20892-2320
800-241-1044
TTY 800-241-1055
www.nidcd.nih.gov

· · · · · · · · · · · · ·
Visual Impairments

American Foundation for the Blind
11 Penn Plaza, Ste. 300
New York, NY 10001
212-502-7600; 800-AFB-LINE
www.afb.org

American Printing House for the Blind
P.O. Box 6085
Louisville, KY 40206
502-895-2405; 800-223-1839

Association for Education and Rehabilitation of the Blind and Visually Impaired
1703 N. Beauregard St., Suite 440
Alexandria, VA 22311
703-671-4500
888-492-2708
www.aecbvi.org

National Association for Parents of the Visually Impaired
P.O. Box 317
Watertown, MA 02272
1-800-562-6265
www.spedex.com/napvi

National Association for Visually Handicapped
22 W. 21st St.
New York, NY 10010
212-889-3141
888-205-5951
www.navh.org

National Organization of Parents of Blind Children
1800 Johnson St.
Baltimore, MD 21230
410-659-9314
www.nfb.org/nopbc.htm

Appendix  E

Toy Manufacturers Cited in This Book

Battat, Inc.
2 Industrial Blvd. West Circle
P.O. Box 1264
Plattsburgh, NY 12901
518-562-2200
www.battat-toys.com

> Octopus*
> Soft Cubes*
> Big Band Set*
> Farm House and farm figures*
> Magnetic Sketch Board*
> Stethoscope*
> Electronic Calculating Cash Register*
> Magnetic Dress Up with Storage Closet*
> * Registered trademark of Battat, Inc.

Discovery Toys
6400 Brisa St.
Livermore, CA 94550
1-800-341-8697
www.discoverytoysinc.com

> Picture This Crib Bumper*
> Animal Tower*
> Bear Blocks*
> Opposite Pairs*
> Money Money*
> Stencils and Pencils*
> * Registered trademark of Discovery Toys

Fisher-Price, Inc.
636 Girard Ave.
East Aurora, NY 14052
1-800-432 KIDS (5437)
www.fisher-price.com

  Ocean Wonders*
  Sparkling Symphony Gym*
  Kick and Learn Piano*
  Smart Magnets*
  Sparkling Symphony Stacker*
  First Blocks*
  See and Say*
  Fun Sounds Garage*
  Little People School Bus*
  Rescue Fire Truck*

  * Registered trademark of Fisher-Price, Inc.

International Playthings, Inc.
75D Lackawanna Ave.
Parsippany, NJ 07054
1-800-631-1272
www.intplay.com

  Puppy Play card game*
  Time to Rhyme*
  Pets Mini Block Puzzle*
  What Time Is It?*
  Baseball Card Game*
  Get Up and Go Games*
  Spin-a-Shape Elephant*
  Baby Farm Friends Bowling*
  Step a Sound Mat*
  Village Vet Set*

  * Registered trademark of International Playthings, Inc.

Klutz
455 Portage Ave.
Palo Alto, CA 94306
1-650-857-0888
www.KLUTZ.com

  The Fabulous Book of Paper Dolls*

  * Registered trademark of Klutz, Inc.

Lego Systems, Inc.
555 Taylor Rd.
P.O. Box 1310
Enfield, CT 06083-1310
1-800-453-4652
www.LEGOshop.com
> DUPLO^R Basic Bucket*
> * Registered trademark of Lego Systems, Inc.

Lillian Vernon Corporation
Virginia Beach, VA 23479
1-800-545-5426
www.lillianvernon.com
> Magnetic Ball*
> * Registered trademark of Lillian Vernon

The Little Tykes Company
2180 Barlow Rd.
Hudson, OH 44236
1-800-321-0183
www.littletikes.com
> Shopping Cart*
> * Registered trademark of Little Tykes Co.

RC2 Corporation
800 Veterans Parkway
Bolingbrook, IL 60440
CS@rc2corp.com
Distributors for:
> *Learning Curve*
>> Wrist Rattle Assortment
>> Sherberts™ Hippo
>> Humpty Dumpty Musical Pull Toy
>> Dressable Madeline
>> Genevieve and Carrier
>> Thomas and Friends Wooden Railway
>> Conductor's Figure 8 Set
> *FeltKids*
>> Zoo Trip
> *Play Sports*
>> Play Ball

Small World Toys

P.O. Box 3620

Culver City, CA 90231-3620

www.smallworldtoys.com

Power Transport*

Discovery Circle*

Unit Blocks of Fun*

All Shapes and Sizes*

Musical Surprise Bear*

Fruit basket*

Croquet set*

Foam paddles and ball*

Magnifying lens*

Clown bop bag*

Musical Activity TV (by Tolo)

* Registered trademark of Small World Toys

Appendix

Other Sources of Toys

Achievement Products, Inc.
P.O. Box 9033
Canton, OH 44711
800-373-4699
Email: achievepro@aol.com
> Catalog of special education and rehabilitation equipment for children with special needs birth to eighteen.

ADCO
5661 South Curticee St.
Littleton, CO 80120
1-800-726-0851 V/TTY
www.adcohearing.com
> Catalog of TTYs, novelty gifts related to deafness, captioner

Antoni Toys and Products for the Physically Challenged
232 SE Oak St., Suite 103
Portland, OR 97214
800-826-8664

Carolyn's
P.O. Box 14577
Bradenton, FL 34280
800-648-2266
> Catalog with adapted board games for children who are blind or have low vision.

Communication Skill Builders
555 Academic Ct.
San Antonio, TX 78230
800-228-0752
210-949-4452
> Books, videos, games, activities to help professionals who work with children with special needs.

Crestwood Communication Aids for Children and Adults
6625 N. Sidney Place
Milwaukee, WI 53209-3259
414-352-5678
www.communicationaids.com
> Catalog of assistive devices to talk for individuals with disabilities, communication board materials, adapted toys for children with special needs, and voice-activated materials.

Dragonfly Toy Co.
291 Yale Ave.
Winnipeg, MB R3M 0LA
Canada
800-308-2208
www.dftoys.com
> Catalog of adapted battery toys, adapted art equipment, textured toys, adapted playground equipment.

Ernie's Toys and Switches
7 Melbourne Ct.
Buffalo, NY 14222
716-883-5621
> Modifies off-the-shelf toys.

Flaghouse-Special Populations
150 N. MacQuestern Pkwy.
Mt. Vernon, NY 14222
800-793-7900
> Catalog of adapted toys.

HearthSong
P.O. Box 1050
Madison, VA 22727
800-533-4397
www.hearthsong.com
> Creative and educational toys, built to last.

Kapable Kids
P.O. Box 250
Bohemia, NY 11716
800-356-1564.
> Catalog of switches and toys that are adaptable for all children with special needs.

Learning Resources
380 North Fairway Drive
Vernon Hills, IL 60061
888-800-7893
www.learningresources.com
> A source of educational games and teaching materials for learners of all abilities.

One Step Ahead
P.O. Box 517
Lake Bluff, IL 60044
1-800-274-8440
www.onestepahead.com
> Toys and clothes for babies and toddlers.

Oriental Trading Co., Inc.
P.O. Box 2308
Omaha, NE 68103-2308
1-800228-0475
www.orientaltrading.com
> Source of inexpensive stickers, crafts, and assorted novelties.

SmarterKids
800-293-9314
www.smarterkids.com
> Educational toys and teaching materials.

Toys "R" Us Guide for Differently Abled Kids
P.O. Box 8501
Nevada, IA 50201-9968
www.toysrus.com/differently.abled
> Catalog to help choose toys for children with a variety of special needs.

Young Explorers: Creative Educational Products
1810 W. Eisenhower Blvd.
P.O. Box 2257
Loveland, CO 80539
1-800-239-7577
www.YoungExplorers.com

References

American Academy of Pediatrics. *Caring for Your Baby and Young Child Birth to Age 5.* New York: Bantam Doubleday Dell,1998.

Ames, Louise Bates and Ilg, Frances L. *Your Five Year Old.* New York: Dell Publishing, 1981.

Anderson, W., Chitwood, S., and Hayden, D. *Negotiating the Special Education Maze.* Bethesda, MD: Woodbine House, 1997.

Atack, M. Sally. *Art Activities for the Handicapped.* Englewood Cliffs, NJ: Prentice-Hall, Inc., 1986.

Bangs, Tina. *Birth to Three: Developmental Learning and the Handicapped Child.* Hingham, MA: Teaching Resources Corp., 1979.

Barber, W. Lucie and Williams, Herman. *Your Baby's First 30 Months.* Tucson, AZ: Fisher Publishing Co., 1981.

Bernard, Susan. *The Mommy Guide. Real Life Advice and Tips from over 250 Moms and Other Experts.* Chicago, IL: Contemporary Books, 1994.

Bondy, Andy and Frost, Lori. *A Picture's Worth: PECS and Other Visual Communication Strategies in Autism.* Bethesda, MD: Woodbine House, 2002.

Brazelton, T. Berry. *Infants and Mothers.* New York: Dell Publishing Co., 1983.

Brazelton,T. Berry. *Touchpoints. Your Child's Emotional and Behavioral Development.* Boulder, CO: Perseus Press, 1994.

Breger, Louis. *From Instinct to Identity: The Development of Personality.* Englewood Cliffs, NJ: Prentice-Hall, Inc., 1974.

Bruni, Maryanne. *Fine Motor Skills in Children with Down Syndrome.* Bethesda, MD: Woodbine House, 1998

Buck, Pearl S. *The Child Who Never Grew*. Bethesda, MD: Woodbine House, 1992.

Burtt, Kent Garland and Kalkstein, Karen. *Smart Toys for Babies from Birth to Two*. New York: Harper and Row Publishers, Inc., 1981.

Caplan, Frank and Theresa. *The Power of Play*. Garden City, NY: Anchor Press/ Doubleday, 1973.

Cary, Elizabeth and Casebolt, Patti. *Pick Up Your Socks and Other Skills Growing Children Need!* Seattle: Parenting Press, 1990.

Cary, Elizabeth. *Without Spanking or Spoiling*. Seattle: Parenting Press, 1990.

Cole, Joanna and Calmenson, Stephanie. *Anna Banana and Jump Rope Rhymes*. New York: William Morrow and Co., 1989.

Cole, Joanna and Calmenson, Stephanie. *The Eensy Weensy Spider Fingerplays and Action Rhymes*. New York: William Morrow and Co., 1991.

Durkin, Lisa Lyons. *Parents and Kids Together*. New York: Warner Books, 1986.

Einon, Dorothy. *Play with a Purpose: Learning Games for Children 6 Weeks to 2-3 Years Old*. New York: St. Martin's Press, 1985.

Eliason, F. Claudia and Jenkins, Loa Thomson. *A Practical Guide to Early Childhood Curriculum*. St. Louis: The C.V. Mosby Co., 1993.

Erickson, H. Erik. *Childhood and Society*. New York: W.W. Norton & Co., 1963.

Faber, Adele and Mazlish, Elaine. *Siblings Without Rivalry: How to Help Your Children Live Together So You Can Live Too*. New York: Avon Books, 1998.

Faber, Adele and Mazlish, Elaine. *How to Talk So Kids Will Listen and Listen So Kids Will Talk*. New York: Avon Books, 1999.

Fairy, Jim and Cline, Foster W. *Parenting with Love and Logic: Teaching Children Responsibility*. Colorado Springs, CO: Navpress, 1990.

Ferber, Richard. *Solve Your Child's Sleep Problems*. New York: Simon and Schuster, 1986.

Garvey, Catherine. *Children's Talk*. Boston: Harvard University Press, 1984.

Geralis, Elaine (Ed.) *Children with Cerebral Palsy: A Parent's Guide*. Bethesda, MD: Woodbine House, 1998.

Goldberg, Sally. *Teaching with Toys*. Ann Arbor: The University of Michigan Press, 1981.

Gordon, J. Ira. *Baby Learning through Baby Play.* New York: St. Martin's Press, 1970.

Gordon, J. Ira. *Baby to Parent, Parent to Baby.* New York: St. Martin's Press, 1977.

Gordon, J. Ira. *Child Learning through Child Play: Learning Activities for 2-3 Year Olds,* New York: St. Martin's Press, 1972.

Greene, Ross W. PhD. *The "Explosive Child": A New Approach for Understanding and Parenting Easily Frustrated, Inflexible Children.* New York: HarperCollins, 2001.

Greenspan, Stanley and Greenspan, Nancy. *The Essential Partnership.* New York: Penguin Books, 1989.

Haerle, Tracy. *Children with Tourette Syndrome.* Bethesda, MD: Woodbine House, 1992.

Hagerston, Julie and Morrill, Joan. *Games Babies Play and More Games Babies Play.* New York: Pocket Books, 1981.

Harland, Kelly. *A Will of His Own: Reflections on Parenting a Child with Autism.* Bethesda, MD: Woodbine House, 2002.

Heins, Marilyn and Seiden, Anne. *Child Care/Parent Care.* New York: Doubleday, 1987.

Hendrick, Joanne. *The Whole Child: Developmental Education for the Early Years.* New York: Macmillan, 1991.

Holbrook, M. Cay (Ed.) *Children with Visual Impairment: A Parents' Guide.* Bethesda, MD: Woodbine House, 1996.

Houghton, Janaye Matteson. *Homespan Language.* Whitehaven Publishing Co., Inc. 1982.

Ilg, L. Frances, M.D., Ames, Louis Bates, Ph.D., and Beeker, Sidney M., M.D. *Child Behavior.* New York: Harper and Row, 1981.

Johnson, Doris McNeely. *The Creative Parenting Toy Guide.* Self-published, 1980.

Jones, Claudia. *Parents Are Teachers Too.* Charlotte, VT: Williamson Publishing Co., 1988.

Kaban, Barbara. *Choosing Toys for Children from Birth to Five.* New York: Schocken Books, 1979.

Karnes, B. Merle. *You and Your Small Wonder. Book 2: 18-36 Months.* Circle Pines, MN: American Guidance Service, 1982.

Kindlon, Daniel J. *Raising Cain: Protecting the Emotional Life of Boys.* New York: Ballantine Books, 2000.

Kranowitz, Carol Stock. *The Out of Sync Child Has Fun*. New York: Berkeley Publishing Co., 2003.

Kranowitz, Carol Stock. *The Out of Sync Child*. New York: Berkeley Publishing Co., 2003.

Kumin, Libby. *Classroom Language Skills for Children with Down Syndrome: A Guide for Parents and Teachers*. Bethesda, MD: Woodbine House, 2001.

Kumin, Libby. *Early Communication Skills in Children with Down Syndrome: A Guide for Parent and Professionals*. Bethesda, MD: Woodbine House, 2003.

Kunchinko, Mary Sheehy. *Raising Your "Spirited Child": A Guide to Parent whose Child Is Intense, Sensitive, Perceptive, Persistent and Energetic*. New York: Harper Perennial Library, 1998.

Leach, Penelope. *Your Baby and Child: From Birth to Age Five*. New York: Knopf, 1997.

Lutekenhoff, Marlene. *Children with Spina Bifida: A Parent's Guide*. Bethesda, MD: Woodbine House, 1999.

Markun, Patricia Maloney. *Play: Children's Business*. Washington, DC: Association for Childhood Education International, 1974.

Masi, Wendy S. and Leiderman, Roni Cohen. *Baby Play*. Chanhassen, MN: Creative Publishing, 2001.

Masi, Wendy S. *Toddler Play*. Chanhassen, MN: Creative Publishing, 2001.

McClannahan, Lynn, Ph.D. and Krantz, Patricia J., Ph.D. *Activity Schedules for Children with Autism: Teaching Independent Behavior*. Bethesda, MD: Woodbine House, 1999.

McConkey, Roy and Jeffree, Dorothy. *Making Toys for Handicapped Children*. Englewood Cliffs, NJ: Prentice Hall, 1983.

Meyer, Donald J., Ed. *Uncommon Fathers: Reflections on Raising a Child with a Disability*. Bethesda, MD: Woodbine House, 1995.

Miller, Karen. *Things to Do with Toddlers and Twos*. Chelsea, MA: Telshare Publishing, Inc., 1984.

Miller, Karen. *More Things to Do with Toddlers and Twos*. Chelsea, MA: Telshare Publishing, Inc., 1984.

Millnard, Joan and Behrmann, Polly. *Parents As Playmates: A Games Approach to the Preschool Years*. New York: Human Sciences Press, 1979.

Monsees, K. Edna. *Structured Language for Children with Special Language Learning Problems.* Washington, DC: Children's Hospital of the District of Columbia, Children's Hearing and Speech Center, 1972.

Munger, Evelyn Moats and Bowdon, Susan Jane. *Child Play Activities for Your Child's First Three Years.* New York: E.P. Dutton, Inc., 1983.

Musselwhite, Caroline Ramsey. *Adaptive Play for Special Needs Children: Strategies to Enhance Communication and Learning.* Austin, TX: Pro-Ed, 1986.

Oberlander, June. *Slow and Steady Get Me Ready.* Fairfax, VA: Bio-Alpha Inc., 1989.

O'Neill, Mary. *Hailstones and Halibut Bones.* New York: Doubleday, 1989.

Oppenheim, Joanne F. *Kids and Play.* New York: Ballantine Books, 1984.

Oppenheim, Joanne and Oppenheim, Stephanie. *The Best Toys, Books, and Videos for Kids.* New York: HarperCollins Publishers, 2003.

Phelan, Thomas W. Ph.D. *1-2-3-Magic Effective Discipline for Children 2-12.* Glen Ellyn, IL: Child Management, 1996.

Powers, Margaret Hall. "Functional Disorders of Articulation/Symptomotology and Etiology," In *Handbook of Speech Pathology, and Audiology,* edited by Lee Edward Travis. Englewood Cliffs, NJ: Prentice Hall, 1971.

Powers, Michael (Ed.). *Children with Autism: A Parents' Guide.* Bethesda, MD: Woodbine House, 2000.

Pushaw, David. *Teach Your Child to Talk.* New York: CEBCO Publishing, 1976.

Schoenbrodt, Lisa. *Children with Traumatic Brain Injury: A Parent's Guide.* Bethesda, MD: Woodbine House, 2001.

Schwartz, Sue (Ed.). *Choices In Deafness: A Parents' Guide.* Bethesda, MD: Woodbine House, 1996.

Scott, Eileen P., Jan, James E., and Freeman, Robert D. *Can't Your Child See? A Guide for Parents of Visually Impaired Children.* Austin, TX: Pro-Ed, 1985.

Screiber, Lee R. *The Parents' Guide to Kids' Sports.* Boston: Little, Brown, and Co., 1990.

Sears, William and Sears, Martha. *The Discipline Book: How To Have a Better Behaved Child from Birth to Age Ten.* Boston: Little, Brown, and Co, 1995.

Segal, Marilyn. *Your Child At Play. Birth-One, One-Two, Two- Three, Three-Five.* New York: Newmarket Press, 1985.

Severe, Sol. *How To Behave So Your Children Will, Too!* New York: Viking Press, 2000.

Smith, Romayne (Ed.). *Children with Mental Retardation: A Parents' Guide.* Bethesda, MD: Woodbine House, 1993.

Sobol, Tom and Harriet. *Your Child in School: Kindergarten through Second Grade.* New York: Arbor House, 1987.

Stern, Daniel, M.D. *Diary of a Baby.* New York: Basic Books, 1990.

Sternlicht, Nancy. *Games Play.* New York: Reinhold Co., 1981.

Stray-Gundersen, Karen (Ed.). *Babies with Down Syndrome: A New Parents' Guide.* 2nd ed. Bethesda, MD: Woodbine House, 1995.

Tannen, Deborah. *I Only Say This Because I Love You: How the Way We Talk Can Make or Break Family Relationships throughout Our Lives.* New York: Random House, 2001.

Volkmar, Fred R. and Wiesner, Lisa A. *Healthcare for Children on the Autism Spectrum: A Guide to Medical, Nutritional, and Behavioral Issues.* Bethesda, MD: Woodbine House, 2003.

Warner, Penny. *Baby Play and Learn.* Minnetonka, MN: Meadowbrook Press, 1999.

Warner, Penny. *Preschooler Play and Learn.* Minnetonka, MN: Meadowbrook Press, 2000.

Weber, Jayne Dixon. *Children with Fragile X Syndrome: A Parents' Guide.* Bethesda, MD: Woodbine House, 2000.

Weisbluth, Marc. *Healthy Sleep Habits, Happy Child.* New York: Fawcett Books, 1999.

Weiss, Mary Jane and Harris, Sandra L., Ph.D. *Reaching Out, Joining In: Teaching Social Skills to Young Children with Autism.* Bethesda, MD: Woodbine House, 2001.

Winders, Patricia. *Gross Motor Skills in Children with Down Syndrome: A Guide for Parents and Professionals.* Bethesda, MD: Woodbine House, 1997.

Index

Address, teaching, 102
Adverbs, 179
All Shapes and Sizes™, 104-105
Alternative communication systems, 17, 18.
   See also Computers
American Speech Language Hearing
   Association, 21
Animal Tower™, 60-61
Art materials, 149-51. *See also* Coloring
Articulation, 12-13
Assessment, speech and language, 21-23, 171
Attention, 175
Autism, 187, 224-25
Babbling, 9, 10, 49
Baby Farm Friends Bowling™, 106-107
Baby talk, 54
Balloons, 215
Balls
   bowling, 106-107
   early interest in, 10
   foam paddles and, 179
   large play ball, 63
   magnetic, 62-63
   playdough, 131
   tennis, 85
Barn toy, 105-106
Baseball Card Game™, 182-83
Basic Skills™ puzzle, 88-89
Bear Blocks™, 126-27
Bedtime, 121
Behavior management, 37-39, 101
Big Band Set™, 78
Bilingual families, 19
Blanket, texture, 46-47
Blocks, 54-56, 58, 65-66, 82, 127

Board games, 122-23
Books
   for birth to twelve months, 70-73
   for the second year, 92-96
   for the third year, 112-16
   for the fourth year, 134-42
   for the fifth year, 163-66
   for the sixth year, 189-92
   homemade, 67-68, 92
   introducing at early age, 66-67
   on computers, 205
   sources for information about, 221-22
Bowling game, 106-107
Boxes, as toys, 79-80
Bubbles, 83-84
Calculating Cash Register™, 178-79
Candyland™, 122-23
Captions, 210
Car rides, 196-97
Card games, 158-59, 182-83
Catalogs, 207-208, 235-38
Cause and effect, 51, 52, 64, 199
Cereal Box Puzzles, 90
Chalk, 151
Choices, giving, 101
Choices in Deafness, 19
Chores, talking about, 196
Clown Bop Bag™, 151-52
Cognitive skills
   delays in, 17-18
   development of, 28-29
   milestones in, 76, 99, 118-19, 145-46, 169
Cohen, Sanford, 203
Coins, 177-78
Color Match, 90

Coloring, 81, 148. *See also* Drawing

Colors, 43, 55, 65, 90, 104-105, 122-23, 129-30, 175-76

Communication board, 36

Communication skills. *See* Language; Language development; Speech

Computers, 199-204, 205-208

Concepts. *See* Single concepts

Consistency, 101, 121

Cookie cutters, 132

Corduroy, 112

Counting, 123. *See also* Numbers

Crayon Rock, 132

Crayons, 81, 132, 150

Crib bumper, 45-46

Croquet, 181-82

Danielle's story, 67-68

Deaf blindness, 225

Deafness. *See* Hearing loss

Descriptive video, 211

Development. *See* Cognitive skills; Emotional development; Language development; Physical development; Social development

Developmental age, 6, 7

Developmental milestones (charts),
    for first year, 74-76,
    for second year, 97- 99,
    for third year, 17-19,
    for fourth year, 143-46
    for fifth year, 167-69

Discovery Circle™, 45

Dolls, 124-25, 154-55, 159-60

Down syndrome, 17, 226

Dramatic play. *See* Pretending

Drawing, 148-49, 175-76. *See also* Art materials; Coloring

Drooling, 22

Duplo Blocks™, 65-66

DVDs, 209-10

Dysfluency, 14-15

Electronic toys, 199-200

Emotional development, 26-27

Emotions, 77, 122, 151

Epilepsy, 226

Evaluation. *See* Assessment

Expressive language. *See* Language, expressive

Eye gaze frame, 36

Fabulous Book of Paper Dolls™, 159-60

Facial differences, 226

Fairy tales, 110

Fantasy, 122

Farm House and farm figures, 105-106

Fascination Station™, 107-108

Fears, 122

Feelings. *See* Emotions

FeltKids Zoo Trip™, 153-54

Fetal alcohol syndrome, 227

Fine motor skills, 8, 149, 150, 172, 174. *See also* Physical development

Fire truck, 129

First Blocks™, 82

Flannel Board, 109-110, 153

Flashlight Fun, 53

Foam Paddles and Balls™, 179

Focus, baby's ability to, 43

Fragile X syndrome, 227

Friends, 174, 194-95. *See also* Play; Social development

Fruit Basket™, 123-24

Fun Sounds Garage™, 103

Generalization, 35

Genevieve, 124-25

Get Up and Go Games™, 180-81

Grasp, 8, 150, 174

Grocery shopping, 194

Hailstones and Halibut Bones, 18

Hearing loss, 19, 35, 78, 126, 203, 225-26

Highchairs, 34-35, 54

Hippo, stuffed, 64-65

Hoban, Tana, 68

Holder, Wayne, 175

Idiomatic expressions, 147-48

Imitation, 11, 49, 86

Intellitools, 201, 207

IQ, 17

Jargoning, 10

Keyboards, 201, 207-208

Kick and Learn Piano™, 51

Kids and Computers, 202

Knock Knock Blocks™, 58

Language. *See also* Language development; Speech; Words
    disabilities, 229
    expressive, 3-4, 15, 22, 81-82
    need for, 1-2
    receptive, 3, 15, 19, 21-22, 81
    signs of problems with, 20
    teaching through daily activities, 193-97
    techniques for teaching, 37

Language development
  "normal," 5-6
  in first year, 7-9, 49, 54, 86
  in second year, 10-13
  in third year, 13-14
  in fourth year, 14-15
  in fifth year, 15
  in sixth year, 15-16
  milestones in, 74, 97, 117, 143, 167
  reasons for delays in, 16-20
Learning disabilities, 203, 227-28
Lekotek Centers, 218
Letters, alphabet, 52, 172, 186-87. *See also* Reading
Libraries, 218
Little Engine That Could, The, 112
Little People School Bus™, 103-104
Madeline, 124-25
Magnetic Sketch Board™, 148-49
Magnetic Dress Up with Storage Closet™, 154-55
Magnifying Lens™, 176-77
Matching games, 126, 158-59
Math concepts. *See also* Shapes
  counting, 123
  money, 177-78, 186
  numbers, 158, 186-87
  time concepts, 179-80
Mental retardation, 228
Mickey Mouse™, 65
Milestones, developmental. *See* Developmental milestones
Mirrors, 45, 58
Mobiles, 44, 47-48
Money Money™, 177
Motor skills. *See* Physical development
Mouth, 22
Music Blocks Maestro™, 108-109
Musical Activity T.V.™, 57
Musical Surprise Bear™, 57
Musical toys, 50, 51-52, 57, 64, 78-79, 108-109, 132
Newspaper Fun, 67
Nonfluency, 14-15
Numbers, 158, 186-87. *See also* Counting
Ocean Wonders™, 50, 200
Octopus toy, 44
Omissions, 22
O'Neill, Mary, 18
Opposite Pairs™, 156-57
Organizations, disability, 223-30

Orthopedic impairment. *See* Physical disabilities
Packing Peanuts Play, 160
Paper box tunnel, 59
Paper dolls, 159-60
Peek-a-boo, 58, 59
Pets, 128
Pets Mini Puzzle™, 157-58
Photos, 67-68, 92
Physical development. *See also* Fine motor skills
  encouraging, 27
  friendships and, 174
  in first year, 8-10, 54, 86-87
  in second year, 10-13, 81
  in third year, 14
  in fourth year, 15
  in fifth year, 15
  in sixth year, 16, 173-74
  milestones in, 75, 98, 118, 144, 168
Physical disabilities, 36, 181, 228
Phrases, 11, 13, 20
Piaget, Jean, 28
Picture This™, 45-46
Play
  as means to develop language skills, 30-31
  importance of, 25-26
  on floor, 35
  stages of, 27
Play groups, 39, 121
Playdough, 129-32
Playground activities, 87
Pouring practice, 80
Power Transport™, 152
Pretend Restaurant, 184-86
Pretending, 126, 184-86, 220
Pronouns, 11, 15
Punching bag, 151-52
Puppy Play Card Game™, 158-59
Push toy, 66
Puzzle Rhymes™, 155-56
Puzzles, 11, 14, 88-89, 90, 155-55
Rattles, 8, 50-51
Reading. *See also* Books
  at bedtime, 121
  captions and, 210
  language experience approach to, 173
  precursors to, 150, 210
  readiness activities, 156, 172, 184-85
  typical age for beginning, 15
Receptive language. *See* Language, receptive

Repetition, 34, 197
Rescue Fire Truck™, 129
Rhymes, 102, 124, 155-56
Roller Ball, 161
Routines, 101, 121
Rules, 175
Salpeter, Judy, 202
Sandpaper numbers and letters, 186-87
School bus toy, 103-104
See N' Say Animals™, 79
Seesaw, 87
Self-help skills, 81, 88
Sensory integration disorders, 187
Shape concepts, 62, 82-83, 104-105,
    108-109, 110, 172
Shape Lunch, 110
Shape sorters, 82-83
Sharing, 121, 123, 175
Sherberts Hippo, 64-65
Shopping Cart™, 123-24
Sign language, 36, 211
Single concepts
    colors, 65-66
    "crawl," 59
    "down," 108-109
    "empty" and "full," 85
    "hard" and "softly," 179
    how to use, 34
    "inside," 106
    "pour," 80
    "roll," 63
    "round," 82
    "round and round," 58
    "shake," 64
    "slow" and "fast," 132
    "top" and "bottom," 161
    "up" and "down," 55
    "vest," 127
Size concepts, 104-105
Sleeping position, 53
Smart Magnets™, 61
Social development, 27-28, 39, 174.
    See also Friends; Play
Soft Cubes™, 54-56
Software, 201-202, 207-208
Sparkling Symphony Gym™, 51
Sparkling Symphony Star Beads™, 64
Special Olympics, 174
Speech. *See also* Language; Words
    baby talk, 54
    definition of, 4

disabilities, 229
signs of problems with, 20
sounds, 12-13, 22
Speech-language pathologist, 14, 21, 171
Spin-a-Shape Elephant™, 82-83
Sports, 174, 175
Stencils, 149, 175-76
Stencils and Pencils™, 175-76
Step-a-Sound Mat™, 87-88
Stethoscope, 183-84
Stuffed animals, 44-45, 64-65, 124-25
Stuttering. *See* Nonfluency
Substitutions, 22
Sunshine Symphony™, 52, 200
Swings, 87
Symphony in Motion™, 44
Syntax, 15
Tea sets, 89
Telephones, for deaf, 204-205
Television. *See* TV
Tennis Time, 85
"Terrible twos," 101
Tests, speech and language, 21-23
Texture blanket, 46-47
Textured toys, 46, 47, 58
Thomas and Friends Wooden Railway™,
    125-26
Time concepts, 179-80
Time out, 38-39
Touch, 8. *See also* Textured toys.
Toy boxes, 40-41, 215
Toy dialogs
    teaching with, 33-35
Toys. *See also* Specific names or types of toys
    electronic, 199-200
    manufacturers of, 231
    materials for making, 219-20
    safety concerns and, 40, 213-16
    selecting, 40-41
    sources of, 217-18, 235-38
    storing, 40-41, 215
    value of, in teaching language, 30-31
Trains, 125-26
TTY, 204-205
Tugging Fun, 84
Tummy Time, 53
Turn taking, 49, 84, 123, 126, 175
TV, 125, 210
Typewriters, 205
Unit Blocks™, 127

United States Consumer Product Safety
   Commission, 213
Videos and DVDs, 125, 209-10
Village Vet Set™, 128
Vision problems, computer-related, 203
Visual impairments, children with
   arts and crafts and, 150
   computers and, 203
   grocery shopping and, 194
   helping adjust to new environment, 60
   homemade books for, 68
   organizations for, 229-30
   using other senses to teach, 18-19,
   using toys with, 35, 41, 46, 58, 105, 110,
      176, 177
   videos for, 211
   visual tracking and, 84
Vocabulary. *See also* Words
   for first year, 69-70
   for second year, 91-92
   for third year, 111
   for fourth year, 133-34
   for fifth year, 162-63
   for sixth year, 188-89
Vocal play, 7-8
Voice inflections, 77
Wait technique, 39
Websites
   as sources of toys, 218, 235-38
   related to computer or electronic
      technology, 205-207
   software review, 202
Weitbrecht, Robert, 204
What Time Is It?™, 179-80
Wheelchair, 103, 181
Words. *See also* Reading; Vocabulary
   average number at eighteen months, 10
   average number at five, 15
   average number at two, 11
   first, 9
   repetition of, 34
Wrist rattles, 50-51
Writing, 150, 176. *See also* Fine motor skills
Young Soccer Player, The, 175

About the Author

Sue Schwartz has a Master's degree in Speech and Hearing and a doctorate in Curriculum and Instruction with an emphasis in Family Counseling. As the developer of the Parent Infant Program in the Programs for Deaf and Hard of Hearing Students in the Montgomery County, Maryland Public Schools and as a presenter in workshops across the country, Dr. Schwartz has taught hundreds of parents and professionals how to help develop language skills in children with special needs. She is the editor of *CHOICES IN DEAFNESS: A PARENTS' GUIDE* (Woodbine House, 1997) and a contributor to other publications. She lives in Silver Spring, Maryland.

All Shapes and Sizes™—*Small World Toys*

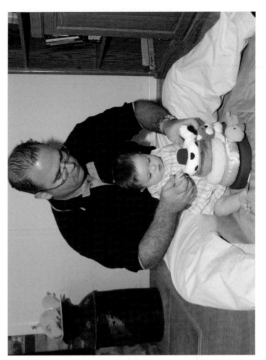

Animal Tower™—*Discovery Toys*

Baby Farm Friends Bowling™—
International Playthings

Baseball Card Game™—
International Playthings

Bear Blocks™—*Discovery Toys*

Big Band Set™—*Battat*

Calculating Cash Register™—*Battat*

Clown Bop Bag™—*Small World Toys*

Croquet Set—*Small World Toys*

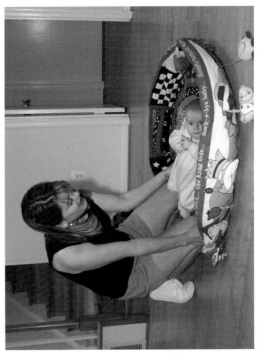

Discovery Circle™—*Small World Toys*

Duplo Blocks™—*Lego*

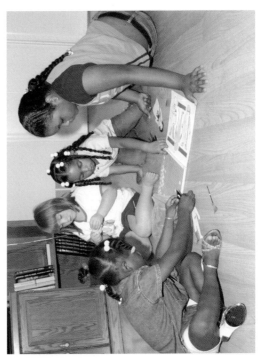

The Fabulous Book of Paper Dolls™—
Klutz

Farm House and Farm Figures™—*Battat*

Fascination Station™—*Discovery Toys*

FeltKids – Zoo Trip™—*Learning Curve*

First Blocks™—*Fisher-Price*

Foam Paddles and Balls™—
Small World Toys

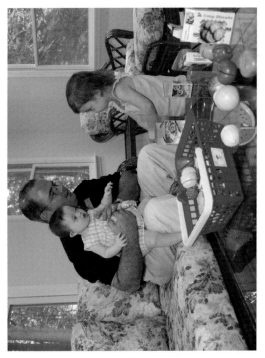

Fruit Basket™—*Small World Toys*

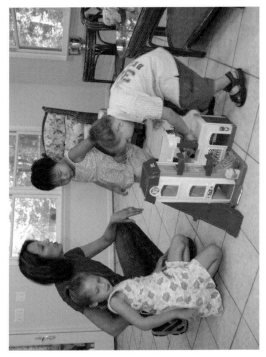

Fun Sounds Garage™—*Fisher-Price*

Get Up and Go Games™—
International Playthings

Kick and Learn Piano™—*Fisher-Price*

Knock Knock Blocks™—*Small World Toys*

Little People School Bus™—*Fisher-Price*

Madeline and Genevieve™—
Learning Curve

Magnetic Ball—
distributed by Lillian Vernon

Magnetic Dress Up with Storage
Closet™—*Battat*

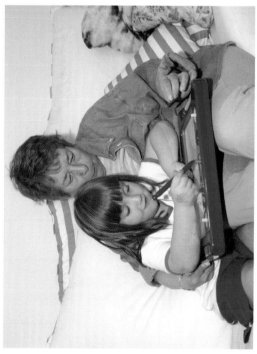

Magnetic Sketch Board™—*Fisher-Price*

Magnifying Lens™—*Small World Toys*

Money Money™—*Discovery Toys*

Moon Assortment Wrist Rattles™—
Learning Curve

Music Blocks Maestro™—*Neurosmith*

Musical Activity TV™—*Tolo*

Musical Bear™—*Small World Toys*

Ocean Wonders™—*Fisher-Price*

Octopus™—*Battat*

Opposite Pairs™—*Discovery Toys*

Pets Mini Block Puzzles™—
International Playthings

Picture This Crib Bumper™—
Discovery Toys

Play Ball—*Learning Curve/Play Sports*

Power Transport™—*Small World Toys*

Puppy Play™ card game—
International Playthings

Push Toy—*Playskool*

Puzzle Rhymes™—
International Playthings

Rescue Fire Truck™—*Fisher-Price*

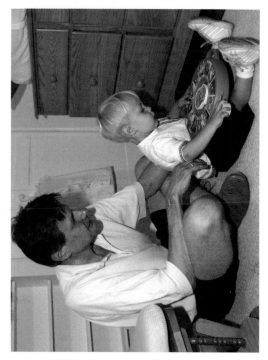

See 'N Say Farm Animals™—*Fisher-Price*

Sherberts Hippo™—*Learning Curve*

Shopping Cart™—*Playskool*

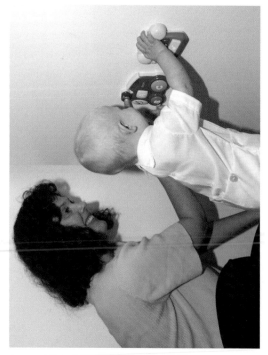

Smart Magnets™—*Fisher-Price*

Soft Cubes™—*Battat*

Sparkling Symphony Gym™—*Fisher-Price*

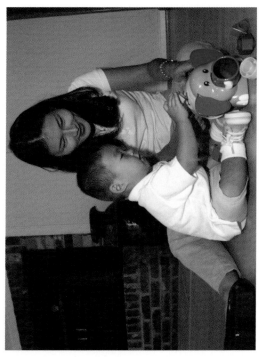

Spin-a-Shape Elephant™—
International Playthings

Star Beads™—*Fisher-Price*

Stencils and Pencils™—*Discovery Toys*

Step-a-Sound Mat™—
International Playthings

Stethoscope—*Battat*

Stuffed Mickey Mouse™—*Disney Products*

Sunshine Symphony™—*Neurosmith*

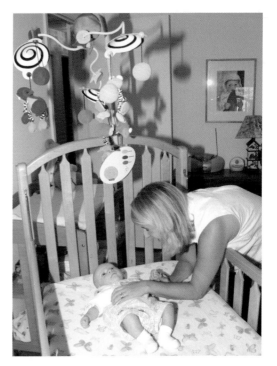

Symphony in Motion™—*Tiny Love*

Thomas and Friends Wooden Railway™—
Learning Curve

Tea Set

Unit Blocks™—*Small World Toys*

Village Vet Set™—*International Playthings*

What Time Is It?™—
International Playthings